THE WOMEN ARE UP TO SOMETHING

THE WOMEN ARE UP TO SOMETHING

How Elizabeth Anscombe,
Philippa Foot, Mary Midgley,
and Iris Murdoch
Revolutionized Ethics

Benjamin J.B. Lipscomb

OXFORD
UNIVERSITY PRESS

OXFORD
UNIVERSITY PRESS

Oxford University Press is a department of the University of Oxford. It furthers
the University's objective of excellence in research, scholarship, and education
by publishing worldwide. Oxford is a registered trade mark of Oxford University
Press in the UK and certain other countries.

Published in the United States of America by Oxford University Press
198 Madison Avenue, New York, NY 10016, United States of America.

CIP data is on file at the Library of Congress
ISBN 978-0-19-754107-4

DOI: 10.1093/oso/9780197541074.001.0001

3 5 7 9 8 6 4

Printed and bound by CPI Group (UK) Ltd, Croydon, CR0 4YY

To Mary Lipscomb, Susan Lipscomb, and Josephine Lipscomb, and to the memory of Barbara Lipscomb

CONTENTS

Preface   *ix*

Acknowledgments   *xv*

A Note on Names   *xxv*

A Note to American Readers   *xxvii*

1. Facts and Values   1

2. Oxford in Wartime   22

3. Daughters of 1919   50

4. The Coming Philosophers   76

5. Murdoch's Diagnosis   103

6. Elizabeth Anscombe versus the World   135

7. The Somerville Senior Common Room   171

CONTENTS

8. Slipping Out Over the Wall   200

9. "Time, Like the Sea . . ."   238

Notes   277
Image Credits   309
Bibliography   311
Index   321

PREFACE

On a chill March morning in 2010, I found myself just north of the Newcastle city center, walking a path along the bottom of Jesmond Dene, pausing sometimes to see what was stirring. Birds and more birds, mostly—the Dene is famous for its dawn chorus—but a few mammals, too: squirrels, a lone urban fox. I had an invitation for lunch, just west of the ravine. But I was already enjoying Mary Midgley's hospitality.

I had written to Midgley in December through her publisher, asking if she would be willing to talk. I explained I was planning a book about her and three of her friends: Elizabeth Anscombe, Philippa Foot, and Iris Murdoch. I'd been reading these four philosophers for years before learning that they'd all been at Oxford together. Now I thought there should be a book about them. I was interested not only in their beginnings and their friendships but also in their ideas: how they had challenged the anti-realist ethics of their male contemporaries and developed an alternative. I told her I would be in England for the next several months, teaching in my college's honors semester in London. I didn't know yet what I should ask, but: would she be willing to meet?

Midgley did more to inspire this project than anyone. I began thinking about it while reading her memoir, *The Owl of Minerva*. Midgley could have been a novelist, like her friend Iris Murdoch. *The Owl of Minerva* is as vivid and funny and wise as a good novel. It first made me aware of the story I tell here: four women with wildly different backgrounds and temperaments doing something revolutionary— and doing it together, as friends. At one point, reflecting on how she and Anscombe and Foot and Murdoch all ended up in philosophy when they had almost no role models, Midgley remarks: "in normal times a lot of good female thinking is wasted because it simply doesn't get heard."[1] There was nothing normal, though, about the time when she and her friends were at university. The Second World War was on, depleting Oxford of men. The best teachers who remained no longer had many advanced male students. They gave their full attention to Midgley and her friends, some of the most brilliant women in England or in the whole Western world.

I owe as much to Midgley's personal generosity as to the prompting of her memoir. As soon as my letter arrived, she emailed to say she'd be happy to talk. If I took the train up from London, I could visit her at her home, the ground floor of a terraced house near the Dene. She said she'd feed me before I returned home. We fixed a date. Thinking that, for a nonagenerian interviewee, I'd better be available whenever she preferred, I booked an early departure from Kings Cross to Newcastle and a late return.

Midgley was a little surprised when I told her I would be in Newcastle by 9. She had supposed, reasonably, that I wouldn't arrive until past noon. I assured her I was happy to take in the local sights until she wanted to meet; I had never been north. At which point, she threw herself into sketching my itinerary:

[I]f the weather's fine, you should surely start by going down to the quayside—which is only 5 minutes from the station—and looking at the bridges, which range from Stephenson's 1842 two-level affair to the fascinating recently built Millennium Bridge. And if you can come up from the quayside via The Side and Grey Street, you will see the fine classical town centre, topped by Lord Grey of the Reform Bill on a whacking big pillar.[2]

She also reviewed the local art museums, but concluded, "I'll expect you when I see you." Later, she mentioned about the Dene.

When I finally arrived at the end of the morning, the first thing Midgley did was serve me lunch, cheese on toast with lentil soup. We began talking at the wall-mounted table in the small kitchen in the back of the house, then made our way forward to the library looking out onto the lane. All afternoon, she urged tea on me, and biscuits from a plaid tin. We both lost track of time—either that, or she was just being generous.

My notes from that day aren't terribly useful. Again, I didn't yet know what to ask. But she welcomed me back twice over the next two-and-a-half years. At one point, she sent me off to the local library with a pile of documents from her filing cabinet to scan for my use. Each time, we had lunch, and tea, and biscuits.

This book is about the joint power of circumstance and character: about four people who were in the right place and time—and in the right company—to do unprecedented and transformative things. How did Anscombe, Foot, Midgley, and Murdoch all follow a path that was virtually unmarked? How did they stick together, different as they were? And how did they work their way toward a set of ideas sharply at odds with what nearly everyone around them thought?

For these four were doubly outsiders. Besides being women in an almost exclusively male discipline, they were advocates of an approach to ethics that was deeply out of fashion. As they began their careers, the dominant view among moral philosophers was that nothing is objectively good or bad, right or wrong, important or unimportant. Rather, all such values are projections, a thin glaze we paint onto an otherwise valueless world. On this view, there are no objective moral truths. As the leading theorist of the time, Richard Hare, wrote: "I have myself chosen, as far as in me lies, my own way of life, my own standard of values, my own principle of choice. In the end, we all have to choose for ourselves; and no one can do it for anyone else."[3] This wasn't just a view about ethics; it was a view about the kind of world we inhabit—about what's real. It was widely supposed to be the only acceptably modern thing to think.

These four friends diagnosed this as an intellectual fad. And they articulated an alternative: there are moral truths, grounded in the distinctive nature of our species—in facts about what human beings need if they are going to thrive. They drew on neglected ancient resources—Plato, and especially Aristotle—but also on Charles Darwin and Jane Goodall, to explain how we are less exceptional than we imagine, and more at home in the world. More than one thing about these women bears explanation, then. Yes, how did they imagine their way into philosophy at all? But also, what prepared them to resist intellectual conformity? And notwithstanding their many differences, how did they build on one another's work? Because they were more than a *cluster*; without any of them exactly intending this, they became a school.

There are really two stories in this book, then: first, a story about four women, their overlapping friendships, and their struggle to establish themselves as philosophers in an often-hostile context; second, a story about two conflicting approaches to ethics. The two are connected. Murdoch, Anscombe, Foot, and Midgley's struggle to establish themselves was in part a struggle to get a hearing for their ideas.

Over the following nine chapters, I trace the intertwining lives of these four characters: a Bohemian novelist and spiritual seeker; a zealous Catholic convert and mother of seven; an atheistic daughter of privilege; and a stay-at-home mother who finally wrote the first of her 16 books in her 50s. But I also sketch the implicit project I see in their work.

Because the project itself has to be *narrated*. It was an unfolding one, not something these four devised one day over tea in the late 1940s, when they were all back together in Oxford as postgraduates. This is unsurprising, because what they eventually accomplished involved an imaginative leap outside what their contemporaries and predecessors thought. Maybe some great imaginative leaps happen all at once. More commonly, though, as Thomas Kuhn describes and illustrates, people first raise new questions about a dominant paradigm, freeing their audience to consider that it could be wrong; next, others begin to try out alternatives: or perhaps just bits and pieces of alternatives. Only later does it become possible to develop these.[4] The leap outside the picture that captivated philosophers in the first half of the twentieth century—a picture on which facts and values had little to do with one another—was that kind of leap. It was a paradigm shift.

This is the story, then, of four women mapping a route for themselves where none existed. It is the story of sometimes intimate, sometimes fraught friendships among four people with a shared history and shared affection but also profound differences. And it is the story of how four relative outsiders felt their way to a set of controversial insights about the world and how to live in it. Their insights make us seem, perhaps, a little less godlike—but they also put us more in touch with the needy, reflective creatures we are.

ACKNOWLEDGMENTS

It has been a dozen years since I started this project. As Alan Jacobs observes, we don't really think alone. Nor do we work that way. Even writing books, we are social animals. And I have accumulated so many debts.

W. David Solomon, my *Doktorvater* at the University of Notre Dame, was also the first person to recommend each of these philosophers to my attention. It was at his house, on a trip through Indiana in the mid-aughts, that my eye first lighted on Midgley's memoir. I stayed up too late that night reading it. There is much more to say about David's contributions to this book, but he knows. I gesture toward an inexpressible debt by thanking him first.

I was interested in philosophy before I met my undergraduate mentor, John Hare. But he modeled for me what it is to *be* a philosopher, and made me want to be like that. He was magnanimous in encouraging me even as I began to work on a group of thinkers who had steadfastly opposed his beloved father, Richard Hare. Among many other things, he guided me to resources in his father's papers at the Balliol College archives and facilitated a wonderful afternoon's conversation with his mother, Catherine.

Alan Jacobs, when I floated this idea to him in the late aughts, said something like "Well, it's about time someone wrote that book." Which was confirming, since I admire his work. If *he* thought the project worthwhile, then probably I wasn't imagining things. I was gratified, too, to get the same reaction from two leading figures in my guild. When I was first contemplating this book, I Googled "Anscombe Foot Midgley Murdoch" to see what was out there already. Among the top hits was a 2008 blog post by Kieran Setiya, "Unwritten Books." My first thought was, "oh, no." But there was no cause to worry. Kieran was tossing off ideas for books he knew he'd never write, and offering the titles and concepts for appropriation by anyone. He would have titled this book *Oxford's Hypatias*, and said that all he wanted was a line in the acknowledgments and a complimentary copy. In the end, my editor and I preferred the title suggested by Candace Vogler when I mentioned the project to her. But it felt like things coming full circle when I learned that Kieran had done the final review of the manuscript for Oxford.

While I've been at this, I've had significant support from several institutions. I began the project in earnest with a 2010–11 sabbatical leave from Houghton College. I am grateful to my chair at the time, Kristina LaCelle-Peterson, for vigorously supporting my proposal, and to President Shirley Mullen, then-Dean Ron Mahurin, and the then-members of the College's Faculty Development Committee (FDC) and Board of Trustees for approving a whole year's leave rather than the usual one term. I am especially grateful to my colleagues Carlton Fisher and Chris Stewart, whose attitude about the gaps I created by going away was, "we'll figure it out," and to my student assistant at the time, Ed Linnecke, who downloaded and printed for me lots of obscure writings by my subjects and who transcribed my first interview with Mary Midgley. Kristina and the FDC also supported my application for funding to travel to England for archival research and interviews in March 2011. Though it was a grief that

by the time I had this idea, Philippa Foot's health was failing, my visit
to England in 2011 coincided with a memorial symposium in her
honor, at which I met a number of people who became crucial to my
work: in particular, Mary Geach Gormally and Sir Anthony Kenny,
each of whom was more than generous with their time and insight
over the following years. On that same visit, Pam Manix arranged for
me to meet Basil Mitchell, which was an honor and a gift.

In 2012, a National Endowment for the Humanities Summer
Stipend made it possible for me to return to England for six weeks,
which I mostly spent at Somerville College. I was welcomed there
as an Academic Visitor and found everyone keen to help me with
a project so closely connected to the College's history. I especially
want to thank College historian Pauline Adams, Liz Cooke of the
Somerville Association, and Librarian Anne Manuel. Anne in particular dug up lots of interesting documents and invited me to join
her staff for their twice-daily tea breaks. Numerous long-term faculty
made time that summer to talk with me in the Somerville Senior
Common Room: notably Miriam Griffin, Barbara Harvey, and Julie
Jack. More than anyone else at Somerville, I am indebted to Lesley
Brown, Anscombe's student and Foot's literary executor, who spon-
sored my application as an Academic Visitor, making my time at
Oxford possible. During my visit, Mark Rowe and Fanny Mitchell
arranged for me to meet Fanny's mother, Jean Coutts Austin. That
was a precious conversation, and just in time. And I would be remiss
if I didn't mention my landlady in the Jericho neighborhood, Mrs.
Elphick, who, when she was in good spirits, regaled me about the
history of north Oxford and when she wasn't, fumed about the
"second-rateness" overtaking the world. I have tried to work in a
manner she could approve.

Finally (I was speaking of institutions), my alma mater Calvin
College—now Calvin University, though I cannot adjust to it—
invited me to spend several weeks in residence during the summer of

2014. The Philosophy Department set me up in an interior office they call "the windowless monad," and it was, truly, excellent for concentration. I had especially fruitful conversations with Ruth Groenhout and with my former professor Lee Hardy while in Grand Rapids, and gave a talk there that turned into chapter 2.

I had other opportunities to talk and write about my subjects along the way, which helped me start to put my thoughts in order. I first produced a version of chapter 6 for the Houghton College Faculty Lecture Series in late 2011. In 2012, I delivered a *very* early version of chapter 5 at Kingston University, at the biannual conference of the Iris Murdoch Society. In 2014, I was privileged to speak at Notre Dame at a conference in honor of David Solomon, and presented there a version of chapter 7. It was energizing to talk that weekend with so many people who were interested in the same figures and topics—of course they were!—especially my old friend Margaret Watkins and a new acquaintance, Peter Wicks. In 2016, I worked up a version of chapter 3 for an International Women's Day conference at the University of Durham. That event was the inspiration and work of Luna Dozelal, Clare MacCumhaill, and Rachael Wiseman. Clare and Rachael are co-directors of the imaginative and energetic In Parenthesis project, promoting the story and legacy of Anscombe, Foot, Midgley, and Murdoch across a variety of media. They, too, have a book in the works about this quartet, which I am eager to read. Chapter 8 grew out of a contribution to a *Festschrift* for Mary Midgley, *Science and the Self*, edited by Ian Kidd and Liz McKinnell. I am grateful to Ian and Liz for being such excellent editors and to Routledge for allowing republication here of some passages from that book. Finally, at the invitation of Anthony O'Hear (with logistical support from Adam Ferner and James Garvey), I kicked off the Royal Institute of Philosophy's 2018–19 London lecture series with a talk that was a *precís* of this book. Every time I traveled, Houghton College footed the bill.

Many, many people sent me articles or photographs or clippings I could use, or shared their recollections or expertise. Some of these people are acknowledged above, but many more aren't. I fear I am going to miss someone, even now. I am grateful anyway to Cameron Airhart, Jimmy Altham, Heather Bennett, Philip Bess, Justin Broackes, Sarah Broadie, John Campbell, Alister Chapman, Gaby Charing, Anne Chisholm, Gillian Clark, Prophecy Coles, Nicholas Denyer, Gillian Dooley, Paul Dummett, Nat Dyer, Kyla Ebels-Duggan, Joel Ernst, Michael Foot, Elisa Grimi, John Haldane, Jane Heal, Sheila Himsworth, Laura and Walter Hopkins, Lydia Howard, Glyn Hughes, Rosalind Hursthouse, Jennifer Jackson, Louis Jeffries, Ian Johnson, Jessy Jordan, Michael Kremer, Mark LaCelle-Peterson, Anton Leist, Myfanwy Lloyd, Alasdair MacIntyre, Gregory McElwain, David Midgley, Martin Midgley, Rob Miner, Anselm Mueller, André Muller, Madison Murphy, Cari and Josiah Nunziato, Meic Pearse, Michael Regan, Jean-Louis Roederer, Frs. Dominic Ryan and Nicholas Edmonds-Smith, Mark Satta, John Schwenkler, Caleb Seeling, James Stockton, Elijah Tangenberg, Christopher Taylor, Roger Teichmann, Honus Wagner (not that one; the young, Catholic, international-development worker), Brian Webb, Patricia Williams, John Wilson, and a trio of people who helped me begin to concretely imagine Foot's childhood in north Yorkshire: Robert Taylor, Stewart Ramsdale and, above all, Jan Hawthorn. Christopher Coope, John Lucas, Miranda Villiers, and Baroness Mary Warnock were particularly generous, hosting me as well as talking with me. It is painful to reflect that three of those four are now dead. I am glad Christopher at least will get to see the book.

I also owe much to the archivists and librarians who assisted me in my research: Anne Rowe, Frances White, Katie Giles (earlier) and Dayna Miller (more recently) at Kingston University; Jessica Hogg, Fallon Lee, and Louise North at the BBC; Daniel Cheely, Jessica Sweeney, and José Perez-Benzo at the Collegium Institute; Marion

Messenger and Portia White at the British Academy; Andrew Gray at Durham University; and Anne Thomson at Newnham College, Cambridge. At Oxford, I received help from Anna Sander and Bethany Hamblen of Balliol College, Clare White of St. Anne's College, Amanda Ingram of St. Hugh's College, and Colin Harris from the Bodleian Library. I already mentioned Anne Manuel at Somerville College, and am not sorry to do so again. More recently, I benefited a lot also from the sleuthing of Somerville archivist Kate O'Donnell. Finally, David Stevick and Michael Green at the Houghton College library must have spent a disproportionate share of their Inter-Library Loan budget in recent years on my sometimes-obscure requests. I am in their debt, too.

A crowd of friends and colleagues read and commented on proposals, preparatory exercises, and parts of the manuscript in draft. Morgan Flannery commented on various proposals, and John Berkman, Bob Black, Christopher Coope, Christian Esh, Cathy Freytag, Luke and Mary Gormally, Dave and Lori Huth, Sunshine Sullivan, and Abigail Bruxvoort-Wilson read and commented on individual chapters. Four people deserve special thanks for reading *everything*, from proposal to manuscript, and commenting in detail on all of it. Susan Bruxvoort Lipscomb read each chapter aloud before anyone else got to see it. Though my instinct for subordinating clauses runs deep, Susan helped me curb it. If this book is recorded someday, it will read (and play) a lot better because of her. Susan's and my dear friends Anna Schilke and Brad Wilber read and commented on everything, too. Each of them is a skilled writer (watch for *their* books in future!) but, more than that, each of them has a gift for combining encouragement with honest critique. The final draft is so much stronger thanks to their suggestions. The fourth person who read and responded to the whole is my editor, Lucy Randall.

I owe Lucy for more than just reading and commenting on my work. In early 2020, with the publishing world (like everything) in disarray, Lucy took a chance on an author without a platform, writing his first book. Then, that summer, she bent her usual procedure and gave me comments on each chapter as it reached her like the installments of a Victorian serial. It was hugely reassuring to know that she thought the work was on track. I am grateful for her flexibility in guiding someone writing in a new genre. I should say too: I owe Rob Tempio of Princeton University Press for suggesting that I show my proposal to Lucy.

You have no idea until you write a book like this how very many nuisance jobs must be done to bring it to publication. The stress of all this was greatly reduced because of the patient professionalism of Lucy's assistant, Hannah Doyle, and that of my own temporary assistant, Katherine Stevick. The pandemic left this exceptionally sharp, detail-oriented person improbably unemployed, and she took on a host of things that would have crushed me to think about. Katherine pursued permissions, assembled my bibliography and index, drafted abstracts, and more. Hannah for her part answered I-don't-know-how-many emails from Katherine and me. I am indebted too to the reviewers Lucy arranged for my initial proposal and final manuscript. I was delighted when one of the initial reviewers outed himself: Midgley scholar Gregory McElwain. I wrote above of my delight in learning that Kieran Setiya had reviewed the manuscript for the Press, but did not say how appreciative I was of his encouraging and probing comments. I was and am.

There are two people whose contributions to this book refuse to be categorized. One is Peter Conradi, Iris Murdoch's authorized biographer, who agreed early on to meet with me, gave me dozens of anecdotes and impressions lying *outside* his 700-page account of Murdoch's life, pointed me toward important sources, and checked in regularly to see how I was doing. Later, he read and commented on several chapters. Graduate school in philosophy is no preparation for life-writing, and as Peter knew so much about the biographer's art and about my subjects, I appealed to him at every turn: about publishers, about style, about how to conduct interviews and manage my burgeoning files, about how to handle some of the less-flattering things you turn up about any human being, even one you admire. If you haven't read Peter's *Iris*, and this book intrigues you: do.

Then there is Mary Midgley, the only one of my subjects who lived long enough for me to talk with her. I said more about Mary in the Preface, so here I will just add, I was so glad to know her.

Every substantial book by a person with a family acknowledges their contributions, or at least their longsuffering patience. If it doesn't, it should. Books are jealous of their authors' attention, and people are finite. Maybe there are writers who can get a lot done without accepting gifts of time from their loved ones. I couldn't. So I express my gratitude and love to Susan, Josephine, Ernest, and Ralph, who dealt with my being away in England for a couple of stretches in the early teens, with my missing a family trip to Idaho in 2014, and with my being out in the backyard cabin day after day through the final push in the summer of 2020, and then again for a string of days in early 2021. Susan has her own scholarship to pursue, about George Eliot and empathy and models of the natural world in literature, but she dedicated a summer and more to helping me bring this project to completion. I don't know whether Iris Murdoch endorsed what Bradley Pearson writes early in *The Black Prince*: "Writing is like getting married. One should never commit oneself until one is amazed at one's luck." But it fits my experience both of this book and of my marriage.

My parents and Susan's parents took our children sometimes, so that (for instance) Susan could come visit me in Oxford for our 15th anniversary. And they asked and asked and asked how the book was going, whether I was making progress, whether I'd found a publisher. So did my grandmother Barbara Lipscomb, who was of the same generation as Anscombe, Foot, Midgley, and Murdoch. She was looking forward to reading the book, or to having it read to her. She died the day I finished the last chapter. And so I dedicate the book to her memory, and to three other colorful, sharp, imaginative, opinionated Lipscomb women: my mother Mary, my wife Susan, and my daughter Josephine. *Sine qua non.*

A NOTE ON NAMES

I decided early in the writing process that I should use last names to refer to my subjects. It is an old dilemma. Iris Murdoch, writing to her producer at the BBC about a talk she was preparing on the French mystical writer Simone Weil, asked, "Is it too matey to call her Simone?"[5] First names could make my subjects seem more vivid as characters, and would sidestep the problem of married and unmarried names. But in consultation with people I trust, I decided it *was* too matey, at least for me. That left me with the problem of changing names. Elizabeth Anscombe, Philippa Foot, Mary Midgley, and Iris Murdoch all married, but Anscombe and Murdoch kept their unmarried names—not only professionally but also in private life. Both Foot and Midgley, however, took their husbands' last names. As this group biography reaches back to my subjects' university years and even their childhoods, I knew Foot would have to be Bosanquet before 1945 and Midgley would have to be Scrutton before 1950. I hope to forestall confusion by highlighting this here. One last word on this topic: I *do* use first names in one particular (but recurring) context. I use them whenever writing about one of my subjects and her mother or father or husband, or about her mother *and* father— any two people sharing a last name. I switch then to first names.

A NOTE TO AMERICAN READERS

A diverting instance of how Americans and Brits are "divided by a common language" is the differing terminology they use to talk about formal—especially higher—education. On top of some general differences in terms, Oxford has a vocabulary all its own, which will be unknown to some readers. I have prepared a short glossary, then, so that readers who find themselves puzzling over a term can flip back to remind themselves what it means.

College in Oxford usage refers to one of the constituent, semi-autonomous institutions that make up the University. The University of Oxford is the sum of its dozens of colleges, plus some facilities and administrative offices that serve them all. In the mid-twentieth century, Oxford's colleges were considerably more autonomous than they are today. Still today, though, a student wishing to study at Oxford applies to and is accepted by a college or colleges, and faculty too are affiliated with particular colleges, though some carry university-wide responsibilities. Though students are sometimes sent out for instruction ("tutoring"—see below) to faculty from colleges other than their own, the usual thing is for a student to be taught mainly by her college's own faculty. Elizabeth Anscombe was an alumna of St. Hugh's College.

First (or *second*, or . . .) is short for "X-class degree" or "X-class marks." In final degree examinations at Oxford, students are placed in numerically descending classes based on the quality of their exam performance. Getting a first (at a university full of very bright people) is a mark of particular distinction, both for the individual and for her college and tutors.

Going up means matriculating at Oxford (or Cambridge). Iris Murdoch and Mary Midgley went up to Oxford (or even just "went up") in 1939. The reciprocal term is "went down." They went down in 1942. If people get into trouble at Oxford and are suspended or expelled, they are *sent* down (or, in a revealing usage, "rusticated").

Greats is a synecdoche for Oxford's four-year, two-part degree course in what is generally known as classics. Strictly speaking, "Greats" refers only to the second half of the course, but is commonly used as a shorthand for the whole. Greats is a longer course than most (most Oxford degrees take three years). The full title is "Honour Moderations [or 'Honour Mods,' or just 'Mods'] and Greats." (The *formal* title is Latin: *Literae humaniores*, "more humane letters.") At the time my subjects were at Oxford, the first part of the course (taking slightly under two years) was focused on classical languages and literature, while the second part (taking slightly over two years) was focused on ancient history and ancient and modern philosophy. The curriculum has become more flexible in recent years.

Michaelmas, Hilary, and *Trinity* are the three terms in the Oxford academic calendar. Michaelmas term runs from mid-October to mid-December, Hilary term from mid-January to mid-March, and Trinity term from late April to late June.

Paper refers to a written examination, whether for entrance or a degree. Philippa Foot revised (not "reviewed" or "studied") for her logic paper (among others) at the end of her undergraduate career.

PPE is short for Philosophy, Politics, and Economics, a multidisciplinary degree introduced at Oxford in the 1920s.

Professor has historically meant something different in the United Kingdom (and elsewhere in Europe) than in the United States. In the United States, it refers to any fully credentialed, established member of the faculty of a college or university (in traditional Oxbridge lingo, a "don"). UK usage is shifting, but during the careers of my subjects, "Professor" meant the holder of one of the few most distinguished positions at a university, carrying not just higher pay and prestige but different responsibilities than those shouldered by other faculty. Such positions often bear the name either of the donor who endowed them or of some especially distinguished former holder of the professorship. Elizabeth Anscombe was Professor of Philosophy at Cambridge University from 1970 until her retirement.

Reading is the British equivalent of the American "majoring in." Philippa Foot read PPE at Oxford.

School refers to pre-university education, or to an institution providing this. So, Iris Murdoch went to Badminton School, and Lady Anne Piper was one of Mary Midgley's school friends at Downe House. At the time, they were schoolgirls. One more point: "public schools" in the United Kingdom are a set of especially distinguished, wealthy *private* schools that have long served as funnels toward Oxford and Cambridge (they are "public" in that they do not draw solely from the children of a particular parish, religious denomination, or profession). Richard Hare attended Rugby, one of the most famous public schools.

Schools (short for "Examination Schools") refers to a building on High Street ("the High") in Oxford where many lecture courses are given during term, but can also refer to the degree examinations conducted there. The building takes its name from this function.

Tutorial system (or, "tutorial and examination system") refers to the distinctive pedagogical system of the Universities of Cambridge and Oxford, where it evolved. Term by term, students are assigned to tutors in the various subfields compassed by their degree examinations. In (standardly) one-hour, once-a-week sessions with each of their tutors, students present short essays they have written on reading the tutor has assigned and receive live critique of their work. These are often small-group sessions, but can be one-on-one. In preparing for degree examinations, then, students examine some texts intensively with their tutors, but also attend lectures in which faculty from across the University give broad overviews of material beyond what students can cover in tutorials. A student's examination papers are read by faculty other than her tutors, exerting quality control.

Viva is short for *viva voce* ("live oral") examination, a follow-up examination that used to be required when a student's examination papers did not make unarguably clear what class she should be in. Iris Murdoch received a first without a *viva*.

Chapter 1

Facts and Values

They say to me, how can you bear to be alive if everything is so cold and empty and pointless? Well, at an academic level I think it is—but that doesn't mean you can live your life like that.

—Richard Dawkins, in *The Guardian*, October 3, 1998

NOTHING THE SAME

It was the newsreels that broke her open.

September 1945. The war was over, really over, at last. Philippa Foot and her husband Michael had been in London through VJ Day, but now they were back in the place that felt most like home to Philippa: Oxford. If they had been hedging in their minds about the future, not wanting to hope too much or too quickly—it was all right now.[1]

They had married as soon as their autumn plans had come together: a Midsummer's Day ceremony at the Caxton Hall register office in Westminster. Philippa's Oxford roommate Anne Cobbe stood up for her. It wasn't the grand wedding her parents would have chosen for their daughter, but in the desperate excitement of looking forward again, no one judged. And why wait? Philippa could only get so much time off during her final months at Chatham House, and—frail though he still was—there was no guarantee Michael wouldn't have to report for a final stint in Army Intelligence before being demobilized. They had a brief honeymoon in the West Country and a short working holiday in Oxfordshire—Philippa teaching a Workers Educational Association summer course—before returning to London to wait out the summer, to pack, to think ahead. And now here they were: in a little eighteenth-century house just outside the New College walls. It was supposedly where Halley lived when he discovered his comet. Home.

The preceding year had been a sickening, exhilarating ride: Michael captured in France in August 1944; escaping only to be brutally retaken, sustaining a broken skull and spine; exchanged to the Allies months later, his survival far from certain. But survive he did, and he and Philippa were finally reunited in late February, Philippa nursing him slowly back to health at his flat a few blocks east of Victoria station. As it began to be possible to think beyond the war, Philippa began inquiring about a discharge from her post so she and Michael could return to Oxford. In 1942, she had been offered a place as a graduate student at her undergraduate college, Somerville; the offer stood. And Michael could finish his interrupted degree.

That spring, as Michael was rebuilding his strength—practically relearning to walk—Philippa was doing four things at once: her day job, assisting a research group on postwar economic reconstruction; caring for Michael; applying for scholarships; planning for their wedding and beyond. They were aware—the whole country was—of the first newspaper pictures and newsreel footage from the Nazi concentration camps. But their minds and days were so full, they had no time for what a growing chorus was calling a moral duty: confronting the images from Buchenwald and Bergen-Belsen.

The cultural impact of the first newsreels from the concentration camps was seismic. Nothing remotely like this had been shown to the British public since the aftermath of the Great War. The Ministry of Information had not permitted publication of graphic images during the war, to safeguard morale but also to maintain public trust. The memory of Great War propaganda about the "Rape of Belgium"—and the skepticism it later provoked—remained sharp. In the case of the footage from the camps, there was even discussion among journalists of whether it could be real. The sources on the ground were authoritative, but: could the Nazis possibly have done *this*?[2]

To forestall disbelief, the British government sent a politically diverse delegation of parliamentarians to Buchenwald on April 21. Most never fully recovered from the experience. Footage from the delegation's visit was the source for all the newsreel coverage that came out at the end of April—the most powerful of which was the Pathé production, *German Atrocities*, narrated by Conservative MP Mavis Tate. The authentication provided by images of Tate and other MPs, together with the empathetic connection she and the camera operators encouraged between inmates and viewers (they are "as you and I," Tate said with emphasis) resulted not in disbelief but in a generation-shaping experience. "Do believe me," she said, "when I tell you that the reality was indescribably worse than these pictures." And viewers did. Though some cinema proprietors worried that people would not stay past the newsreels after viewing such horrific content, they did not suffer economically from showing it. There were queues down the block for weeks. And the newsreels remained in circulation far longer than the usual few days. Hermione, Countess of Ranfurly, saw the footage in London in mid-July, two-and-a-half months after its initial release. Her reaction is typical of many recorded in the popular press and in Mass Observation diaries at the time: "Incredibly horrible. Beyond our wildest imaginations of atrocity and evil. I had to come out before the end I was so upset."[3]

But between VE Day celebrations in London, honeymoon planning, and preparing for the return to Oxford, Philippa didn't look at the images of the camps—*really look* at them, as her friend Iris Murdoch would say—until she and Michael were settled in their new lodgings. Then one day she too went to the cinema and took in the piles of bodies, the remains charred in ovens or tangled in electrified wire, the emaciated survivors stumbling around in a daze, the adolescents clutching the bowls of thin soup they'd been given, flinching instinctively as anyone approached. Like so many others, she emerged in shock.

She went afterward to Keble College to see her mentor, Donald MacKinnon. There was no one whose counsel she valued more highly. They had met routinely on her visits to Oxford since 1943. Now she and he sat across from one another again, he in his battered armchair, she in the better one, reserved for pupils and guests. He never had difficulty letting silence linger, and he let it linger now. She said, "Nothing is ever going to be the same again." He looked back at her. "No. Nothing is ever going to be the same."[4]

As they spoke, and as she walked the gloomy passageway back from MacKinnon's rooms in one of Keble's neo-Gothic towers, Philippa Foot was coming to a resolution. She was interested in lots of things. In her renewed application to Somerville, she'd sketched a project titled, "The Idea of Substance in Locke and Kant." But now there was something she wanted to say about ethics, too.

Nothing in the moral philosophy of her time was adequate to what she'd just seen. And if philosophy was to have any point, it had to be able to speak to that horror.

FACTS AND OPINIONS

The trouble with the moral philosophy of Foot's time—though she didn't have words for this yet—was that it was in thrall to a picture, a questionable picture of what's real and unreal. The picture is one that goes back centuries in the modern Western imagination: back to the early-modern period and the scientific revolution. It had been given especially clear and forceful expression in the interwar years by a group of Austrian intellectuals calling themselves the Vienna Circle—and by a young Oxford don who went to Vienna and came back with the zeal of a convert. And it has not faded away. It is all around us: the dichotomy between facts and values.

Every three years, the Organization for Economic Cooperation and Development sponsors an assessment of educational outcomes in 79 countries. The most recent results, from the 2018 assessment, were released at the end of 2019. The results are examined from every angle by participant countries, looking for grounds to celebrate or to reform. One detail from the latest assessment, though, generated an unusual amount of attention, under headlines like: "Only 9% of 15-year-olds can distinguish between fact and opinion."[5] *Forbes*, *The New York Times*, and other high-profile publications ran fretful pieces, highlighting the result. The nine-percent figure is an international average. In the United Kingdom and United States, students fared somewhat better: 11.5 percent and 13.5 percent, respectively. The distinction is, after all, routinely taught in their schools. But it is evidently hard to teach effectively. Perhaps the problem isn't with students or teachers, but with the distinction.

As typically presented in lesson plans and on handouts (many of which are available online), the concept of a fact fuses truth and verifiability. "A fact refers to something true or real, which is backed by evidence, documentation, etc." "A fact is something that is true, real information. It can be proven." Note: "fact" is a "success term." There are no false facts, however compelling the evidence. Facts are true, by definition.[6]

Other widely circulating definitions vary little from these. Some tie facts to "objective reality" or assert that facts are not debatable. But these seem to be elaborations on the definitions already given. To say that facts are objectively real is to say that they are (1) true and (2) can be confirmed by different observers, despite their differences. They are like *objects*, there to be seen.

There is more variety among definitions of the contrast term, "opinion." Opinions, some authors say, are matters of feeling: "an opinion is an expression of a person's feelings that cannot be proven." Sometimes, though, they speak instead of "personal belief" or a "personal view" or a "perception." But there is a shared thought across these definitions: opinions are expressions of subjectivity, the distinctive perspectives of individuals. Opinions, more than one author writes, are expressions of "bias." This contrasts with the objectivity, the perspective-independence, of facts.[7]

Where did the distinction come from?

A distinction between differently credentialed thoughts—grades of belief—goes back to Plato at least. The fact/opinion distinction, though, is more recent. It emerged in the interwar years in America, in connection with a new movement to promote "critical thinking" as part of responsible citizenship. Critical thinking was supposed to be a shield against advertising and propaganda—a newly salient concern after the experience of the first World War and especially after the appearance of Edward Bernays' cheerfully amoral how-to manuals,

Crystallizing Public Opinion (1923) and *Propaganda* (1928). Drawing on his experiences producing wartime and postwar propaganda for the United States—and on the theoretical apparatus of Walter Lippman's 1922 *Public Opinion*—Bernays set himself up as the first public-relations consultant. In his books, he explained how groups can be manipulated by leading them to associate products or organizations with psychologically potent symbols. (It is perhaps relevant that he was Sigmund Freud's nephew twice over.) The books were arresting, attractive, shocking. They demanded a response. Educators and educational theorists complied.

In 1940, Horace Morse and George McCune first published their "Selected Items for the Testing of Study Skills," later retitled "Selected Items for the Testing of Study Skills and Critical Thinking."[8] Among other things, this instrument asked students to distinguish facts from opinions. It may have been the first of its kind; it was certainly the first to become influential. The linkage between the fact/opinion distinction and critical thought remains in fact-versus-opinion lessons today, even when the words "critical thinking" aren't used: "[I]t is . . . imperative that students are able to unravel the threads of what is true from what is mere belief if they are to successfully navigate the deluge of media they will encounter in their lifetimes. Whether on the news, in advertising, or a history book, distinguishing between what is fact and what is opinion is crucial to becoming an autonomous person with the critical abilities necessary to avoid being manipulated easily."[9] To be able to distinguish opinion from fact is to be ready for responsible citizenship. To mistake opinion for fact is to be duped, to take smoke and mirrors—spin, propaganda—for reality.

There is an obvious point to such a distinction. In a polarized and manipulative media environment (nothing new under the sun), there is clear value in teaching people to seek and identify shareable starting points—claims that opposed parties can be reasonably expected to acknowledge—and to distinguish these from plausible conjectures, competing interpretations, and outright propaganda.[10] However difficult to achieve—in courtrooms, in journalism, or in live debate—greater objectivity is a valid goal.

The fact/opinion distinction as usually presented to children, though, is a bundle of confusions. For starters, neither part of the definition of "fact" is actually used as a criterion by children doing their exercises. Recall, facts are standardly defined as truths (1) that can be proven (2). The "truths" part of that definition is idle, though, because the only way to assess what's true is by considering grounds for believing it. There is no such thing as verifying a claim and *then* checking to see if it's true. So truth isn't really a criterion. The real criterion is verifiability. Or it should be.

Curriculum authors seldom say much about what counts as adequate verification. Perhaps this is wise, as anything they said would embroil them in old and difficult debates. Is a philosophical argument verification? How about a mathematical proof? Inference to the simplest explanation? Encouraging early experimental results? The testimony of a trustworthy witness? Anything they said about this would inevitably count as, well, opinion. So just as with truth, these authors make no real use of the idea of verification, turning instead to linguistic tests that distinguish fact-type statements from non-fact-type statements by the kinds of adjectives they use. So children aren't taught to consider the merits of claims, but to judge them by how they are expressed.[11]

This brings us to the tests themselves. Numerous authors supply helpful lists of "clue words" or "indicator words" that readers can use to distinguish facts and opinions in the field—like guidebooks for birders. One tells children to watch for adjectives related to "quantity, size, age, shape, color, origin, material"—"information about something that can be proven." These are the marks of the common fact. The wild opinion, by contrast, may be recognized by these signs: adjectives like "beautiful," "ugly," "best," "worst," "expensive," "tired," "yummy," or "gross." All describe "how you feel about something."[12] Or here's another, even more revealing list of "clue words" for opinion statements: "should, think, best, worst, good, right, wrong, better, believe, feel, character trait words." Looking at these lists, and at the sorting exercises that accompany them, it is clear the conclusion children are supposed to draw. Lesson plans often start out with easy samples, to help students pick up the distinction. Opinions are statements like, "the sun is pretty," "the cake was delicious," or "Friday is the best day of the week." But the application is plain: any evaluative statement is an opinion, no matter how well-grounded: "Abraham Lincoln was eloquent"; "She's in better shape than I am"; "It is wrong to deliberately kill the innocent."

To believe this, though, is to believe that there is no point in reasoning about evaluative matters—conflating distinctions between well-grounded and poorly grounded, evaluative and non-evaluative, real and unreal. To believe this is to be captive to a picture. On this picture, judgments of good and bad, better and worse, should and shouldn't, right and wrong, are all mere subjective responses, like appetite or nausea. (No one reasons about whether their nausea is well-grounded.)[13] On this picture, nothing counts as getting an evaluation right, because there's nothing for evaluations to get right. On this picture, values can never be facts.

THE BILLIARD-BALL UNIVERSE

This is the picture Foot was resisting, not yet realizing what it was, as she tried to process what she had seen at the cinema. Again, it is an old picture, first emerging in the early-modern period.

It began with the transition in early-modern natural philosophy (or, as we now call it, "science"), away from Aristotle's picture of the natural world. Aristotle too had a "picture" in the sense in which I'm using the word: a set of background assumptions, seldom explicitly formulated, that shapes and constrains our intellectual imagination.[14] To bend the metaphor slightly, pictures like this frame our thought.

As scientists and historians alike are starting to appreciate, Aristotle was an empirical researcher of the first rank.[15] But he thought very differently about the order of nature than moderns reflexively do. We tend to think and frame our theories in terms of inert material bodies acted on by outside forces. Our paradigm, since the early-modern period, has been billiard balls on a table. Aristotle, by contrast, was a biologist first to last. Even when doing what he called physics (by which he meant the study of nature in general; *physis* means "nature"), and especially when doing ethics or political science, he thought in terms of organisms, like plants.

Plants too are material bodies. But the material is *alive*. It begins as a seed or an embryo and then, if conditions are right, it develops in a self-directed way until it reaches maturity and reproduces itself. Eventually it diminishes and dies, and its material is incorporated into other living beings. Lots of things can interrupt the process along the way. But that's the normal progression: what will happen, if (as we still say) "nature takes its course." Impressed with the explanatory power of this pattern, Aristotle generalized it and used it to interpret all natural phenomena: everything in nature, he thought, is somewhere along an arc of self-directed development from immaturity to maturity to senescence to death. He thus says that heavy bodies are trying to reach the center of the earth—which sounds absurd to modern ears. (We still say, "the plant is reaching toward the sun," which doesn't sound absurd. We are still thus far Aristotelians.) Aristotle's natural philosophy is a case study in a compelling pattern of explanation being turned into a paradigm. To a man with a hammer, the proverb goes, everything looks like a nail. To Aristotle, after grasping the pattern of a self-directed life cycle, everything looked somewhat like a tomato plant.

The picture increasingly adopted by the natural philosophers of the sixteenth and seventeenth centuries, and handed down to us, is very different. It pictures material reality—the stuff of this world—as inert, not directing itself anywhere or trying to achieve anything. It sits motionless (or continues in its present motion) until something external imparts energy to it—like a cue stick striking a billiard ball. The world is matter in motion, impelled from without by external forces.

There were multiple motives for the formation of the new picture. There was, first, the suffocating orthodoxy of late-medieval and early-modern university culture, which had long since abandoned the fearless disputation and visionary system-building of a Thomas Aquinas in favor of unquestioning defense of a few approved texts—including, ironically, Thomas's own.[16]

But resentment at oppressive university cultures was not the only motive to reevaluate Aristotle's authority. There was also the European discovery of the Americas. This immediately rendered every world map obsolete. But just as importantly, it turned up biological and anthropological phenomena unknown to Aristotle and his medieval followers, making everything these authors had written seem parochial. What authority could a philosopher have, whose theories took no account of the New World? Meanwhile, Gutenberg's press lowered the barriers to authors putting their ideas before readers and lowered the barriers to readers having a look. With the moveable-type press spewing out hundreds of millions of volumes in the sixteenth century alone, the cacophony of new voices was impossible to ignore. Michel de Montaigne's reaction in the late sixteenth century is emblematic: "What do I know?" he asked. (Precious little, he concluded.) Under these conditions, fewer and fewer intellectuals were willing to put their faith in an author who had been dead for nearly two thousand years. An *anti*-Aristotelianism began to take hold among Europe's intellectual elite, equal and opposite to the dogmatic Aristotelianism of the universities. A vacuum was created, for new pictures to fill.[17]

As the intellectuals of Europe abandoned its universities, where did they go? For this partly explains the picture they embraced. These were men of the world, mostly: diplomats, doctors, the leisured rich, soldiers of fortune. Many were, like the artists of the high Renaissance and the Baroque, under the patronage of queens, kings, and lesser nobles. Many, too, began to band together in informal societies outside the universities to share and test their ideas. Even when they did not explicitly organize, they were better known to one another than any group of innovators could have been in an earlier age, thanks to the culture of print.

These worldly figures readily embraced Bacon's dictum that knowledge is power. From their positions close to power, they saw knowledge as a way of manipulating the world to human ends, "for the . . . relief of man's estate."[18] If one wishes to manipulate the world, matters are simpler if the world is not bent on fulfilling its own, conflicting ends. But there are clearer motives to the new, "mechanical" picture of nature in an idea we encountered earlier, looking at fact-versus-opinion lessons: objectivity.

In the cacophony of voices that was the new culture of print, some reacted like Montaigne: with a genial skepticism toward all the competing claims being urged on them like samples at a farmer's market. But for men of the world seeking power, or for those like Descartes who simply shared Aristotle's desire to understand? Skepticism was unsatisfactory. They sought instead a means—a method—for transcending conflicting impressions and interpretations: a method for attaining objectivity.

It is a familiar thought that the method of hypothesis and experiment helps us pursue objectivity. When different observers replicate one another's results, they bring us nearer to descriptions of the world that are not perspective-dependent: descriptions that can be shared by all. If lots of observers, from lots of perspectives, see the same thing, that suggests that it's there for anyone to see—that it's objectively real.

But this was a thought with momentum. If one's aim is to produce perspective-independent descriptions of the world, why not try to eliminate the human perspective entirely, describing the world in ways that make no reference to how things look or sound or smell or taste or feel—to anyone? One might, say, identify features of the world that correlate with and seem to prompt color perceptions—is this dress blue and black or gold and white?—but which can be described without reference to color. This was the next step in objectivity: striving to eliminate human subjectivity entirely, describing the world in ways that would make sense to intelligent bats.

So early-modern natural philosophers, starting with Galileo, embarked on a program of banishing from scientific discourse references to qualitative aspects of human experience: colors, flavors, smells, sounds, and so forth. They began to distinguish such "secondary qualities" from "primary qualities" (number, shape, size, position, motion) and to try to produce descriptions of the world entirely in terms of the latter. What these primary qualities have in common, besides being less directly and obviously tied to sensation, is that they are readily quantifiable. Thus the ideal of mathematization joined the ideal of experimentation and that of applying science for the relief of the human estate, all three tied in different ways to the overriding ideal of objectivity—a leading theme in Shakespeare's great tragedies, the obsession of the age.*

What does this have to do with ethics, though—with values? Just this: whether they intended it or not (Bacon, anyway, seems to have welcomed the result), proponents of the distinction between primary and secondary qualities ended up excluding more than just colors and smells from the language of science. They also excluded all talk of purposive movement, of natural goal-directedness, of nature taking its course (or having one).

The result was overdetermined. As we've seen, a whole generation of intellectuals had become reflexively anti-Aristotelian. In 1686, Leibniz—like a democratic socialist in McCarthy's America—felt the need to defend his integrity after making the least use of an Aristotelian notion, protesting that he was not an obscurantist, that he had "devoted much time to experiments in physics and to the demonstrations of geometry...."[19] But nothing was more intimately associated with Aristotle's thought than natural teleology (goal-directedness). Moreover, goal-directedness was hard to capture in the now-preferred language of mathematics. It's difficult framing a mathematical description of billiard balls moving about on a table. The thing is possible, though, with enough ingenuity (and especially with the aid of the new calculus). But a mathematical description of

---

* Consider how Othello and Lear both come to disaster when subjective biases lead them to misinterpret what they see and hear: Othello through jealousy, Lear through a pusillanimous hunger for affirmation. Or how Hamlet sets up an experiment to determine if he should trust the apparition he saw on the ramparts of Elsinore. Or how Macbeth, once he embarks on his campaign of murder, is too blinded by fear and ambition to seriously question his interpretation of the witches' prophecy. The same theme is present in *Romeo and Juliet, Much Ado About Nothing,* and elsewhere.

a bunch of entities striving toward their cross-cutting goals, which they will achieve to the extent that conflicts and unforeseen accidents don't occur? It's not that you couldn't use numbers to describe such a scene. (Contemporary social scientists do.) But the Aristotelian picture is far more resistant to mathematization. Meanwhile, a thrilling prospect had come into view, thanks to the work of Galileo, Kepler, and others: the prospect of a comprehensive mathematical description of nature. This description excluded talk of natural goals and purposes.

This created two problems for ethics. First, the received theory of ethics was Aristotle's, and it was bound up with his picture of the natural world. According to Aristotle, there is an ideal for human life, a state in which we realize our natural potential. The task of ethics is to describe this ideal as far as possible (Aristotle himself says that precise mathematical representation of the ideal is impossible). Having grasped the ideal, rational animals can direct themselves toward it. In the prevailing anti-Aristotelian atmosphere of the early-modern period, that theory, with its attendant vocabulary of virtues (qualities that help people realize the ideal) and vices (qualities that frustrate its realization), was no longer acceptable and had to be replaced by something new.[20]

At a deeper level, the exclusion of goal-directedness from the new picture of nature made the task of replacing Aristotle's ethics daunting—maybe even impossible. On the new picture, the world consists of inert matter. For simplicity's sake (that is, for the sake of mathematization), this matter is treated as all-of-a-kind. It is a world of gobs of undifferentiated stuff, moving or altering its movement only in response to impulsion from without. Varying quantities and arrangements of this stuff are set in a field (the universe), where they occasionally collide and transfer energy to one another according to invariant, mathematically representable laws. Value is not part of this description of the world.

I said earlier that Aristotle made a paradigm—a picture—of his favorite explanatory pattern. He looked at the movements of the heavens or a falling stone and saw the same sort of process at work as in the life cycle of a tomato plant. Early moderns, reacting against all things Aristotelian and desperately seeking objectivity in a context of endemic pluralism, came up with a new pattern of explanation: billiard balls, the lawlike interaction of inert bodies in space. Like Aristotle's pattern, this analogy had tremendous explanatory power. Whatever simplifications it involved, it brought astonishing clarity to human understanding in astronomy, in physics generally, and beyond. Kepler's judgment was bold but understandable when he wrote that God had waited 6000 years for someone to perceive His work.[21]

Moderns, too, made a paradigm out of their new pattern. To a man with a hammer, everything looks like a nail. It is an easy transition from "this is a helpful pattern of explanation" to "this is an all-competent pattern of explanation." Likewise, it is an easy transition from "I have excluded flavors from my descriptions of nature" to "flavors are not part of nature." As powerful and fruitful as the new pattern was, and as excited as European intellectuals became about it, it was understandable that they would come to equate the elements of a deliberately simplified description of nature with what nature *really* is.

Just as it was always a stretch making Aristotle's pattern cover the movements of the heavens, it has been a stretch making the pattern that emerged during the modern scientific revolution cover plant and animal life, and especially the lives of human beings: their psychology, their politics. But set that thought aside. My immediate point is this: moderns took their pattern for a paradigm. They took their theoretical simplification for reality. When they had done that, then value became something unreal. A picture began to emerge.

THE DAWKINS SUBLIME

The epigraph to this chapter is a quote from evolutionary biologist and popular science writer Richard Dawkins. It is a crystalline expression of the picture Foot needed to escape.

The picture was not quite complete at the end of the seventeenth century. Most of its elements were in place, but one more was needed to give it the power it would exert on Foot and her contemporaries. It is a picture that remains potent today in the Western imagination. But as is characteristic of such pictures, it typically operates below the level of conscious affirmation. As Charles Taylor puts it, "we have trouble often thinking ourselves outside of [such pictures], even as an imaginative exercise," precisely because they are the background to our thought.[22] Indeed, this picture can be *especially* difficult for those captive to it to recognize as a picture. That is because this picture includes the idea that it is not a picture, that people who think in terms of this picture have forsworn all pictures and are simply confronting reality as it is. I call this conceit "the Dawkins sublime."

Only a few years after the 1748 discovery of the remains of Pompeii, Edmund Burke gave a name to the aesthetic experience many Europeans had, contemplating Pompeii's final hours. Why was it so fascinating? Why did it become such an arresting subject for engravers and poets? Strangely but truly, the contemplation of something overwhelming, even horrifying—something lethally powerful and hard to wrap one's mind around—can produce . . . pleasure? Not, of course, if one is directly exposed to the power of whatever it is. But if one is merely contemplating it and not in immediate danger? Consider the characteristic thrill many people feel looking down from a cliff edge (not clinging to a root, but from behind a wall!), or looking out into a blizzard from inside a warm cabin, or looking at magazine pictures of the wreck of the Titanic strewn across the Atlantic seabed, under the crushing weight of two miles of black water. People seek out these experiences. Burke labeled this phenomenon—both the emotional reaction and the objects that provoke it—"the sublime." Here is how he articulates it: "Whatever is fitted in any sort to excite the ideas of pain, and danger, that is to say, whatever is in any sort terrible, or is conversant about terrible objects, or operates in a manner analogous to terror, is a source of the sublime; that is, it is productive of the strongest emotion which the mind is capable of feeling."[23]

It is hard to know how much the late eighteenth century's and early nineteenth century's hunger for the sublime—in gothic novels, in the art of Joseph Wright of Derby (who produced more than 30 paintings of Vesuvius), in Hector Berlioz's *Symphonie Fantastique*, and so on—was prompted by having a word for it. Whether Burke was shaping the *Zeitgeist* or carried along by it, this much is clear: the sublime was one of the principal aesthetic preoccupations of the next several generations. And throughout the nineteenth century, as Westerners came to terms with new developments in geology and biology, the universe at large came to seem to many like the ruins of Pompeii: sublime. Westerners began to describe in elevated if melancholy terms the human condition in a lethal and indifferent universe. Alfred Tennyson was crying out in grief when he gave these words to personified Sorrow:

"The stars," she whispers, "blindly run;
A web is wov'n across the sky;
From out waste places comes a cry,
And murmurs from the dying sun;

And all the phantom, Nature, stands—
With all the music in her tone,

A hollow echo of my own,—
A hollow form with empty hands."[24]

The rest of *In Memoriam* traces Tennyson's re-ascent from those depths. But this passage articulates the remaining feature needed to complete the picture I am talking about.

Note the language: blindness, death, hollowness, emptiness. This vocabulary, endlessly repeated by authors from the nineteenth century onward, became a trope. The world is cold, pitiless, bereft. But however grim it sounds, we are also recognizably in the domain of the sublime: there is exaltation in beholding the bleakness of it all, or in having steeled oneself to look without flinching. Here is Matthew Arnold:

"Ah, love, let us be true
To one another! for the world, which seems
To lie before us like a land of dreams,
So various, so beautiful, so new,
Hath really neither joy, nor love, nor light,
Nor certitude, nor peace, nor help for pain . . . ."[25]

It is comprehensible that people would take comfort in one another in the face of a gloomy prospect. It is comprehensible too, especially for graduates of the type of public school that both Tennyson and Arnold attended, that ideas of bravery and manly self-mastery would become associated with views like this. Thus Steven Jay Gould: "[I]t's a tough life and if you can delude yourself into thinking that there's . . . some warm fuzzy meaning to it all, it's enormously comforting."[26] Some of us, though, are man enough not to delude ourselves. Partly on these grounds, bravery and self-mastery have become powerfully associated with scientific inquiry in the modern imagination.

There is a tension in such views, though. Take Arnold's lines: "Ah, love, let us be true/To one another! for the world, which seems/To lie before us like a land of dreams,/ . . . Hath really neither joy, nor love, nor light . . . ." Ah love, let us love one another, for there really is no love. Either the speaker and his beloved are exempted from the general picture of the world he is presenting, or he is contradicting himself. So too in the Dawkins quote at the outset. How can he bear to go on, he says people ask him, "if everything is so cold and empty and pointless?" Conceding that that's just the way it is, he allows that he doesn't—can't—live "like that." He goes on to explain how doing science gives his life meaning, all the while maintaining that it can't, really.

The tension comes from the fact that the Dawkins sublime is grounded in the billiard-ball picture of the universe. Purpose, value, love, meaning—these are not primary qualities. They are unreal. This is one of the primary inspirations for the Dawkins sublime. The world is devoid of value, value is all in our heads, and understanding the world is like gazing into an abyss. As Steven Weinberg writes, "The more the universe seems comprehensible, the more it also seems pointless." But ah, love, let us face this with whatever dignity we can, though notions like dignity are mere projections of ours. So Weinberg continues, "The effort to understand the universe is one of the very few things which lifts human life a little above the level of farce and gives it some of the grace of tragedy."[27] Or, put in terms of the language-arts lessons that so many schools now use: character-trait words like "courage" are clue words for groundless opinions, mere subjective likes and dislikes; but it is courageous to think critically.

Philippa Foot had studied a version of this picture—officially hostile to any real basis for ethical distinctions, though contemptuous of anyone cowardly enough to deny it—in the modern philosophy portion of her undergraduate curriculum. On the theories she had encountered as a student, moral judgments merely expressed the approval or disapproval of the speaker.

But now she had seen the newsreels, had seen what camp commander Josef Kramer and his underlings had done at Bergen-Belsen. As she stepped through the Keble College gates onto Parks Road, she knew what she wanted to say, if only she could find the words: that what the Nazis had done was wicked. As she put it years later, looking back on the moment of realization: "this is not just a personal decision . . . or an expression of disapproval. There is something objective here."[28]

She wouldn't have to find the words alone. She had friends.

Chapter 2

Oxford in Wartime

NUMBER TWO, BRADMORE ROAD

Philippa Foot only really met Iris Murdoch as they were each preparing for their final examinations in June 1942. Their shared tutor, Donald MacKinnon, suggested to Murdoch that "Philippa might appreciate a friendly visit."[1] Housebound and discouraged—however good a front she was showing—Foot (then Bosanquet) did need company. Still, it wasn't the introduction she would have chosen. Ever self-conscious about whether she truly belonged at Oxford, and intimidated by the older, more glamorous Murdoch, Bosanquet wouldn't have chosen for their first real conversation to happen while her torso was encased in plaster.

Bosanquet had been a frail child, contracting abdominal tuberculosis around age 8. The prescription she got was a year sleeping in the open air. So summer and winter that year, she slept on a balcony outside the nursery window. This was in Kirkleatham, in northernmost North Yorkshire; icy winds swept in from the nearby coast through the winter months. Whether or not this had any real effect on Bosanquet's TB, it certainly toughened her. But this hard-earned toughness didn't stop her from being nervous about her place at Somerville or from fretting about the quality of her work.

Now her back was acting up at the worst possible moment. Was it a recurrence of TB? Some other sort of spinal inflammation? Given Bosanquet's history, her doctors were taking no chances, and ordered her to spend the summer in a spinal cast. Her tutors had agreed to the extraordinary measure of teaching her in her lodgings, and the Principal of Somerville had arranged for her exams to be administered there, too. But she was seeing almost no one apart from her tutors, her landlady Mrs. Muir, and her roommate and best friend Anne Cobbe. She couldn't go to lectures. She couldn't visit the Bodleian. She couldn't even go to the University Parks (only a block away!) to take her mind off her endless revisions.

MacKinnon often nudged people to support one another. Murdoch wouldn't otherwise have looked in on Bosanquet. Their most significant interaction until then had been when Bosanquet opposed Murdoch's candidacy for the presidency of the Junior Common Room the year before. Bosanquet had nominated someone else, fearing that the politically enthusiastic (i.e., loudly Communist) Murdoch would be a nuisance, calling too many meetings. Murdoch didn't take it hard, but still, they hardly knew each other. It wouldn't have made sense for her to pay Bosanquet a visit. Murdoch revered MacKinnon, though, so she went.

It took Murdoch longer to gather a bouquet of wildflowers than to walk from her digs in Park Town to the church-like, neo-Gothic door of Mrs. Muir's house, 2 Bradmore Road. She knocked, went up to Bosanquet's room, and sat down beside her. So began a friendship that would last the rest of their lives.

MARY BEATRICE SCRUTTON GOES UP

In the late 1930s, Oxford's women's colleges (or "societies") may have been the most selective undergraduate institutions in the world.

A number of factors conspired toward this result. The prestige long associated with an Oxbridge education was compounded at Oxford because they now granted degrees to women, while Cambridge still did not. Oxford changed its policy in 1920, the same year British women received the right to vote. Cambridge did not follow suit until 1948. It made Oxford a particularly attractive destination for women.

Not that Oxford's policy of granting degrees to women was uncontroversial. In 1927, fretting that the University was acquiring a reputation as "socialistic, weak in athletics, and be-womaned,"[2] the ancient house of Congregation (Oxford's chief administrative gathering) capped the number of women undergraduates at 840 (out of a total population of over 4,000). It stipulated further that, although the overall quota could rise if any new women's societies were founded, the ratio of men to women could not fall below four to one. A quota remained in force until the late 1950s.[3] So an English schoolgirl in the late 1930s seeking an elite degree was competing with candidates from across the empire for one of about 250 places a year.

If it was difficult to gain admission to any of Oxford's women's colleges, it was particularly difficult to get into Somerville.

Somerville and Lady Margaret Hall were Oxford's first women's colleges, opening together in 1879. From the first, Somerville had both the more scholarly and the more radical reputation. Each of Oxford's four women's colleges was founded by educational reformers, radicals in their way. Nevertheless, differences in charter led over time to differences in reputation and atmosphere. Lady Margaret Hall (LMH) was officially Anglican, and built a reputation as a socially respectable destination for bright young women, making the idea of an Oxford education less threatening to some prospective students and their families. Somerville by contrast was pointedly non-sectarian (there was a minor furor in the early 1930s when an Old Somervillian gave a large donation for a college chapel; what could a Somerville *chapel* be like?), and as proudly bluestocking as any place on earth. Being non-sectarian, it also drew a wider pool of applicants, making the competition for places even fiercer and reinforcing a culture of academic striving. As a popular verse of the 1930s had it, "Lady Margaret Hall for Ladies, St. Hugh's for Girls, St. Hilda's for Wenches, Somerville for Women." (This was certainly unfair to St. Hugh's and St. Hilda's.)* There were other versions, one of which concluded, "Somerville for Freaks." With the elite women of the empire concentrated into a few colleges, and one established as the most rigorous of the group, it was no surprise that Somerville students performed exceptionally. By 1945, the Principals of all four women's colleges were Old Somervillians.

Somerville's application process was certainly the most daunting. Anyway, Mary Scrutton was daunted. Women on both sides of her family had been attending university for a generation, and she was expected to go. Her parents were older than most, and her father was a reasonably well-paid vicar in the Church of England. So they were able—with assistance—to send their two children to good boarding schools and then to university (Mary's older brother Hugh attended Cambridge, like their father). Sitting her entrance examinations in December 1937, it seemed to Mary as if her whole life was riding on the results. She took the exams in a "state of panic."[4]

In the late 1930s, every applicant for admission to Oxford University had to sit for two sets of written examinations. Responsions, the University-wide examinations, required candidates

---

* Another bit of Oxford folklore, reported to me by Old Somervillian Miranda Villiers (conversation with author, July 20, 2012): how would students at each of the four women's colleges respond, on being told there was a man she ought to meet? LMH: "Who are his people?" Somerville: "What does he read?" St. Hugh's: "What games does he play?" St. Hilda's: "*Where is he?*"

to show basic competence in two or three languages—one of them Latin or Greek—and either mathematics or natural science. But there were also college-specific examinations, because every undergraduate at Oxford must be affiliated with one of its dozens of federated colleges or societies. The college-specific exams consisted mainly of a set of papers linked to each applicant's intended field of study. But there was also the "general paper," which removed applicants from their strongholds of special preparation and exposed their capacity (or incapacity) to think seriously on their feet. The prompts for the general paper rewarded a philosophic temperament: an interest in stepping back and looking hard at some concept or piece of conventional wisdom, or in coming at some familiar fact from an unusual direction. Many actual general-paper prompts have been published: "When if ever is it justifiable to break a law?" "Consider the suggestion that the history of a mountain is simpler than the history of a mouse." To her good fortune, Scruton had a history teacher at her preparatory school, Downe House, who knew what the paper was like and prepared her students with prompts like "Nature is too green and badly lighted. Discuss."

All this was intimidating enough. Somerville added a layer. The College examinations were administered off-site. Afterward, candidates who had impressed their examiners were invited to Oxford for an interview, a chance for College staff to assess temperament and fit. The atmosphere conjures itself: the nerves, the posturing, the emotional extremes. Nina (Mabey) Bawden, who went up in 1943, describes the experience:

> I went to Oxford in my school uniform . . . and was ashamed when I arrived at Somerville and found that the other girls waiting outside the Principal's room were wearing what I thought of as 'best' clothes . . . . They all seemed to know each other, they all came from private boarding-schools, and as soon as I heard them

and saw them I knew it had been presumptuous folly to imagine I might be allowed to join this exclusive society. . . . I was last on the list that morning. The other girls went into the Principal's room one by one, and, when their interviews were over, clung to each other. 'Oh my *dear*,' they wailed, 'wasn't she *terrifying*? Of course we haven't an *earthly*.'[5]

Trying to imagine "the gorgon who clearly lay in wait," Bawden steeled herself and went in, but found only a "small, rosy woman, beaming at me with a grandmotherly air." Principal Helen Darbishire coaxed Bawden with small talk until she got her onto a topic that excited her: the condition of the working class in Wales. Darbishire listened interestedly for several minutes, gave Bawden a chocolate, and said, "Dear child, we will be happy to have you." Somerville wanted the Nina Bawdens, not the "healthy young mares" in line ahead of her.

Scrutton's experience five years earlier was similar. She sank into despondency as she waited, listening to "a smart girl who kept telling us all how much she had impressed the interview panel by explaining to them just what made Keats choose the words 'blushful Hippocrene' in the 'Ode to a Nightingale.'" "I wished he hadn't chosen them," she thought, and "expected nothing but disaster."[6] But like Bawden, she would be surprised. The Somerville staff had a good idea what kind of student they wanted. Particularly impressed with Scrutton's general paper, they admitted her to study Classics and offered her a scholarship.[7]

For all Somerville's selectivity, its students did suffer some deficits relative to their male peers. The most distinguished and best-resourced public schools in Britain—Eton, Rugby, Winchester—were male-only. These schools were particularly strong, and schools open to women comparatively weak, in classical languages: one of the prerequisites for admission to the University and the foundation of the famous classics course for which Scrutton had applied. This was no accident. These schools' curricula were built to propel students toward Oxford—and, indeed, toward classics. "Greats" (*Literae humaniores,* or *Lit. hum.*) was by 1938 a standard pathway to academic careers in several fields: philosophy, ancient history, archeology. More importantly, it was a long-standing portal into the male-dominated fields of politics and civil service. Preparing colonial administrators and other civil servants had been Benjamin Jowett's guiding aim when he revised the curriculum in the late nineteenth century.[8]

Lit. hum. remained a prestige degree well into the twentieth century. It took four years, one year longer than a typical Oxford degree. Beginning with just under two years of advanced study in classical languages and literature (Honour Moderations, or "Mods"), it then pivoted to two-plus years of ancient history and ancient and modern philosophy. Though Greats *was* a classics course, it was also intended from its medieval origins as a general course in humane letters—explaining why it was understood as broad preparation for civic life.

Pupils at elite boys' schools received years of preparation translating into and out of classical Greek and Latin; Greats picked up where their school syllabi left off. Few women received comparable preparation. When Scrutton started at Downe House, Greek wasn't even available. A particularly good classics teacher, seeing how well Scrutton and a few others were progressing in Latin, offered to teach them Greek. The girls squeezed it into a corner of their schedules. It thus became possible—just—for Scrutton to aspire to read Greats at Oxford, a course which otherwise would have been closed to her, as it would have been closed to most of her teachers.

There is almost a parable here about the subtle ways in which gatekeeping works. Gatekeepers could suppose that they are simply insisting on baseline competence in relevant subjects. Isn't it obvious to make Greek and Latin prerequisites for a classics course? But in fact, given the way the world is, the effect of insisting on that background is to cut off opportunities for people who might be capable of impressive work, if only a path were open to them that didn't impose those conditions.

The unwitting assumption that all Oxford undergraduates had gone to school at someplace like Eton affected students outside the Greats curriculum, too. Bawden read "Modern Greats" a few years later, a concentration explicitly designed for students interested in the same kind of broad-based humanistic education but who had never seriously studied Greek. Even she found that her philosophy tutor didn't know where to begin with her. "He had not taught girls before," she wrote, "nor any student of either sex from a state grammar school, and could not believe I had never learned Greek. He seemed convinced . . . that I must be concealing this simple and fundamental skill out of some mysterious modesty."[9]

However temperamentally fretful she was, and however academically disadvantaged, Scrutton was always willing to work. She had first thought she would do her degree in English literature, but a teacher advised her to study something she wouldn't study on her own; she took this to heart. Somerville had admitted her on the condition that she get remedial coaching in ancient languages—Oxford coaching—before coming up the following autumn. Scrutton had already started extra languages work the preceding summer, preparing for her entrance examinations. So she and brilliant-but-imperious Old Somervillian Diana Zvegintzov carried on through the rest of 1937 and the first half of 1938. (Zvegintzov's reaction when Scrutton received a scholarship: "Well well, I'd rather lose my reputation as a prophet than my reputation as a coach.")[10]

Scrutton might easily have passed Iris Murdoch on the pavement in front of her tutor's house in Chiswick. Murdoch lived nearby, and was getting tutoring in classical languages herself. Like Scrutton, Murdoch's first thought had been to study English, but she was now having second thoughts and cramming Greek and Latin. It's possible they were seeing the same tutor.[11]

In late September 1938, the girls likely rode the Great Western Railway west and north from Paddington to Oxford and, making their way laboriously over the tracks and across the canal, lugged their things up Walton or St. Giles Streets. Some wealthier girls would have been chauffeured to the College gates. The entrance that received them all, an eclectic but dignified composition in warm yellow stone, is described in the opening paragraph of Old Somervillian Dorothy Sayers' *Gaudy Night*: "built by a modern architect in a style neither new nor old, but stretching out reconciling hands to past and present."

Murdoch and Scrutton settled in at opposite ends of the College, Scrutton in a room with small windows on the top story of the late-Victorian West building (today, Park), Murdoch in an airy new room over the gates. The only two Somervillians in their year who were reading Greats, they were immediately brought together in tutorials with Mildred Hartley, Somerville's classics tutor. And so they finally met, Scrutton plopping down on the floor of Murdoch's room day after day as they began trying to turn themselves into classicists. They too would be friends for life.

THE WOMEN ARE ON PROBATION

Scrutton and Murdoch had much in common: the kinds of schools they attended, their choice of college, their interests, their course of study. The years would reveal more: both became thinkers with large, imaginative temperaments who traced connections others missed. Both would eventually come to feel somewhat confined by and estranged from the academy.

But there was something emblematic, too, in the differences between their rooms. Scrutton's was dim and quiet, as far as possible from the gates on Woodstock Road where the Somervillians came and went—a cell best suited to study or sleep. Murdoch's was above the entrance, sunny and colorful, decorated with posters and a thin, square, art deco cushion in aquamarine.[12] Similarly, as they settled into college life, Scrutton was cautious, conscientious, a person who kept her emotions and her sometimes wry thoughts mostly to herself. She was quiet, sober, and peripheral, like her room. Murdoch by contrast was flamboyant, open, and known to everyone. In Somerville's dining hall, the seats closest to the high table were occupied by the studious and scholarly, while those at the far end of the room were filled by women whose lives centered more on society or sex. Scrutton and most of her friends sat in the middle, between these extremes. Murdoch, though, appeared everywhere. Dressed in dirndl skirts, unconcerned with what others thought, she was magnetic to women and men alike. Her gift for friendship with the widest array of people defined her from then on. Years later, Philippa Foot asked her if she ever found anyone boring. "Never," she said.[13]

Murdoch's teachers adored her, though she was also the sort they worried about. Shortly after their arrival, Dean Vera Farnell sat the first years down and lectured them: "You must seriously realise that you have to be careful how you behave. It isn't a joking matter, the women are still very much on probation in this University. You may think that it doesn't matter if you do something a little wild, but I can tell you that it will."[14] Farnell's admonition didn't stop some Somervillians from slipping over the College walls at night (curfew was 11:15, or midnight "in exceptional circumstances"),[15] but hers was a voice of hard experience. The prejudices and anxieties that had prompted the University to cap the number of women undergraduates were not dead. The sense of precariousness, that women's position as members of the University was unsettled, subsided after the war, but in 1938 it was still deeply felt.

In the short term, the women couldn't win. If they behaved themselves impeccably and overcame all deficits to outclass their male peers, they provoked airy contempt. Christopher Hobhouse's chatty 1939 guidebook, *Oxford*, gives a sense of the prevailing stereotypes:

> Though their numbers are small, a casual visitor to Oxford might well gain the impression that the women form an actual majority. They are perpetually awheel. They bicycle in droves from lecture to lecture, capped and gowned, handle-bars laden with note-books, and note-books crammed with notes. Relatively few men go to lectures, the usefulness of which was superseded some while ago by the invention of the printing press. The women, docile and literal, continue to flock to every lecture with mediaeval zeal, and record in an hour of longhand scribbling what could easily have been assimilated in ten minutes in an armchair.[16]

Hobhouse goes on to fantasize about the life of women "undergraduettes": "[a]fter dark, in their own college libraries or in their comfortless little rooms, they huddle for hours on end, stooping and peering over standard text-books." He contrasts this imagined female servility with the "lordly" life of male undergraduates, commanding college scouts to produce breakfasts and lunches in their rooms, not merely skipping lectures but taking short-cuts where they find the syllabus "wasteful or slow." Hobhouse grudgingly acknowledges the fruits of the women's "stupefying assiduity," even as he tries to represent it as a fault: "The results of this obsession are clearly seen in the examination class-lists."

Heedless of the Farnells and the Hobhouses—as diligent as she was ecstatic—Murdoch threw herself into every aspect of university life. She dragged Scrutton with her into much of it: a "hurricane of essays and proses and campaigns and committees and sherry parties and political and aesthetic arguments."[17] Soon she would be involved too in theatricals and publications. In particular, both Murdoch and Scrutton promptly got involved in local politics. That fall, with Chamberlain's strategy of appeasing Hitler at the forefront of national conversation, they canvassed for A.D. Lindsay, Master of Balliol College, who was running as an Independent Progressive against Conservative Quintin Hogg. Then as now, student political opinion leaned left (as Scrutton would later recall, the only question was, "how far left do you want to go?").[18]

Living with the sense of threat and decay that typified the interwar years, they longed as much as any generation before or since to give themselves to a redemptive cause. Not having been old enough to do anything about the horrors of the Spanish Civil War, students threw themselves into the Lindsay campaign as if it were a crusade. Scrutton, a principled but instinctively moderate and pragmatic thinker, suspected that vocal Communist support was doing the Lindsay campaign no good. She listened with disquiet one day as a fellow student explained how she had been out campaigning for Lindsay—and defending the Marxist theory of the state. The students were shocked when the Oxford electorate narrowly elected Hogg. They represented the defeat in Manichean terms: "the creative, the generous, the imaginative" versus people dominated by "selfishness, stodginess, and insincerity."[19]

Murdoch, more prone than Scrutton to radical devotion, became a proselytizer for the Communist Party almost from the moment she arrived at Oxford. This was a dominant part of her Oxford experience, not shared with Scrutton. Writing to a friend from Badminton School in April 1939, she told her, "Ann, you *must* see, that this is the only way . . . . We've got to reorganize society from top to bottom—it's *rotten*, it's inefficient, it's fundamentally unjust, and it must be radically changed, even at the expense of some bloodshed." After some more remarks about the "carefully planned, scientific" character of the coming revolution, she adds, "About Christianity—I'm glad you are finding it good and a help to you. And I hope that it will lead you to what I consider its only logical conclusion—communism. . . . My religion, if I have one, at the moment is a passionate belief in the beautiful, and a faith in the ultimate triumph of the people, the workers of the world."[20] She held on to this faith until close to the end of the war, when it was (for a time) displaced by her friend's faith, Christianity.

Murdoch's capacity for friendship and for passionate devotion fused in a remarkable number of love affairs already during her first year at Oxford. In the same letter, she remarks that she is "in love with about six men all at once." After graduation, sharing a flat in London with Philippa Bosanquet, they agreed one night to tell one another about the proposals of marriage they'd each received. Bosanquet went first, then Murdoch. As Murdoch's list went on and on, Bosanquet asked, annoyed, whether perhaps it would save time to list the men who had *not* proposed to her. The length of the list is partly a reflection of circumstance; she was surrounded her first year by men about to be called away, perhaps to their deaths. But it is partly too an index of Murdoch's capacity to display and inspire devotion.

Somehow, Murdoch was able to give herself no less fully to her studies—though her and Scrutton's Mods tutorials with Mildred Hartley arguably confirmed one of Hobhouse's criticisms: that women dons (faculty) applied extreme pressure to their pupils to equal or outdo their male counterparts. The reputation of the women's colleges, he writes, is "a scourge" used by "the female don" to "drive her pupils to ever more exaggerated efforts."[21] Determined that her students would match their male peers stride for stride, no matter their starting point, Hartley insisted that Murdoch and Scrutton do Greek and Latin translations and even compositions in prose and verse—a typical feature of boys' school curricula. These verse compositions taught the young women nothing. Scrutton later likened them to "a rather desperate kind of crossword puzzle."[22]

Happily, there were other aspects of scholarly life that were more rewarding. Murdoch sketched ancient Greek vases in the basement of the Ashmolean Museum, and both she and Scrutton attended lectures from E.R. Dodds on Greek tragedy and on Plato. Scrutton had discovered Plato as a 16-year-old at Downe House and loved the fusion of reason and imagination in his dialogues. Murdoch reacted against his politics. At Hartley's instigation, both Murdoch and Scrutton participated for a time in German-Jewish émigré Eduard Fraenkel's legendary, years-long seminar on Aeschylus's *Agamemnon*.

Fraenkel's presence highlights something noteworthy about the Oxford atmosphere at the turn of the 1940s; Oxford was full of displaced persons. Murdoch wrote to a friend in 1941 describing Oxford as "a gentle civilised city full of elderly German Jews with faun-eyes & Central European scholars with long hair & longer sentences."[23] Led by Helen Darbishire, Somerville took in a cluster of refugee scholars, the College's modest finances notwithstanding. And they were not unique in this.

Fraenkel's personal influence in Oxford was complex. He acted with shocking impropriety toward women students, inviting them to his rooms in Corpus Christi College and groping them while discussing Greek literature. This was widely known and did not pass unremarked. Isobel Henderson, Scrutton and Murdoch's Roman history tutor, warned Murdoch that Fraenkel would "paw [her] a bit, but never mind."[24] The "never mind" at the end is telling. The general opinion on Fraenkel by the women of Oxford seems to have been that he had an aggravating habit, like a tendency to interrupt, not that he was a predator.*

Murdoch adored Fraenkel despite the pawing, and remained in correspondence with him for years. Scrutton, who was less prone than her friend to radical discipleship, seemed not to attract Fraenkel and got off without pawing, but also without much of a connection. Both, though, glimpsed for the first time in Fraenkel's seminar what a scholarly life could mean.

The seminar was a new pedagogical specimen at Oxford, transplanted from the soil of the German university. For two hours a week, in a ground-floor room at Corpus Christi, Fraenkel inducted participants, colleagues and students alike, into a kind of thoroughness and exactitude they had never known. Each week, an undergraduate and a member of the faculty would be assigned to comment on the next small bit of text. The undergraduate would open discussion and then, once he or she was reduced to confusion, the don would take over. When the don, too, inevitably faltered under Fraenkel's inquisition (the seminar was once likened to a gathering of rabbits, addressed by a stoat), Fraenkel would take charge. From there, "the discussion . . . might go on for weeks, citing other relevant passages and ranging over most of European history."[25] A generation of eminent

---

* Was this just the different outlook of a different era? Can we comprehend Henderson's attitude, though we would not accept it? Henderson did not live in College and had a reputation as more worldly than her colleagues. Perhaps she didn't think sexual expression mattered much (within wide limits), and thus if it enabled a woman to get ahead in the world, "never mind." Perhaps she was willing to give Fraenkel a pass because he kept his demonstrations within limits. Perhaps, too, she pitied him—fired from his position in 1933, slurred by his former colleagues as an "uppity Jewboy," forced to flee for his life. Fraenkel also suffered from a painfully deformed right arm, the result of a childhood bone infection, and may have seemed more sad than threatening on that account. Certainly detectable in Henderson's remarks is her respect for Fraenkel's position and work (the sort of respect that has shielded many men from accusations of harassment or assault). Not everyone was so tolerant. In her *Memoir* (Duckbacks, 2002), Mary Warnock relates conversations with an array of Fraenkel's women students. Several were indignant or horrified.

classicists—Hugh Lloyd-Jones, Kenneth Dover—pointed back to the seminar as modeling for them what their own work should be like. Mary Warnock, though her career would be in philosophy and then politics, saw an inheritance in her own work: the "deep desire to get things right, even quite small things . . . ."[26]

Agamemnon—indeed, the entire *Oresteia*—is a profound meditation on evil, suffering, and retribution, from the first great chorus with its hymn to Zeus. Scrutton remembered the seminar returning, again and again, to these words:

> Zeus has led us on to know,
> The Helmsman lays it down as law
> that we must suffer, suffer into truth.[27]

Perhaps no one could read a work of this kind with a great scholar and not be affected. But Scrutton recalled a moment in which she and Murdoch brought something to the tragedy that their Eton and Rugby-educated peers did not—maybe precisely because they'd been less cloistered. They were talking with a fellow student about a passage one of them had been assigned. Scrutton was struck by "how much better equipped than us he seemed to be about the language, and how much less idea he had of the point of what was being said."[28] In the time that an elite public-school curriculum might have given to Greek, she and Murdoch had delved instead into history and literature and politics. And that mattered, too. Murdoch wrote perhaps her best poem about the experience of the seminar. They sat in the ancient-looking room at sunset, week after week, everyone half-knowing what might lie ahead—that, like Iphigenia and Cassandra, like Achilles and Agamemnon, their lives might be cut short: "Did we expect the war? What did we fear?/First love's incinerating crippling flame,/Or that it would appear/In public that we could not name/The Aorist of some familiar verb."[29]

AN OPENING

In the 1938–39 academic year, with another war looming, it was a live question, inside and outside the University, whether Oxford should simply shut down. Limited conscription of 20- to 22-year-old men began in April 1939, following the German invasion of Czechoslovakia. In September, conscription was extended to all able-bodied men between 18 and 41 who were not conscientious objectors—and many objectors were assigned to national service work. The exodus raised practical questions. Who would lecture? If there were lectures, who would attend? Would there be enough to justify maintaining the organizational life of the University?

It helped that there was precedent. Oxford had weathered the Great War with a skeleton crew of the very young, the old, the infirm, pacifists, clergy—and women, already part of the life of the place, though they were not yet eligible for degrees. In 1914, people did not anticipate how long and bloody the conflict would be, so it was natural to carry on in the hope that all would soon return to normal. As a result, those who held the decision in 1939 knew that the University could carry on under such circumstances.

They knew, too, that they could count on the strength of the women's colleges, each of which had a long waiting list. The quotas of course went out the window. In June 1939, a few months before the invasion of Poland, Oxford awarded BAs to 1025 men and 226 women. In June 1940, just after the evacuation of Dunkirk and the fall of Paris, the numbers were 377 and 215. Many of the men who stayed were completing degrees judged to be of strategic importance—in the sciences, for instance. In June of 1941, there were as many women graduating as men; by 1942, women were the majority.

This does not mean that women were the majority of the student body as a whole. Beginning in 1939, a number of teenaged men came up to Oxford for shortened courses, or to begin courses they hoped to finish after the war. Meanwhile, until several years into the war, women were encouraged to complete their degrees so that they could fill white-collar positions being vacated by men. For a brief window, then, from 1939 to 1942, many of the classrooms and lecture halls of Oxford were populated mostly by women, accompanied by a thin and unrepresentative sprinkling of men: "conscientious objectors, the disabled, and a few ordinands."[30] The women began to fill another kind of vacated position, too: as the protégés of their remaining teachers. This was the world in which Murdoch and Scrutton transitioned from the first to the second part of their Greats course, and in which Bosanquet began her three-year course in Modern Greats—that is, Philosophy, Politics, and Economics (PPE).

What were the effects of this sudden transformation of Oxford from "a man's University with a certain number of women in it" to one in which men and women were on an equal footing or in which (among advanced students) women even predominated?[31] Scrutton later wrote,

> The effect was to make it a great deal easier for a woman to be heard in discussion than it is in normal times. Sheer loudness of voice has a lot to do with the difficulty, but there is also a temperamental difference about confidence—about the amount of work that one thinks is needed to make one's opinion worth hearing.[32]

A summary of facts is suggestive. Whereas prior to the war, men had been a dominant majority in all courses except English literature and modern languages, suddenly they were a clear and consistent majority only in the natural sciences (where policy welcomed men to continue toward their degrees), jurisprudence, and theology. The change was most dramatic in *Literae humaniores* and PPE—traditionally among the most male-dominated courses. Suddenly, there was an unprecedented preponderance of young women in these courses. Suddenly—at the exact moment when Bosanquet came up, and when Murdoch and Scrutton's syllabus turned to philosophy—most of Oxford's philosophy students were women. From autumn 1940 through 1942, women were frequently a majority at meetings of the Jowett Society, the undergraduate philosophical society. The presidency was held by Somervillian Jean Coutts, a Greats student a year ahead of Murdoch and Scrutton. Then by Elizabeth Anscombe of St. Hugh's College. Then by Philippa Bosanquet.

Missing and fretting about many of their friends, wondering what on earth they were still doing in university with a war on, Murdoch and Scrutton revised for their Mods exams through the historically bitter winter of 1940. Equipped with hot-water bottles that went cold long before the end of their three-hour exams in the grand, fan-vaulted—but unheated—Divinity School, they each managed to grind out second-class marks. Certainly, they'd dreamed of getting firsts. But given where they'd begun, they were unashamed. Now the curriculum would shift back to their native tongue. And they would discover what they wanted to do with their lives.

DONALD MACKENZIE MACKINNON

The philosophical climate of the late 1930s was turbulent, but not in a way likely to inspire anyone who wasn't already a philosopher. During the first three decades of the twentieth century, Cambridge had been the vital center of Anglophone philosophy, home to Alfred North Whitehead, Bertrand Russell, and Ludwig Wittgenstein as they produced groundbreaking works in logic and the philosophy of mathematics. No one of comparable significance was at Oxford, and Oxford was not associated with any philosophical movement—unless it was the tail end of nineteenth-century Hegelianism.

This began to change in the 1930s, as a rising generation of Oxford philosophers began to engage with their Cambridge peers and with others beyond. Most influential of all, inside and outside the academy, was a brash, attention-seeking young lecturer, Alfred Jules Ayer. In 1936, Ayer published an improbable book: a philosophical best-seller, *Language, Truth and Logic*. Ayer was a Greats student at the turn of the decade, and on the recommendation of his Christ Church tutor Gilbert Ryle began to explore a new philosophical school based in Vienna. The Vienna Circle, which Ayer joined for a time, was devoted to the picture traced in the last chapter. The Circle aspired to banish from science—and philosophy—any talk that went beyond empirical observation, beyond the "facts." Taking their stand against the spirit of "metaphysics," they embraced "the opposite spirit of enlightenment and *anti-metaphysical factual research*."[33] They attempted this in part through a purification of language, seeking to eliminate from our descriptions of the world all traces of human subjectivity. They advocated and tried to produce "a neutral system of formulae, for a symbolism freed from the slag of historical languages; and also . . . a total system of concepts."

Ayer returned from Vienna inflamed with what he had seen and heard. He began to connect it with his earlier reading of the British empiricist tradition: Hobbes and Locke and (especially) Hume. Prodded by another rising Oxford philosopher, his friend Isaiah Berlin, Ayer put his thoughts into book form, and the book became a sensation, drawing both praise and denunciation in the academic and popular press alike. It was, among other things, an attack on all philosophy that had ever been written in Oxford.

The opening sentence lays down the challenge: "The traditional disputes of philosophers are, for the most part, as unwarranted as they are unfruitful."[34] The reason, Ayer says, is that philosophers have not policed their language to make sure that their statements are even *meaningful*. And what kinds of statements are meaningful? Just two: (1) statements about the world that could be confirmed or disconfirmed by observation, and (2) statements about the logic of our language. There are statements of fact, open to verification or falsification by experience. There are statements defining words for use in statements of fact. All else is sophistry and illusion.

Ayer acknowledges nothing as a statement of fact—even if it seems to be one—if the speaker does not know "what observations would lead him . . . to accept the proposition as being true, or reject it as being false."[35] Ayer's chapter on ethics and theology is instructive on this point. Consider someone who says that there is a God. Is she reporting an observation? (If so, of what? A sunrise? A feeling? *The whole world*?) Or are there observations she can imagine making that would lead her to retract her statement? If she does not understand her faith as an observation-report, and if she cannot say what observations would lead her to renounce her faith, Ayer says that her statement is meaningless. She is saying *nothing*—despite how it seems to her or to others. Or consider someone who says that some action is wrong. Again, Ayer asks, is he reporting an observation? Or are there observations he can imagine making that would lead him to retract his statement? Neither, Ayer supposes. Moral judgments, he thinks, simply *praise* or *blame*; they neither report nor predict anything. Ayer concludes, "If now I . . . say, 'Stealing money is wrong,' I produce a sentence which has no factual meaning—that is, expresses no proposition which can be either true or false. It is as if I had written 'Stealing money!!'—where the shape and thickness of the exclamation marks show, by a suitable convention, that a special sort of moral disapproval is . . . being expressed."[36]

There are serious problems with Ayer's view, some of which we will take up later. For the moment, it is the legacy of Ayer's view that matters. Ayer's tone of breezy dismissal was all too easy for undergraduates to adopt. More importantly, Ayer's view, with its restrictive conception of a fact, helped harden the dichotomy that had been emerging since the early-modern period, between "fact" and "value." Again, according to this dichotomy—this picture—values are human projections onto a purposeless or "value-free" reality.

Ayer embraced this picture, drew out its implications, and gave it swaggering expression. It didn't matter how many details of his views were later rejected. Ayer more than anyone established the terms in which young philosophers in the late 1930s and early 1940s approached their discipline. He rendered suspect virtually all pre-modern moral philosophy, which did not sunder fact and value. Again, Ayer: "the traditional disputes of philosophers are . . . as unwarranted as they are unfruitful."

Language, Truth and Logic was reprinted in 1947, selling even more copies the second time around. For an extended period before and after the war, then, philosophers developed their theories in response to Ayer. In a letter to Bosanquet, immediately after their graduation, Murdoch wrote that she was looking ahead and contemplating the significance of life, but added glibly that of course such expressions were strictly meaningless. Ayer was in the air.

As Murdoch's letter illustrates, the effect of Ayer's work was essentially destructive. It did not help people think about their most urgent questions, such as what to do with their lives. It undercut such thinking. As Murdoch would later recognize, Ayer's work *did* imply judgments about better and worse ways to live. It glamorized what I called the Dawkins Sublime: a self-congratulatory toughness in facing a world where the words "God" and "good" have no meaning. But it was incompatible with the political idealism of Murdoch and her peers—with the judgments they were making every day about right and wrong, just and unjust.

Ayer's philosophy offered little to the rising generation. Though Scrutton, Murdoch, and Bosanquet each had a philosophical temperament—all three won scholarships with distinguished general papers—idealistic young people like them were unlikely to find Ayer's philosophy helpful. They found it unsettling, even dumbfounding. But not constructive. If philosophy meant "what Ayer did," what could it say about Franco and Hitler?

Philosophy was salvaged for the Somervillians when—Somerville having no philosophy tutor on staff—they were assigned for tutorials to young theologian-philosopher Donald MacKinnon. More famous now in theological circles, MacKinnon was a philosopher before he was a theologian, and was one of the most impressive minds of his generation. A Winchester pupil, he did so well in Greats at New College that he was quickly brought back—still only in his twenties—to be a Fellow at Keble. The hulking Scotsman was promptly invited to join "the Brethren," a small coterie of rising philosophers convened by Isaiah Berlin and J.L. Austin.[37] The group included Ayer. Less than a decade later, at the remarkable age of 34, MacKinnon was snatched away for a professorship at Aberdeen.

MacKinnon was deeply interested in the eighteenth-century thinkers Joseph Butler and Immanuel Kant—indeed in the whole history of philosophy. He taught his students to engage seriously with figures whom Ayer had consigned to irrelevance. But as evidenced by the impression he made on Austin, Berlin, and the rest of the Brethren, MacKinnon also kept up with contemporary philosophy. He took seriously Ayer's charge that his own inquiries—in ethics and theology—were meaningless. MacKinnon identified especially with Kant. As MacKinnon interpreted him, Kant showed skeptics like Ayer how to leave room for transcendent realities, even in the face of their skepticism.[38] In his portrayal of Kant—as a thinker determined to reconcile the seemingly irreconcilable—MacKinnon could have been writing about himself.

MacKinnon wanted to reinvigorate theological reflection in the face of Ayer's challenge because he found such reflection necessary to address the ethical and political issues of the moment. Like Kant, he was fixated on human evil, and on our responsibilities in the face of it. Like Dostoevsky's Ivan Karamazov—indeed, like Dostoevsky himself—MacKinnon drew examples from newspapers of the terrible things people did to one another. He believed that any adequate philosophy or theology must be capable of speaking to these examples.

When MacKinnon is not remembered for these things—his brilliance, his preoccupation with the special challenges to theology of his mid-twentieth–century moment—he is remembered as a tormented eccentric. His eccentricity was real. Dennis Nineham recounted how MacKinnon gave him a make-up tutorial in a pub one Sunday morning, pacing up and down for minutes on end, practically shouting: "You see *WHEN* Kant says this, he *MEANS* to say that, and *THIS* is *CRUCIAL*." The other patrons fell silent witnessing this performance, then broke into applause. MacKinnon blushed. He had lost track of his surroundings and had no notion of the scene he was creating.[39] The stories that still circulate about him—sucking on razor blades, chewing up pencils or lumps of coal, rolling himself up in a rug—date predominantly from his Keble years and probably reflect the stresses he was under during the war. Scrutton wrote:

> MacKinnon often made strange unpredictable movements and, in particular, strange grimaces, which . . . seemed to express profound anguish. A lot of the stories about him are true enough. He did wave pokers and other things about in an alarming way . . . . He did lie on the floor or beat the wall violently . . . . He was

prone to long silences, sometimes not seeming to hear at all what was said to him.[40]

If MacKinnon suffered from a condition like Tourette's, it may have been exacerbated in those days, when—disqualified from military service by his asthma—he threw himself into teaching as if to justify his existence, taking as many pupils as would ordinarily be divided among three or more fellows. Like Uriah in the book of *Samuel*, he refused to sleep at home with his wife while other men were stationed across the channel and overseas. He slept in his rooms at Keble when he wasn't on duty as a fire lookout, a post in which he took great pride. He sometimes gave tutorials dressed in his coveralls from the night before. Years later, recalling his tutorials, Scrutton found MacKinnon's generosity unfathomable. One day, having spoken with her for two hours (the standard was one), MacKinnon said, "I don't think we've really got to the bottom of this. Come back on Thursday."[41] As Bosanquet would later remark, he had no sense of proportion.

He understandably took some getting used to. But he also inspired devotion: by his intelligence and insight, by the attention he lavished on students and his tendency to worry over them (he wrote to Bosanquet daily as she waited for news about Michael Foot's release), by the depth of his engagement with both the material he taught and the crises of the time. Many students, from one end of his career to the other, credit him with setting the direction of their lives. He was the obvious person for Bosanquet to seek out in her grief after seeing the footage from Buchenwald and Bergen-Belsen. By the end of their undergraduate years, Bosanquet, Murdoch, and Scrutton were all considering philosophy as a path. Bosanquet later described MacKinnon as "holy" (this from a committed atheist) and as having "created" her.[42] MacKinnon appeared recurringly in her journals until the end of her life. In 1945, Murdoch wrote about MacKinnon, "After meeting him one really understands . . . how those people at Galilee got up & followed without any hesitation."[43]

There was danger in this. I have remarked on Murdoch's penchant for devotion—for discipleship. Peter Conradi traces this to her childhood, to her deep, only-child's attachment to her "quiet bookish" father.[44] Ever after, she sought out father figures. Whatever the cause, Scrutton and Murdoch diverged in their relationship to MacKinnon just as they had in their relationship to Fraenkel. There was no harassment here, and no affair. But Murdoch's connection with MacKinnon became far more intense than Scrutton's. She wrote to Frank Thompson about him, "It's good to meet someone so extravagantly unselfish, so fantastically noble . . . . He inspires a pure devotion."[45] Was the dramatic, unguarded Murdoch more attractive to her teachers? Did she seek such connections? Scrutton certainly admired MacKinnon—her later philosophical work shows his influence as deeply as any of her friends' does—but it was Murdoch and Bosanquet who formed adult friendships with MacKinnon. The friendship with the intense, demonstrative Murdoch would become a problem. And MacKinnon never did the obvious, necessary thing, introducing his students to his wife.

MacKinnon did not offer his students a philosophical program like Ayer's. Insofar as MacKinnon had a program, it was to attend to perennial human questions and to the philosophers who addressed them. He did not ignore Ayer's critique. But neither did he cease to ask questions that he found meaningful, even if Ayer would have called them "pseudo-questions." He went on teaching philosophy as something integrally connected to life, when this conception had nearly been abandoned by his peers. A month before the letter quoted above, Murdoch wrote to Thompson, "I had almost given up thinking of people & actions in terms of value—meeting [MacKinnon] has made it a significant way of thinking again."[46]

Murdoch's, Scrutton's, and Bosanquet's studies inevitably came to feel unreal, as the war and their university years ground on; it is a recurring theme in Murdoch's letters to both Thompson and David Hicks. Murdoch especially longed for more direct engagement with the world. But philosophy at least was not pointless. And thanks to MacKinnon's tireless instruction, all three came away with first-class marks in their final exams—even Bosanquet, encased in plaster.

MISS ANSCOMBE

Sometime in 1940, as they were all beginning to study philosophy, all three Somervillians became casually acquainted with a peer as undeterred by intellectual fashion and as committed to the philosophical enterprise as MacKinnon was: Elizabeth Anscombe.[47] Anscombe was at St. Hugh's, not Somerville, and was a year ahead of Murdoch and Scrutton. But she was friends with Somervillian Jean Coutts, and so came to Somerville a lot. Intimidatingly brilliant, sometimes curtly dismissive, but also capable of immersing herself with complete self-forgetfulness in a philosophical problem, Anscombe would become as much icon as friend to each of the others. She also baffled them.

During her own final exams in 1941, Anscombe appeared one night in the doorway of Scrutton's room. Anscombe was due to sit for her political theory exam the following morning. She wanted Scrutton's take on a thought that had occurred to her as she looked for the first time at books she was supposed to have read long before. Scrutton recalled how Anscombe "said thoughtfully in her beautiful quiet voice, 'some of the stuff is actually quite interesting. But there's one thing here that I don't understand. As far as I can see, this man,' and she drew out Hobbes' *Leviathan*, 'is just saying that you mustn't revolt unless you can. Can that be what he means?'"[48] Scrutton swallowed her astonishment and told her friend that this was indeed a standard scholarly take. Anscombe too got a first.

How did Anscombe turn into that person, the person she was at 22?

Well, how did any of them?

Chapter 3

Daughters of 1919

"WHAT DID YOU EXPECT?"

When Oxford's 1938 spring recess ended and Elizabeth Anscombe settled in for Trinity term, she didn't know what to expect when—or if?—she returned home.

Elizabeth and her parents had quarreled all through her secondary-school years, during her steady march toward Catholicism. To be fair, they quarreled about lots of things, not just religion. Allen Anscombe was often overwhelmed by his daughter. Why couldn't she be like the twins? John was now a schoolteacher, like his father. Tom was a curate in the Church of England. Allen had no use for religion, not since the War, but Tom's becoming a minister wasn't an offense. Tom was a touch enthusiastic, but at least it was the state church, not Rome—not popery. But Elizabeth, oh his dear Bessie. What had become of the little girl who stood beside him and recited Latin verbs in her clear voice while he worked on carpentry?[1]

Elizabeth had been about 12, just starting secondary school, when she picked up a book about the English Catholic martyrs: Richard Challoner's *Memoirs of Missionary Priests and other Catholics of both Sexes who suffered Death or Imprisonment in England on account of their Religion, from the year 1577 till the end of the reign of Charles II*. Challoner sent her looking for more. At 15, she spent a summer with an aunt and uncle in Normandy, reading book after book by G.K. Chesterton. She told an interviewer later, "In the course of reading one of these, *The Everlasting Man*, it came to [me] that I believed in God and ought to pray." She sought out a priest.[2] Her fights with her parents intensified on her return; these didn't go well for her parents. Young Elizabeth was increasingly, obnoxiously skilled at verbal combat. She excelled in debate at Sydenham High School. Allen did physics and woodworking, not politics or religion. He used to make a gesture like cranking an engine when Elizabeth started in on him or his wife.

Elizabeth had her independent spirit partly by inheritance. Gertrude Thomas Anscombe was a decade older than her husband, had had part of a university education from the University of Wales Aberystwyth, and had spent years, before she married, teaching classics. She did not follow the scripts society handed to her. Literally, even. At her and Allen's wedding in 1914, she refused to recite the traditional Anglican vows, promising to love and cherish him, but *not* to obey.

Allen and Gertrude first tried to argue Elizabeth out of her nascent Catholicism. It didn't help that their real objections stemmed from prejudice: Catholicism was unrespectable, even repulsive. Such anti-Catholicism remained strong in Great Britain through mid-century. As one turn-of-the-century observer wrote, the "opinion of the religious people I knew and loved was that Roman Catholic worship is idolatry, and that it was better to be an Atheist than a Papist."[3] Elizabeth's parents had internalized the prevailing repugnance. At one point, family lore has it, Gertrude and Allen's will excluded any Catholic child from inheriting. Unsurprisingly, they knew little about the faith their daughter was embracing or about its history, even in England. Once, Allen picked up a volume of Challoner and started thumbing through it. He became perplexed. He had assumed that

Catholics had all left England or converted when Henry had his Reformation. If he knew any martyr stories, they were from the more famous, anti-Catholic *Foxe's Book of Martyrs*. Wasn't it Catholics who had imprisoned people and burned them for their faith? Weren't they all foreigners? "But these are all English names," he said. "What did you expect?" retorted Elizabeth.

Getting nowhere, her parents asked an Anglican priest to talk to her. This was unkind to the poor man. He had scarcely sat down and offered a few pleasantries when Elizabeth began grilling him on his understanding of the Eucharist. He scrabbled for common ground, expressing his conviction that the consecrated host is in *some* sense the body of Christ. Elizabeth was unimpressed. She wanted to know if the priest was committed to the same miracle that she was. "Is it bread?" she demanded.[4]

Finally, Gertrude and Allen issued an ultimatum. Elizabeth had won a scholarship to St. Hugh's College, Oxford. Like Murdoch and Scrutton, she planned to read classics. (And with a mother who taught her children Greek at home, she didn't need an extra year to prepare.) But though the Clara Evelyn Mordan award was St. Hugh's top scholarship, it was not all-inclusive. Gertrude and Allen told Elizabeth that if she joined the Church, they would cut off her support.

Didn't they understand who they'd raised?

Elizabeth went up in the fall of 1937 and promptly presented herself for catechesis at Blackfriars Priory, the Dominican study house in Oxford. Fr. Richard Kehoe found himself with, surely, one of the most advanced catechumens he had ever known. Elizabeth had considered herself a Catholic since 1935, and had read everything she could get her hands on.[5] Her questions were not elementary ones about Mary or the Pope. She wanted to know whether she was required to accept a philosophical claim she had encountered in Bernard Boedder's

Natural Theology, to the effect that God knows what people would have done under circumstances contrary to fact. Kehoe told her, no, she didn't need to believe that.

On April 28, 1938, during the first week of Trinity term, Elizabeth was received into the Church under the grand, rounded vault of the Oxford Oratory, next door to Somerville.

So, what then? She had gone and done it, the thing her parents had forbidden. Now she had to go home and face the consequences— her own small martyrdom, perhaps. She didn't *want* to be estranged from her parents—or her brothers. The siblings fought too, natu- rally,* but love goes deeper than rivalry, and there was talk of another war. Elizabeth rode back to London at the end of term and found herself again at her parents' home on Trewsbury Road.

She soon knew it was going to be all right. It was now full sum- mer, and she needed a skirt altered. Gertrude had Elizabeth stand on a table and went to work. Neither said much. But as her mother tucked and pinned the new hem, Elizabeth knew there was no break between them. Gertrude had had to drop out of university when her own father died. She could no longer afford it. Elizabeth baffled and infuriated her mother. But there was no way Gertrude Thomas Anscombe—classics scholar, feminist—was going to stop her daugh- ter from finishing her degree.

---

* Anscombe related to Mary Midgley a childhood memory of sitting in her family's back garden in a stick-built fort, feeling furious. As one of the twins started clambering in, she thought, "do I have a log I can whack him with?" (Mary Midgley, conversation with author, March 7, 2011.)

A BIG DARK HILL

Anscombe was Gertrude and Allen's daughter. She was the daughter of a Church she first discovered in books. She was also the daughter of those books: Challoner, whose stories of persecuted recusants inspired her devotion; Chesterton and Shaw, whose polemics shaped her style; Boedder and Aquinas, who introduced her to philosophy and taught her that it could be an offering to God.

Scrutton, Murdoch, Bosanquet: whose daughters were they?

They were all, before they were anything else, daughters of the Armistice. Anscombe, Murdoch, and Scrutton were all born within six months, between mid-March and mid-September 1919. Bosanquet was born just over a year later. They were at the leading edge of the post–Great War baby boom, as the war's survivors were demobilized, returned home, and started families.

In every case but Murdoch's, their parents were married before the end of the war, and all but Murdoch had an older sibling or two. Anscombe, the oldest, was born where her father was still stationed, in Limerick, Ireland. But if they weren't daughters of homecoming *marriages*, they were nevertheless daughters of the so-called "lost generation."* Their fathers were all officers in the British Army. All

---

* Taken literally, rather than as a metaphor for existential disorientation, the label is an exaggeration. I do not belittle the effects of the war. But the British specifically lost around 700,000 troops in the conflict—roughly 12% of their mobilized force. Nearly everyone lost a friend or family member. The casualty rate among junior officers was especially high, around 17%. Nevertheless, 1919 saw a record number of marriages in England, Scotland, and Wales. This would have been impossible if the great majority of the forces had not returned. It is not astonishing that A.W. Anscombe, W.S.B. Bosanquet, W.J.H. Murdoch, and T.B. Scrutton all survived. The odds of four randomly selected junior officers all surviving the war were roughly even.

saw combat and came home altered. Allen Anscombe was wounded in February 1917, precipitating his transfer to Ireland. Thomas Scrutton, a chaplain, was also wounded, in 1918. Unlike Allen Anscombe, he kept his faith. But Scrutton's attempts to explain to the young men of his regiment the importance of all the killing and dying converted him to pacifism.[6]

Though Mary Scrutton was not a Catholic—nor a Christian of any sort—it is impossible to talk about her origins without talking about faith. Her parents' world centered on it. Thomas Scrutton had not grown up a Christian. His father, a famous judge, had been hostile to religion, directing that when he died, he should not be given a church funeral. (His dictate was not followed, because it wasn't discovered until too late.) But Thomas converted to Christianity in early adulthood after a series of dramatic spiritual experiences and became an Anglican priest. His daughter Mary would partly—but not entirely—reverse this movement. She drifted away from her parents' faith during adolescence. She expected something more to happen when she prayed, and when it didn't—when she didn't have the kind of experiences that had been central to her father's conversion—she felt let down. In interviews late in life, she likened Christianity to an engine she couldn't start. But she retained great respect for her parents' "imaginative, humane and liberal" creed and lives.[7] She would acquire a reputation for impatience with dismissive critics and caricatures of religion. She had seen how thoughtful and constructive it could be.

Thomas and Lesley Hay Scrutton met before the war but became close in 1914, just after the start of hostilities, when economic panic put lots of people out of work in Thomas's southeast London parish. Lesley responded to a call for volunteers, and she and Thomas began working side by side, doing whatever needed to be done, as they would for the rest of their shared life. They were engaged within a year and married in 1916. Much of their work in Greenford, where they moved in 1924, was of a similar sort: helping new neighbors in that burgeoning suburb connect with one another and get vital services that had not yet been established nearby. Some people would have been resentful at the transformation of their sleepy rural parish. But Lesley organized gatherings for women who had no friends and no venues in which to make them. Thomas won a seat on the local council and pushed developers to do right by the waves of newcomers. At the same time, thanks to the Scruttons' involvement with Quaker Relief, the Anglican Pacifist Fellowship, and other such organizations, their home was a way station for missionaries, relief workers, and refugees. There was always talk about politics and current events around the Scrutton dinner table, and it was *engaged* talk. Mary was surprised later to meet people who didn't think of politics as a part of life, people who "regard[ed] the occasional intrusion of political events into real life as an unfortunate mistake."[8]

Even Thomas's preaching carried him out of the sanctuaries of his churches. The church he served during Mary's late adolescence opened onto the marketplace in Kingston-on-Thames. Thomas would stand on a chair outdoors after evening services and invite questions. England was rapidly secularizing in these years, and he always drew a crowd of curious non-churchgoers, asking questions like whether everything in the Bible is true. (His answer: "no.")

Mary's parents both came from well-to-do professional families: Lesley Hay's father David helped engineer the first underground rail lines in London. And Thomas and Lesley's life was comfortable, too. They could afford a domestic servant. Of the modest privileges the family enjoyed, the most significant for Mary—apart from private schooling—was the scope and character of her childhood home. From ages 5–15, she had the run of the Greenfield rectory grounds.

The rectory had been a hobby farm, encompassing fields and ponds and a number of outbuildings, now mostly in disrepair. Following, watching, sometimes trapping and tending frogs, toads, newts, and mice, Mary became ardently zoophilic. It would be a decade into her career before she began to connect this love with philosophy, but the foundation was laid during her primary-school years. From as far back as she could recall, Mary hated dolls and wanted only stuffed animals for toys.

Notwithstanding her admiration for her parents, Mary reflected later on a lack of closeness between her and them (particularly between her and her father). She attributed this to a generational divide. As engaging as she found their tea-time conversations about the rising menace of fascism, and the extent to which it was rooted in the punitive measures of the Treaty of Versailles, the Great War stood between them:

> All through my childhood, that war loomed steadily in the back-
> ground like a big dark hill overshadowing the landscape. Our
> ideas of what it meant were not very clear. But because this hill
> was a place where only adults went, we gradually came to feel
> that it was not as real as the places that we ourselves could visit.
> Our elders' concentration on it began to make them seem alien,
> removing them from the rapidly changing world that we thought
> we understood.[9]

Then too, Lesley and Thomas belonged to a generation who had radically lost faith in their elders—and carried this loss of faith into their parenting. The elders had recruited their generation to a glorious cause. And those who fought the war had believed what they were told. Instead, their experience was Thomas's: crouched beside the broken and dying, trying and failing to explain how all the blood and filth, degradation and loss were worthwhile. When they returned home and began raising their own children, they were much more hesitant than their own parents had been to use the tones of authority. Or so it seemed to Mary later, looking back.

Though her parents were reluctant to impose on her, this couldn't keep Mary from developing her own crisis of confidence. She was constantly pestered by parents and teachers alike on account of her daydreamy sloppiness. Though she was bright, she always felt she was failing to live up to people's expectations: her grandparents', her maiden aunts', her teachers', her father's. Ponds and fields and books were places of escape. When Mary left for Downe House School in 1932, the thing she liked best about it was the way its founder and headmistress, Olive Willis, minimized rules, encouraging students to sleep outdoors in summer or to hike to the horizon to see what was there. There was plenty of time, too, to learn languages or mathematics—or history from Jean Rowntree, the teacher who coached her students on how to write the general paper for Oxford. But there were also whole afternoons to embark on impromptu picnics, to sit and listen to visitors like novelist Charles Williams, or to stand between the stacks in the library discovering for the first time the fusion of thought and imagination in the dialogues of Plato.

"A PERFECT TRINITY OF LOVE"

Scrutton, Murdoch, and Anscombe all grew up in suburban London: Anscombe in Sydenham to the southeast, Scrutton and Murdoch to the west. They were all more or less middle class, though the Scruttons were considerably better off. Murdoch's father was a minor civil servant. Like all the fathers in this story, he was not especially young—29—when his philosopher-daughter was born. From a once-successful line of Irish farmers but born just as the farm was about to fail, Hughes Murdoch lost his father when he was 13. His mother and her three children retained their respectability, and they weren't penniless—but they weren't far from it, either. The family were of mixed English and Irish ancestry and evangelical Protestant, so neither young Hughes nor his mother objected to his sailing off to London at 16 to apprentice himself as a clerk at Scotland Yard. This laid the groundwork for his later career.[10]

His wife-to-be, too, was Irish and English, Protestant (Church of Ireland), and lower middle class, having been orphaned at five and taken in by her grandfather. Irene (Rene)* Richardson had a beautiful singing voice and had begun to establish herself in the Dublin opera scene when she met Hughes Murdoch, now back in Ireland. It would later bother their daughter Iris more than it ever bothered Hughes or Rene that Rene had given up singing after she and Hughes fell in love, conceived Iris, and married. Within a couple of years, they left behind the fraught political situation in Ireland and moved back to London. Hughes landed a good-enough clerical position in the Ministry of Health, and that was that.

Hughes and Rene were thus displaced persons—a category that would fascinate and attract Iris throughout her life. However sensible—even welcome—it was to get away from the War of Independence and its aftermath, the Murdochs faced intense prejudice back in England. Anti-Irish prejudice, like anti-black prejudice, was strong even later than anti-Catholic prejudice (as Peter Conradi notes, landlords put up signs, into the 1950s, reading "No blacks, no dogs, no Irish"), and the English did not always distinguish between Irish Protestants and the Catholics whom they especially despised.

Apart from their extended families back in Ireland, whom they saw during the summers on holiday, Iris's parents were largely cut off from the world. Hughes, an unassuming man, went to the office, did his work, and returned home. Rene looked after their daughter, puttered

* Pronounced "ree-nee."

indifferently around the house and, once Iris was in school, joined a local choir and a swimming club. Even before the war, Hughes had become a freethinker, and though Rene sang Sunday-school songs to young Iris, she did not press the matter. She sang Irish Nationalist songs, too, without any more-fervent commitment. The Murdochs had no church. They had no party. They had no friends. Instead, they turned inward and made their home their world. Hughes doted on Rene, who adored him in return. They both doted on Iris, their only child. Hughes read Iris *Treasure Island* and other adventure stories, and Rene sang her songs. Iris later recalled her family as "a perfect trinity of love."[11]

Hughes' income was a modest £400 a year, but it sufficed; the Murdochs had only a few priorities. They put most of their resources into their small, semi-detached house in Chiswick and into Iris's schooling. This was initially at the experimental (even eccentric) Froebel Demonstration School, near the Murdochs' home. Hughes would bring Iris to school on his way to work, giving them extra time together. At Froebel, in addition to all the standard subjects and some study of "affairs" (contemporary politics), there were elaborate put-ons of courtly life, overseen by the headmistress, Miss Bain (a.k.a. "King Bain"), with Knights, Ladies, Squires, and Dames arrayed beneath. This involved a great deal of dress-up and solemn ritual. It sounds comic, but Iris loved it, and it is not difficult to see how, together with all the Robert Louis Stevenson and Lewis Carroll at home, it began to prepare her for a life spent as much in fiction as in philosophy. One of her first pieces of creative writing was "a fairy play with a chorus for rabbits,"[12] probably performed at a school concert.

Like many families who build their world around an only child, what they couldn't face was childhood's end: Hughes and Iris especially. When the time came for Iris to leave Froebel, and she won a scholarship to a good boarding school (Badminton), the rupture was terrible. Scrutton had been mildly apprehensive about her transition to boarding school, but quickly fell in love with the surrounding woods and Miss Willis and the library. Iris, by contrast, "ran round and round the playground with her hair all over her face, weeping," then went and cried in a cloakroom.[13] A kind classmate witnessing her misery formed a small society for "The Prevention of Cruelty to Iris."[14] Only Iris's absolute faith in Hughes, who was no less miserable but believed that Badminton School was what Iris needed, saw her through. On holidays, the family would count down their remaining meals together.

Badminton *was* what Iris needed. The young woman who took Oxford by storm six years later is unimaginable apart from the influence of Badminton headmistress Beatrice May Baker, known to her pupils as "BMB."

Baker was a tough, weather-beaten woman, disciplined and demanding, one who lived by her ideals—feminist, Quaker, Socialist—and (sometimes) brought them alive for others. Baker began each day with a cold bath at 7:15 and made her pupils do the same. She did not force her own vegetarianism on students, but they were served vegetarian meals twice a week. Once, in a school chapel service, she preached against hot-water bottles. "We were Athenians but we were Spartans too," Murdoch would later recall.[15]

Baker's imperious demands were not limited to physical discipline. She would swoop down on unsuspecting students and ask what they were reading, to see if it was worthy. "Fill your lives!" she told students and staff alike. ("If I fill my life any more I shall go mad" one staffer muttered in reply.)[16]

However difficult Baker could be, she also inspired some— Murdoch among them—by her pure commitment to a vision of the Good. Baker was a zealous proponent of the League of Nations, and strong-armed her pupils into joining the Junior League. Murdoch's first visit to continental Europe was a school trip to the Palace of Nations in Geneva. Baker's idealism took more down-to-earth forms, too. As the 1930s wore on, she brought a stream of refugee students ("foreign friends") to Badminton. Baker modeled for Murdoch the kind of absolute devotion to causes that Murdoch would later emulate. Murdoch's unyielding undergraduate Communism is a direct inheritance from BMB, in tone if not in substance. Baker was also the first person besides her father Hughes to whom Murdoch attached herself, the way she would go on to attach herself to MacKinnon and other mentor figures afterward. Murdoch remained close to her former headmistress for the rest of Baker's life—Murdoch seeking Baker's approval in the 1950s before she married literature scholar John Bayley.

EXCURSUS: THE MORBID AGE

In her sixties, Murdoch published a poem in a book of remembrances about Baker. Early in the poem, she writes, "*Pure idealism* was what you had to give,/Like no one now *tells* people how to live." She likens what Baker demanded of her pupils to summiting Everest: "How could we have considered this ascent/Had not our cynic hearts adjudged *you* innocent?" But then the poem takes a somber turn:

> Politics too seemed innocent at that time
> When we believed there would be no more war.
> . . .
>
> We lived through the jazz age with golden eyes
> Reflecting what we thought was the sunrise.[17]

Murdoch was recalling her girlhood at a distance of half a century, but the elegiac tone was no less emblematic of the late 1930s. Grief over the twilight of civilization was one of the defining marks of the culture of Anscombe, Bosanquet, Murdoch, and Scrutton's childhood and adolescence. The interwar years in Britain were, in Richard Overy's phrase, a "morbid age."[18]

Revolutionary Marxists *celebrated* this idea of the nighttime of civilization. Most people who spoke of it evinced dread. But they shared with the revolutionaries a powerful sense of living *fin de siècle*. Medical metaphors (senescence, disease, death) emerged as a common language through which to articulate this sense. Consider these titles published between 1919 and Hitler's rise to power in 1933: *The Decline of the West* (1922), *The Decay and the Restoration of Civilization* (1923), *Will Civilisation Crash?* (1927), *The Day After To-Morrow: What is Going to Happen to the World?* (1928), *The Problems of Decadence* (1931), *Can We Save Civilisation?* (1932). The decline and fall of the West was not merely an elite preoccupation, either. The public-minded BBC gave a broad hearing to the doomsday prophecies of scholars like Albert Schweitzer, Oswald Spengler, and Arnold Toynbee. There were popular treatments, too, like H.G. Wells's *The Salvaging of Civilization* (1921).

The power of the theme was its flexibility, its capacity to engage people of radically different circumstances and convictions. There was no widely accepted set of causes or symptoms for civilizational decline, other than the Great War. "Civilization in crisis" was a banner under which Communists and Christians, eugenicists and pacifists, psychoanalysts and traditionalists, could march together. The rhetoric—the metaphor—united them, without anyone having to agree on its meaning. Was the problem the collapse of capitalism, pollution of the genetic pool, the impending destruction of humanity due to ever-more-terrifying military technologies, or something else altogether? This was the subject of vigorous argument. What was agreed on all sides was that something had gone wrong with the West—a sickness had taken hold—and the prognosis was uncertain at best.

Anscombe, Bosanquet, Murdoch, and Scrutton grew up, then, in a culture that understood itself as unstable, living between an unprecedented outbreak of ferocity and something worse to come. Perhaps the morbid anxieties of 1920s and 1930s Britain were a neurotic-if-understandable response to the first war and the social transformations surrounding it. Perhaps they were vindicated by the outcome. These anxieties were, regardless, what the daughters of middle-class and upper-class professionals—school teachers, vicars, civil servants, engineers—would have encountered in magazines and books, and heard on the radio, from the pulpit, from their teachers. They were a consistent background, the *basso continuo* of the interwar era.

As Anscombe, Murdoch, and Scrutton began their secondary education in the early 1930s, things really did begin to tip: the Japanese invasion of Manchuria, Hitler's ascent, the Italo-Abyssinian war, the Spanish civil war, the run-up to a second world war. The whole of Britain—especially those, like Miss Baker and the Scruttons, who were politically engaged—waited with increasing apprehension on the outcome. The controlling metaphor also began to shift, from sickness to a precipice: *On the Rim of the Abyss* (1935), *Europe Into the Abyss* (1938), *Europe: Going, Going, Gone!* (1939).

How did this sense of impending doom manifest in the lives of young women like Scrutton or Murdoch? In addition to working on her Greek and Latin, Scrutton traveled in the year before she went up to Oxford. Her beloved teacher Jean Rowntree urged upon her and her parents the timeliness of learning German. Travel to Germany itself was out of the question. But the Scruttons knew a Jewish family in Vienna, the Jerusalems. The Jerusalems' daughter Lilli had spent a season with the Scruttons, and Mary's brother Hugh had stayed with the Jerusalems in return. So off Mary went to the Austrian capital in March 1938—just in time for the *Anschluss*. Overnight, she recalled, "huge red floating banners marked with swastikas appeared at once, as if by magic.... Jewish shops ... were marked crudely in white paint and were quickly targeted by vandals who looted and smashed everything they could reach. Broken glass was everywhere."[19] When Herr Professor Jerusalem was arrested, the Jerusalems dispatched Mary—who had less to fear in the streets—to the offices of a local Quaker group, to see if they could do anything for him.

The Jerusalems survived; Mary's parents were instrumental in resettling them after Professor Jerusalem was lucky enough to be released. None of what she had seen in Vienna was a surprise to Mary, though. As the daughter of Thomas and Lesley, Mary had spent countless childhood evenings in conversation with refugees. She "knew how these things were done."[20] But as she—and Murdoch—first went up to Oxford that fall, it *was* with a sense of standing at the lip of an abyss. And in their hunger for a healing, restoring cause—a remedy for the morbidity afflicting their society—they were daughters of their time.

"SHE DOESN'T *LOOK* CLEVER"

The daughters of 1919 grew up, too, in a fundamentally altered legal and institutional context.

The mobilization of millions of British men during the Great War had led or even compelled women to leave a limited range of previously "acceptable" occupations—domestic service, dressmaking, laundering, nursing, teaching, and above all homemaking—for jobs in civil service, emergency services, farming, transportation, and munitions manufacturing. The eventual return of more than five million men of working age, then, was an economic crisis at least as serious as their departure had been. Large groups of women were dismissed from positions they had held during the war. No doubt some were pleased to be done handling explosives or working in fields, but many who had enjoyed the greater freedom of the war years were frustrated at being told they had to give up their wartime occupations and the pay that accompanied them. Fewer and fewer women were willing to do domestic work, and with (often informal) "marriage bars" excluding married women from some lines of work, the unhappily unemployed now included many women as well as men.

There isn't a simple, causal relationship between this fraught situation and the string of egalitarian legislative and institutional changes that took place between 1918 and 1920. These changes wouldn't have taken place without decades of preparatory work by activists. But it is equally unbelievable that there was *no* connection. In a two-year period, propertied women of 30 were accorded the right to vote (1918); the Sex Disqualification Act made it illegal to exclude (unmarried) women with comparable qualifications from the major professions (1919); Viscountess Nancy Astor was the first woman seated in Parliament (1919);[21] the report of the War Cabinet Committee on Women in Industry advocated the principle of equal pay for equal work (1919); and women were welcomed as full members of the University of Oxford and permitted to take degrees (1920). In retrospect, these changes look simultaneously like an acknowledgment that women had proved themselves and like a conciliatory gesture, as both private and public action (such as the 1919 Restoration of Pre-War Practices Act) pushed women out of roles they had come to occupy and often prize.

Whatever the motivations behind these reforms, and however delayed or incomplete their effects, they did fundamentally alter the position of women in British society. They established a general presumption of legal and institutional equality. Women like Scrutton, Murdoch, and Anscombe, born shortly after the end of the war, were the first to grow up under this presumption. There was, for them, no need to adjust to the idea that women were allowed (in principle) to pursue any educational or professional goal they wished. They were the first generation of women who could, mostly, take this for granted.

Philippa Bosanquet, however, could not. Her parents belonged to the world that was passing away. Not only was there no expectation that she would pursue educational or professional goals; there was every expectation that she would not.[22]

William Bosanquet, Philippa's father, came from an old and distinguished family. Huguenots, they fled France after the revocation of the Edict of Nantes (1685) and quickly established themselves on the other side of the Channel. They are featured in books like *Burke's Peerage* and *The Plantagenet Roll of the Blood Royal, Being a Complete Table of All the Descendants Now Living of Edward III, King of England.*

William was a younger son of a younger son, and so did not inherit an estate. Like his father, though, he went to Cambridge and afterward secured a prominent, well-paying position: in William's case, as an engineer and supervisor at a steelworks. He made a good marriage too, to Esther Cleveland, daughter of United States President Grover Cleveland (and the only baby ever born in the White House). William and Esther's daughter, however uncomfortable she became with the culture of her parents, never forgot that she was the granddaughter of a US president and never ceased to be intrigued by her mother's family history. William and Esther met in Switzerland in 1915; they became engaged late in 1917 after Esther came to London to work as a nurse at a military hospital. Their marriage at Westminster Abbey on March 14, 1918 was reported on both sides of the Atlantic.

Both Philippa's parents had seen something of the war, then. So decades later, in 1942, when William lost his position, they were not too grand to accommodate themselves to reality. They rented out most of their country house ("the Old Hall") in Yorkshire for storage and took up market gardening. Scrutton visited the Old Hall in that period, and recalled an atmosphere of moth-eaten grandeur. Throughout Philippa's childhood, though, the Bosanquets were distinctly upper-class, with strict ideas about how (and with whom) to conduct themselves. It was proper for Philippa and her sister Marion to befriend Victoria Gore, daughter to a Lady in Waiting, or Rosemary Vane of Raby Castle, but *not* the children of the local physician. Also not proper for Philippa and Marion: formal education.

Indeed, all the primary and secondary education Philippa received—apart from one miserable year at the socially elite St. George's School, Ascot—was in her parents' home. Not that she was, in the contemporary sense, home-schooled. Her parents had no role in her schooling. They saw her only a few hours a day, even when she was desperately sick. As was customary in their circle, William and Esther turned over Philippa and Marion to a nanny, Jennie Baxter, who became like a mother to them both. They were subsequently put in the charge of governesses. Philippa would later remark in an interview, perhaps too flatly: "I had no education . . . . In this milieu, women didn't go to school. They just had a succession of governesses, who didn't know anything . . . ."[23]

So Philippa and Marion got only basic arithmetic and literacy (though Philippa's spelling and handwriting would be lifelong sources of embarrassment to her), French, and the most baroque details of etiquette. Forbidden as they were to play with the children of the village, they spent much of their time in the traditional pursuits of their class: attending dressy occasions with "the great and the good," going on outings with Nanny, and—above all—riding horses, including in the annual fox hunt.

It is impressive that Philippa managed to do as much riding as she did, given the variety of ailments that afflicted her as a child. Together with her TB, she suffered from ear infections. A botched operation on the kitchen table left her permanently deaf in one ear. Small wonder that Nietzsche ("What does not destroy me, makes me stronger")[24] later became one of her favorite authors. Despite everything, young Philippa was an accomplished equestrian. In her riding, as in the brutal winter she spent outside the nursery window, she was forced early to develop inner strength. Years later, in a journal, she mused, "How did they allow a child who was perhaps not even as much as 10 to get up and go out alone [on horseback]? . . . No one seems to have thought to ask 'Does that child know how to ride?' when they bought a half-broken-in 2-yr.-old pony at the fair!" But then, she observed, "I suppose that was how M[arion] & I grew so tough!"[25]

What Philippa conspicuously lacked was a deep connection with her parents—though, like most children, she wanted one. But she had neither the closeness of Murdoch with her parents nor the admiration with which Scrutton regarded hers. The connection Murdoch felt with her parents, Bosanquet felt with her nanny. She and her sister used to leave notes for Baxter in the armpit of their teddy bear. In a late journal entry, Philippa wrote, "Nanny loved me so very much. Never to be forgotten: the look on her face—as if something

<u>unbelievably</u> wonderful had happened—when I walked up to her bed in University College Hospital after her stroke."[26] As Philippa herself lay dying, she said, "Nanny's waiting for me."[27]

Philippa's letters home from London during the latter half of the Second World War survive. They are chatty, witty, faultlessly polite, even effusive ("Lots & lots of love to you dear chickens"), but also guarded.[28] Later in life, Philippa mourned her parents deeply. The terrible sadness is that her love was almost certainly reciprocated, though its expression was constrained by expectations of how upper-class parents behaved. We have Philippa's letters to her mother because Esther kept them, among the things she took with her when she moved back to the United States after William's death. Marion found them when settling Esther's estate. "[Why] were we so <u>overwhelmingly</u> convinced," Philippa wrote in her journal, "that she didn't care about us?"[29]

This highlights the central puzzle of Philippa's childhood: what led her, even before she left home, to set herself against the class-consciousness of her parents—first by applying to university, and later in other ways? Was it seeing comparatively little of them, even as she fought her way through sickness after sickness? Was it a temperamental mismatch: simply not liking the world into which she was being initiated? Philippa did fantasize from early childhood about leaving home. A notebook of juvenilia is preserved in her papers. The bulk of it is given to a long, rambling, largely unpunctuated story about two children, Tom (6) and Mary (5): "TOM AND MARY WERE REALLY VERY NICE CHILDREN BUT THEY WERE GREEDY AND SPOILT MARY WAS SPOILT AND TOM WAS GREEDY MARY HAD A BUNNY AND TOM A PONY THEY WERE VERY HAPPY." The story begins at Christmastime; the great excitement on Christmas morning is the announcement from their mother, Mrs. Hall, that she's sending them both away to school, Tom to "the Priory," Mary to "the Nunery" [sic].[30]

Perhaps it was all of this, plus a positive attraction to the vision projected by her last governess. She "actually had a degree" and said to Philippa, "you could go to university, you know"—mapping out for her the work she would need to do to pass Responsions.[31] Philippa's parents didn't understand, but also didn't try to stop her. Her mother did fret to a friend about what would become of her baby, doing something so common. Her friend consoled her: "Never mind, dear. She doesn't *look* clever."[32]

Philippa Bosanquet plunged into her correspondence work, terrified that she would not meet the standard but desperate to escape. No one could have wanted Oxford more or been more willing to suffer for it. She learned of a woman—a Mrs. Muir of 2 Bradmore Road, Oxford—who coached women for the University entrance exams. She moved to Oxford in 1938, then, at the same time as Scrutton and Murdoch, though she was a year younger. As Scrutton and Murdoch were being lectured by Vera Farnell about the need to preserve Somerville's reputation, Bosanquet and her new friend Anne Cobbe were revising and revising, hoping to be in Murdoch and Scrutton's shoes the following fall.

Someone—the same governess?—had told Bosanquet that Somerville was known among Oxford's women's colleges for being "intellectually but not socially snobby." That suited her perfectly.[33] On her application, Bosanquet expressed interest in being a writer, or perhaps a social worker. Philosophy she only discovered when she was sent to MacKinnon the following year. Her Latin may have been merely adequate and her mathematics little better. But like Scrutton and Murdoch, she wrote a stunning general paper, on liberalism— Somerville classics tutor Mildred Hartley still recalled it, 30 years later—and won a scholarship she didn't need.

MISS ANSCOMBE AGAIN

Anscombe could have easily never come into this story.

She was a year ahead of Murdoch and Scrutton and at a different college, was taught mostly by different tutors, and from her first weeks at Oxford gravitated to a small community of young Catholics and catechumens centered on Blackfriars Priory.[34] The Somervillians saw Anscombe at meetings of the Jowett Society, which she attended faithfully. And her friendship with Jean Coutts brought her to Somerville from time to time. (Anscombe was at St. Hugh's very little, it seems. On one occasion, she was called up before the Principal, Miss Gwyer, for dining too seldom in College.[35]) Anscombe was an impressive figure, but existed mostly at the periphery of Scrutton and Murdoch's world. She was unlike them, too, in that she was a philosopher before she ever set foot in Oxford.

St. Hugh's was the first among the women's colleges to hire a fellow in philosophy, Old Somervillian Mary Glover. Only Lady Margaret Hall had followed suit by 1937. But soon after the war began, Glover began sending Anscombe to tutors in other colleges for most subjects: perhaps because the St. Hugh's site had been requisitioned for a military hospital, perhaps because Glover thought Anscombe needed more than she could provide.* Her tutors' reports offer a vivid picture of her talent and temperament at ages 20–21.

Anscombe's Greek history tutor in the fall of 1939 could get no satisfactory answer from her as to why she had not read the assigned portions of Herodotus over the long vacation, and noted that she

---

* Somerville faced a similar (though less dramatic) fate, as the building where Scrutton lived in 1938–39 was appropriated the following year to house nurses from the Radcliffe Infirmary. (A few rooms on the ground floor were sectioned off for use by medical students. This area was known around Somerville for years to come as "the Isle of Man.") Scrutton and 30 others were sent to lodge in available rooms at Lady Margaret Hall for the 1939–40 academic year.

couldn't be bothered even with the smaller passages she was supposed to be reading week to week. Her father had died of cancer in late August, which seems explanation enough.[36] But if Anscombe was incapacitated rather than simply uninterested, the debility passed quickly. That year, she and her friend Norman Daniel wrote and published a pamphlet criticizing the British government's official justifications for the new war.[37] And that winter, Donald MacKinnon tutored her in Plato and found her work excellent.[38]

Anscombe remained consistently inconsistent for the rest of her undergraduate career. In Trinity term 1940, her tutor in modern philosophy fretted about her "reluctance to give the necessary attention to philosophers who repel her by their personality and/or their writings." The following term, her logic tutor, Martha Kneale, had nothing but praise for her capacity and dedication.[39] This oscillation came to a head in her final examinations in June 1941. Her philosophy papers were excellent—notwithstanding that she had been thumbing through Hobbes for the first time on the eve of her political theory paper. Her Greek history paper, thanks to some remedial work with Marcus Tod of Oriel, was acceptable, but her Roman history paper was bad. This led to a *viva* in which Anscombe simply froze. One of her examiners reportedly asked, "Is there a single fact about the period you are supposed to have studied of which you are able to inform your examiners?" As Michael Dummett remarks, for the philosophy examiners to have prevailed on their historian colleagues to give Anscombe a first, "her philosophy papers must have been astonishing."[40]

Already in her teens, Anscombe was drawn to philosophy, not knowing yet what it was. When she read Boedder's *Natural Theology*, she found she could not get the questions and arguments it raised out of her head. In particular, she found herself unable to stop puzzling about an argument Boedder made for the claim that "anything that comes about must have a cause."[41] Anscombe wrote:

> the proof had the fault of proceeding from a barely concealed assumption of its own conclusion. I thought that this was some sort of carelessness on the part of the author, and that it just needed tidying up. So I started writing improved versions of it; each one satisfied me for a time, but then reflection would show me that I had committed the same fault. . . . I tore them up when I found they were no good, and I went round asking people why, if something happened, they would be sure it had a cause. No one had an answer to this. In two or three years of effort I produced five versions of a would-be proof . . . . In all this time I had no philosophical teaching about the matter.[42]

She was frequently gripped by philosophical questions in this way. She attended Professor H.H. Price's lectures about perception before philosophy was even one of her subjects, and quickly became obsessed with the issues Price raised. As she recalled: "for years, I would spend time, in cafés, for example, staring at objects saying to myself: 'I see a packet. But what do I really see? How can I say that I see here anything more than a yellow expanse?'" She treasured Price's lectures—though, as she wrote, "not because I agreed with him." On the contrary: "I used to sit tearing my gown into little strips because I wanted to argue against so much that he said."[43]

If any of these women was certain to end up in philosophy, like the isolated figures of the preceding decades—Susan Stebbing, Dorothy Emmet, Mary Glover, Martha Kneale—it was Anscombe. Likewise, if any of them was more or less invulnerable to being turned aside by bad teaching—if there was one who needed no one to inspire her—it was Anscombe. Combative, uncomfortable in the role of a leader, she was nonetheless the one to whom the Somervillians would later look for inspiration, the one they were most eager to hear speak when they all made their way back to Oxford after the war. There, as graduate students, they began meeting in Philippa and Michael Foot's parlor at 16 Park Town. They began asking whether they had to believe what Ayer said about ethics—and what anyone might say instead.

They weren't the only ones returning to Oxford after the war, though, and wondering how to go beyond Ayer. There was also an ambitious, conscientious, haunted prisoner of war, against whom they would define themselves for decades.

Chapter 4

The Coming Philosophers

TWO WARS (I)

Late spring is the hot season in Thailand. Temperatures can clear 100 degrees, day after day. And in May 1943, along the Kwae Noi valley, they did. That's when Richard Hare and a party of fellow British officers were packed into box cars and sent from the large POW camp in Singapore to work on the Burma-Thailand railway.[1]

Work on the railway had begun in mid-1942. After the Allies established naval supremacy at the Battle of Midway, Japan needed to send troops and supplies overland in support of their campaign in Burma. The proposed route for the railway—along the Kwae Noi river then up and over the Three Pagodas Pass— was unattractive from an engineering standpoint, but was the best available option. It would connect Rangoon and Bangkok and thus the existing Burmese and Thai rail systems. As 1943 began, and Japanese forces were defeated again at Guadalcanal, the railway project took on increased urgency. Others—chiefly Australian POWs and conscripted locals—had been pounding along for months. Now, fearing what loss of time might mean, Imperial Japanese Army commanders began putting to work every prisoner they held: no matter how unwell, no matter if they had tools, or boots, or food.

Hare and the other officers of the 22nd Mountain Regiment had not been treated *well* at the Changi jail camp, where they were sent in February 1942. They were underfed. They were subject to disease and abuse. But life at Changi wasn't wretched. Temperatures by the sea weren't brutally hot (and were never cold). And as long as they didn't try to escape, the POWs were often left at their leisure.

Not for nothing had Hare been the top classical scholar at Rugby School and then at Balliol College, Oxford. He spent his first 15 months at Changi "improving [his] Urdu, learning some more languages (Persian and Italian)," attending lectures by fellow prisoners, singing in a church choir, growing vegetables they needed but were not getting otherwise—and writing a book.[2]

The book wouldn't have happened without a stroke of luck. After the fall of Singapore, it took the Japanese Army several days to get organized and arrange for direct supervision of their thousands of new prisoners; defeated Allied soldiers were told to go to Changi jail and wait. (There was no point in fleeing; they were 1500 miles from the nearest Allied territory.) While they waited, Hare nabbed "a beautiful ledger" from the prison office and began to record his philosophy.[3] When Hare was ordered to join the work gangs on the railway, over a year later, he strapped the ledger to his back, the way others packed Bibles or pictures of loved ones. Hare had few loved ones. His next of kin was the uncle who had taken him in when he was orphaned at 15. Hare carried his book.

On the ride to Bangkok, in terrible heat, having eaten almost nothing, Hare saw something remarkable. An air-conditioned passenger train pulled up next to the box cars holding Hare and his fellow prisoners. Directly across from him, framed in one of its windows, "as if in an aquarium, was a young Japanese officer, eating an excellent meal with an air of exquisite refinement." Hare would later recall this as a decisive moment in his life. He had been stationed in India before he was sent to Singapore; he reflected how the poor in India "must sometimes . . . have seen me myself doing the same."[4]

The march up the Kwae Noi valley was almost the end of him. Hare estimated that 20 to 40 percent of those who traveled with him from Singapore died and were buried near the grade. Allied medical officers were typically allowed to hold back a few men each day from bushwhacking, from blasting and hauling rock, from carrying baskets of soil. But their overseers also set quotas and limited exemptions. Under increasing pressure from Tokyo, they sent out the "able" (sometimes including those who couldn't keep food down) for shifts of up to 18 hours, working on rations of fewer than 1000 calories a day—mostly maggoty rice. They sometimes had eggs or rancid meat to eat, seldom any vegetables. Their medics sometimes had supplies to treat the men's dysentery and malaria and septic sores, sometimes not. Those who weren't sent out for heavy work were sometimes pressed into service digging pit toilets ("benjos") with the crudest tools, or with their hands. They were beaten for not doing what they were told, or sometimes for no reason at all.

The worst of the heat passed. Monsoon season began. Dozens of men were crowded into each tent, water coming through the roofs, water rising beneath the bamboo pallets where they slept, campsites and worksites turned to mud. Disease in camp increased. Hare willed himself to live. Whenever he was released from work, if he could lift his head and had something with which to write, he penned a few more lines of his book. Decades later, after Hare's death, a fellow soldier wrote to Hare's family, saying that Hare had kept *him* alive—by example and by encouragement. Hare and his fellow prisoners met at night and prayed Psalm 57, as it appears in the *Book of Common Prayer*: "They have laid a net for my feet, and pressed down my soul: they have digged a pit before me, and are fallen into the midst of it themselves. . . . Set up thyself, O God, above the heavens: and thy glory above all the earth."

Somehow, Hare and his book made it back to Singapore. He appended the following epigraph, from the Greek soldier-poet Archilochus:

> My spirit, my spirit, tumulted by griefs beyond repair—
> But rise—*set* yourself to face the foes that dash against;
> your heart, as enemies array to hem you in,
> plant steadfast! And neither in victory openly exult,
> nor in defeat collapse into wails at home,
> but rather delight in the delightful, and in anxious grief
> be moderate: recognize the rhythm that bears along human lives.[5]

TWO WARS (II)

Within a few weeks of the railway's completion, as Hare was returned to Singapore to try to recover his strength, Philippa Bosanquet moved into Iris Murdoch's London flat.[6]

Murdoch leased the flat in September 1942, almost as soon as she arrived in London for her wartime assignment. It was a remarkable place. Number 5 Seaforth Place, known to Bosanquet and Murdoch for the rest of their lives simply as "Seaforth," was the top floor of an abandoned warehouse and stables once used by a cluster of local brewers. There was no number 1, 2, 3, or 4: just the one door off a tiny alley. A steep, open stairway led up to a huge storage area above the old stables, and then up again to a barely divided living space (there was one large archway, with a curtain strung across). The space had had various functions over time: granary, hayloft, a place to sleep for grooms without other lodgings.

With a leaky greenhouse roof over "the kitchen" (that is, the space adjoining the stairs, where Murdoch set up an old gas oven) and "some six square miles of window to guard in blitz and blackout," the flat was blazing in summer, freezing in winter.[7] There was no running water except in the bathroom beneath the stairs, which doubled as a shelter during air raids. The only heat came from the oven and a small gas space-heater; warmth bled away through the windows and through cracks in the ceiling. Murdoch acquired a few bookshelves, a table and chairs, and a pair of armchairs. She slept on a cot. The rest of the furniture was orange-crates. A friend later described it as "like a stage set for a school performance of something by Dostoevsky."[8] The District line of the London Underground ran directly beneath the building. As trains came and went, Seaforth would rumble and shiver like the Bankses' house in *Mary Poppins*.

The first part of 1943 was "hellishly lonely" for Murdoch. In the fall of 1942, Mary Scrutton had been working in London; she and Murdoch had met regularly for lunch. Then Scrutton requested release from her position at the Ministry of Production to go teach at her old school, Downe House. The Ministry had been a bad fit. Scrutton's supervisor hadn't known how best to use her, and the tense atmosphere of an office where she was irritably dismissed whenever she asked for direction began to affect Scrutton's digestion. So now she was gone. Murdoch had exchanged letters with Bosanquet, beginning to cultivate their friendship further. But Bosanquet was still in Oxford, assisting her former tutor (now boyfriend), Hungarian economist Thomas Balogh. Murdoch went up to visit Bosanquet and Donald MacKinnon when she could. She steeled herself to a silent "yes" as she passed the signs posted on every railway platform: "Is your journey really necessary?" All the young men she had known at Oxford were now at war. She wrote to some of them—particularly Frank Thompson, to whom she was increasingly attached. (Thompson would be killed in Bulgaria in 1944.) For someone whose university life had been overflowing with friendship and discovery, it was a profoundly alienating time.

In late January 1943, Murdoch wrote to Thompson, first in a comic spirit about how the mice at Seaforth Place were eating his letters ("I am not on very good terms with the mice, and the fact that I have been careless enough to leave valuables around where they could get at them can be chalked up as a point to them"), but then with a vulnerability she seldom exposed in correspondence: "I wish you would come home . . . you and the others. . . . [I'm] oh so much in need of intellectual intimacy. The patient mind which is prepared to comprehend my own and toss me back the ball of my own thought." She was reading and trying to write, she said, but finding both difficult. With affected casualness, she remarked that she had "parted company with [her] virginity," but added that she didn't love the man.[9] She had written earlier to Bosanquet that she felt "like going out and picking up the first man I meet that's willing, simply for the sake of a more intense relationship of any description with another human being."[10] She *saw* lots of people in then-bohemian Fitzrovia, but connected deeply with none. She offered herself as a low-level spy for the Communist Party, copying Treasury documents and leaving them in a hollow tree in Kensington Gardens for a fellow agent to collect.[11] But that wasn't friendship either. Fearful for Thompson and others, salving the wound with sex, furtively passing along the (mostly dull) documents to which she had access, Murdoch seemed to her colleagues withdrawn.

Bosanquet's arrival at Seaforth in October 1943 was water and life to Murdoch. Now in London working for the Royal Institute of

International Affairs at Chatham House, assisting a group planning toward postwar reconstruction, Bosanquet drew Murdoch out of isolation. Each offered something to the other: Bosanquet brought laughter and conversation to Seaforth. (She also brought more and better furniture.) For her part, Murdoch led Bosanquet into worlds she longed to inhabit. Culture, for one. Even after three years at Oxford, Bosanquet felt desperately undereducated. Murdoch shared her own voracious reading with her new best friend. It was Murdoch's habit to grab a book and sink into an armchair immediately on arriving home, and Bosanquet began doing the same. They read Dickens together, and Proust, and Beckett. Bosanquet's commonplace book from these years is stuffed with quotes from authors who preoccupied Murdoch: Bernanos, Buber, Gorki, Jung, Marcel, and Pascal. Above all, Kierkegaard. Murdoch also took Bosanquet along to parties in Fitzrovia with Dylan Thomas and Arthur Koestler—with whom Murdoch had (of course) struck up casual acquaintanceships. Afterward, the women wended their way back through the foggy streets or on the underground, navigating platforms packed with refugees from the bombed-out East End.

Murdoch welcomed Bosanquet, too, into a frugal, even spartan life that was the antithesis of everything Bosanquet had known growing up. On Bosanquet's first night at Seaforth, Murdoch told her that once the lights were off, she could use the blackout cloth over the greenhouse glass as a blanket; they didn't have others. They sometimes went to bed in their coats, with hot-water bottles at their feet, as Seaforth barely kept the weather out. That winter, Bosanquet wrote to her mother, "the fog even in this room is so thick that I can but dimly discern Iris across the other side."[12] They shared shoes, and wore them out, and then walked around in bad shoes. On their days off, they queued for rush tickets to see the opera or the ballet. Bosanquet began to feel, for the first time in her life, both cultured and unfussy. When a V2 rocket destroyed several houses nearby, blowing out their windows, the women laughed and laughed when the alarm clock rang five minutes later. They headed off to work that morning, picking their way across the new rubble, seeing if anyone needed a hand.

HOMECOMINGS

Hare finished his book in September 1945, on a converted ocean liner sailing home. Fighting recurring malaria, he plunged immediately back into his studies. He too was a child of 1919; he had come up with Anscombe in 1937. Like Anscombe (and Murdoch, and Scrutton), Hare read Greats. He had taken his initial examinations in classical languages the winter before he enlisted, but still had the second half of his course to complete. Like Bosanquet—now Foot— who returned at the same time, Hare came back to an Oxford very different from the one he had left.

Nina Bawden, who lived through the transition, describes Oxford during and after the war:

> In the autumn of 1943, Oxford slept in a strange and timeless silence. No bells rang in wartime, from clock tower or steeple, and there was almost no traffic; the uncluttered curve of the High, the spires of the colleges, slept in the clean, moist, quiet air as in some old don's dream of peace.
>
> When I went back to Oxford for my third and last year . . . Oxford was changing. The ex-servicemen were coming back . . . seeming to us older than their actual years warranted, stern purposeful men with wives and moustaches, taking over

our university and reducing us, by their middle-aged presence, to the status of schoolchildren. . . . Our streets, our cafés, our societies—the whole of our playground was invaded by . . . soldiers and sailors and airmen; . . . the Radcliffe Camera [a reading room for the Bodleian Library], so comfortably adequate for its reduced wartime population, was busy as a mainline station at rush hour.[13]

The influx of ex-servicemen like Hare—both among the faculty and among the students—was certainly the most dramatic change in the Oxford scene. Oxford was once again crowded, and once again dominated by men. Once more, as Scrutton later remarked, "a lot of good female thinking [was] wasted because it simply [didn't] get heard."[14] It is sad but unsurprising that Oxford in the late 1940s trained no women who went on to do the kind of work that Anscombe, Foot, Murdoch, and Scrutton did. That would have to wait until their generation (and others who came up just after them, like Mary Warnock) established themselves in the women's colleges and began mentoring other young women. The return of male dominance in shared spaces was one factor. Another was a shift away from the close mentoring relationships that enabled Foot, Murdoch, and Scrutton to imagine a life in philosophy. This was as much a matter of circumstance as of prejudice. It affected men as well as women—though the better-resourced men's colleges blunted the effect on their students. But the crowded streets and shops and lecture halls meant that most students no longer received the one-on-one tutorials that had been standard through the early 1940s.[15]

On the other hand, the swollen population also meant tremendous enrichment for the mature students and younger faculty coming back: people like Foot and Hare, and soon Scrutton and Murdoch. If combined tutorials became more common, the lecture lists also became more expansive and diverse. As Mary Warnock recalled, faculty "[came] back from the war with their heads full of new books which, before they were written, could be tried out in lectures."[16] Philosophy in particular saw a dramatic revival at Oxford. In the final years of the war, the student-run Jowett Society typically drew around 10 attendees per session. At the first meeting of Michaelmas term 1945, attendance leaped to 74. That was an early show of enthusiasm—attendance at the next meeting was only 26—but subsequent meetings continued to draw dramatically better than during wartime. There were several spikes of 50 or more, even as the faculty-run Philosophical Society began meeting separately for the first time since 1941.

Oxford was quickly becoming the most prominent center of philosophical activity in the English-speaking world. Gilbert Ryle, Ayer's old tutor and now holder of one of the University's three distinguished professorships in philosophy, had everything to do with this. Before the war, as a fellow of Christ Church College, Ryle used to coach crew as well as teach philosophy. After the war, as Waynflete Professor of Metaphysical Philosophy, he brought the spirit he used to build teams of rowers to building a team of philosophers instead. He approached the task no less competitively.[17]

Ryle disagreed with many of Ayer's specific opinions but was convinced that something like the critical analysis of language Ayer practiced was the way of the future.[18] As Hare recalled, Ryle "made it his business to secure the many philosophical jobs that were then vacant for young philosophers of a school that he thought most promising, the analytical."[19] Ryle further promoted the kind of philosophy he valued as editor of one of the premier journals in the discipline, *Mind*. The result, over the coming decade and a half, was the establishment of a distinctive Oxford style: a style that would become more sharply defined over time, especially after the 1952 appointment, on Ryle's recommendation, of J.L. Austin to the White's Professorship of

Moral Philosophy. I will consider the Oxford style more closely in the next chapter.

There would have been a lot of philosophy going on, regardless. Due to the inclusion of philosophy in two of Oxford's best-known courses (Greats and PPE), Oxford had always been home to an unusually large number of philosophers—far more than Cambridge, which employed only a handful. Philosophy at Oxford wasn't just for people who wanted a philosophy degree. All kinds of people whose real interests lay in politics or ancient history ended up studying philosophy along the way, because it was part of the package. PPE, in particular, grew in popularity after the war. Over time, the sheer percentage of Britain's national elite who had studied a little philosophy at Oxford led to Oxford-style philosophy becoming a surprisingly prominent topic of public conversation. In the short term, the percentage of students at Oxford who studied philosophy meant that Oxford needed many, many philosophy teachers.

To cultivate candidates for these positions, Ryle designed and promoted a new graduate course, the B.Phil. Instead of a long thesis, the new degree required a series of examinations and a shorter thesis. The B.Phil. also took just two years, and thus could quickly begin emitting a stream of young philosophers with advanced training. The first term in which graduate classes were listed alongside philosophy lectures was Michaelmas 1946. A year later, there were five graduate classes advertised, up from three. A year after that, there were eleven. The first B.Phil. degrees were awarded in 1948. But in the postwar years, Ryle and his colleagues also trusted their instincts; they didn't require the B.Phil. of the candidates they liked best. Hare was hired to teach at his alma mater, Balliol College, immediately upon completion of his undergraduate examinations in 1947. He was made a fellow of Balliol shortly thereafter.

Into this rich ferment—not yet resolved into anything dogmatic—first Foot returned, then Scrutton, then Murdoch.

Foot returned to Somerville as a graduate student, working on a B.Litt. (the B.Phil. was not yet available). Already in her first two years back, she took pupils on the side. Her husband Michael was still finishing his degree, and they needed the money. Foot was an impressive teacher from the first: "meticulous, imaginative ... inspiring."[20] In 1947, Somerville hired Foot as a lecturer on a trial basis. Two years later, after she had taught herself enough Greek to be able to tutor Greats pupils, the College elevated her to a fellowship. Scrutton too returned to Oxford shortly after the war, though initially she had no formal connection to the University. (From 1945–47, she worked for retired classical scholar Gilbert Murray, assisting him with his memoirs.) The same year Foot became a lecturer, Scrutton began a D.Phil. thesis on the late-classical neo-Platonist, Plotinus. The year after that, matching people with positions like a younger Gilbert Ryle, Foot managed to find a place at St. Anne's College, Oxford for Murdoch.

But Foot's newest friend, the one who would shape her work the most deeply, had never really left.

Anscombe and Foot (then Bosanquet) probably became acquainted in 1941. Anscombe had graduated but was still at St. Hugh's, working on a D.Phil. thesis about "Thomas Aquinas on the identity of bodies."[21] She was a busy woman. She was also taking a few pupils and presiding over the Jowett Society, which Bosanquet had finally joined. She was *also* preparing for her wedding that December. Bosanquet and Anscombe were fixtures at the Society for the next five terms, each reading papers with the other in attendance. In Michaelmas 1942, Bosanquet was secretary of the Society and ascended the following term (as was customary) to the presidency.

For some reason—another bout of ill health?—Bosanquet did not deliver the traditional end-of-term presidential address. Anscombe stood in for her.

That year, Anscombe was awarded the Sarah Smithson studentship at Newnham College, Cambridge. She continued to come and go from Oxford, though, working on her thesis and teaching for St. Hugh's and other colleges even as she moved to Cambridge and began attending lectures by one of most famous philosophers of the twentieth century: the intense, tormented Austrian émigré Ludwig Wittgenstein. Teaching opportunities—more plentiful in Oxford, even in wartime—were one reason for the coming and going. Like the Foots after the war, Anscombe and her new husband, fellow philosopher and fellow convert Peter Geach, needed all the money they could get. They weren't living together, except at brief intervals. Geach, a conscientious objector, had been conscripted into timber production in lieu of military service.[22] Their first child Barbara was born in 1943. Then the Smithson award ran out. Geach and Anscombe had found a landlord in Cambridge who rented to poor families with children and let them sublet.[23] Anscombe earned enough by teaching to justify the commute, but the couple were poor—especially toward the end of the war, when their second child arrived.[24] Addicted to smoking, Anscombe sometimes retrieved cigarette stubs from the pavement.[25]

In 1946, Anscombe "returned" to Oxford as the recipient of the Mary Somerville Research Fellowship at Somerville College. She took lodgings in Oxford while Geach remained in Cambridge. Once again, she found herself commuting: to see her husband and children and to continue her studies with Wittgenstein. And once again, they were poor. Geach did not work during this period, except on his own philosophical research, which would bear fruit in a string of influential articles in the 1950s. He minded the children and studied logic. Anscombe pursued her research, participated in the life of two universities and, by a special dispensation from the usual regulations governing the Mary Somerville Fellowship, did a little teaching on the side. In early 1948, Somerville Principal Janet Vaughan was approached by a Philadelphia-based charity looking to send aid packages to "intelligent, educated, white-collar [families] who . . . [had] been caught between the fixed income and rising prices" of the postwar years. Vaughan offered several names, but highlighted Anscombe as the neediest, describing the family's situation as "really rather desperate": "the children need food, clothing, and anything that can be sent for them." She only warned her correspondent that Anscombe was unlikely to satisfy "the wives of prominent citizens" who hoped to receive photographs and letters from the objects of their charity: "Miss Anscombe is an extremely brilliant philosopher, but . . . [h]er mind only really works on the highest abstract problems, and I doubt if she ever writes a letter to anybody."*, 26

The Mary Somerville Research Fellowship was ostensibly for continued work on Anscombe's D.Phil. project—which she never submitted. She sent with her application *two* complete theses as proof of her ability to produce finished prose, and said that she had written a third. As she had spent her late adolescence writing version after version of a proof that "anything that comes about must have a cause," she had spent the war years writing and discarding versions of her doctoral thesis. She wrote, "I have been in great difficulties in the attempt to bring my work . . . to a conclusion because my philosophical ideas have undergone radical alterations in the last two years." She had not stopped thinking about ancient and modern conceptions of body and soul, and in particular about "Aristotle's

---

* Vaughan was wrong about the last point. Anscombe was an appreciative correspondent with many friends and colleagues over her lifetime. But Vaughan's letter shows the impression Anscombe made in her first years at Somerville. And Vaughan wasn't wrong about the probability of Anscombe sending pictures of her children to the wives of prominent citizens in Philadelphia.

concept of 'life.'"[27] But in the meantime, she had found the person with whom she wanted to think through these things: Wittgenstein. And as Wittgenstein's apostle to Oxford, she would help her friends see an alternative to the theory of ethics ascending there: Hare's.

BEYOND "BOO" AND "HURRAH"

Ethics was generally out of favor in the postwar Oxford scene— notwithstanding how many ethical questions the war had raised. "Moral philosophy was a despised subject," Mary Warnock wrote, "though it had to be taught because 'Morals and Politics' was a compulsory subject in both Greats and PPE."[28]

Part of the problem was Ayer. Whether or not they were sympathetic to his ideas, no one thought they could philosophize about ethics anymore—or about anything "metaphysical"—without addressing Ayer's critique. Ayer's doctrine, again, was that things people say only have meaning when they express either (1) definitions or rules of logic, or (2) actual or theoretically possible observations. If you're using words but not articulating definitions or logic, and not talking about things you (or someone) could see, hear, taste, smell, or touch, you're not saying anything. Your words are meaningless.

The implication for ethical discourse, Ayer concluded, is that it is meaningless. Moral judgments can show feelings of approval or disapproval. But they can't, strictly speaking, *say* anything. They are like cheers or boos at a sporting event. A fan who boos an opposing player shows how he feels, but he doesn't make a *claim*. And if someone responds, "that's false!" or "liar!" they're either joking or have misunderstood. A boo can't be false (or true). It can't be a lie. It's expressive, but lacks what philosophers call "propositional content."

Though Ayer himself didn't liken ethical discourse to fan support, it quickly became a common shorthand for his theory (or anti-theory) of ethics. In January 1940, there was a discussion at the Jowett Society (MacKinnon was one of the discussants) on "The Boo-Hurrah Theory of Moral Judgments." The more technical label for Ayer's theory, taken from a drier, duller elaboration by American philosopher Charles Stevenson, was "emotivism." Ethical language *emotes*, but is otherwise empty.

It wasn't that no one had convictions about how to live; people always do. Nor was it that no one had any philosophical thoughts about ethics. But the dominant view was that ethics was "a subject without an object."[29] As a philosophical topic, ethics was a dead end. There was no point discussing it, other than to explain why the discussion could go nowhere.

I said above that Ayer was only part of the reason that ethics was "despised." Ayer or no Ayer, lots of people had internalized the billiard-ball picture, and with it the idea of a dichotomy between facts and values. Even some of Ayer's signature ideas predated *Language, Truth and Logic*. Writing in 1923, literary critic I.A. Richards and philosopher C.K. Ogden anticipated Ayer at several points. Ogden and Richards contrasted statements like "the height of the Eiffel Tower is 900 feet" with "more primitive," "emotive" uses of language which are not "theoretically verifiable"—exactly as Ayer would a dozen years later.[30] Over the following two decades, this became an intellectual orthodoxy—in Oxford above all. Warnock summarized the *Zeitgeist* of 1940s Oxford like this: people drew a hard distinction "between reality, the facts of science, and subjective emoting . . . . Only the scientific was to be respected as true."[31] Ayer's book was a vivid expression of the billiard-ball picture. But the picture would have gripped the imagination of philosophers and their audiences regardless. And once you're inside that picture, moral philosophy is bound to seem like a waste of effort.

Over time, emotivism proved unworkable as a philosophical theory, notwithstanding how attractive it had been to Ayer and other tough-minded skeptics. A better theory was needed—even by those who merely wanted to dismiss ethics once and for all. It was hard to imagine, though: who would do this thankless work at a time when moral philosophy was passé?

Nevertheless, by 1950, in busy, busy Oxford, someone had done the job. A new theory was available, one that would reign in Oxford and beyond for the next decade. The new theory retained the billiard-ball picture but imbued it with sobriety, even grandeur. It cleverly overcame the flaws of emotivism while linking ethics to the Dawkins sublime.

Only a very particular kind of person could have come up with this theory. Only someone brilliant, who could see his way through a host of technical difficulties. Only someone with considerable self-possession and grit, willing to work hard on "a despised subject." Indeed, only someone deadly earnest, someone who had learned through hard experience "the supreme importance of oneself."[32] Only Hare.

What was wrong with emotivism? Why was Hare's new theory needed? In its crudest form, in *Language, Truth and Logic,* emotivism made nonsense of how people discuss moral questions. Emotivism claims to expose—to unmask—what is *really* going on in moral discourse. But an "unmasking" theory like emotivism *must* persuasively explain the concrete details of the discourse it unmasks. If it can't do this—if its explanations of these details are forced or unilluminating—then it fails as a theory. So it was with emotivism. Because if moral judgments are like "boo" or "hurrah," it is hard to understand what is going on when people argue about ethics, trying to persuade one another. Indeed, is the comparison even plausible? Think of an actual conversation where you were trying to bring someone around on a question of how to behave. Was it remotely like one group of fans trying to shout down another—drowning out boos with hurrahs? Didn't you, rather, bring up facts and principles that you saw as relevant to your case?

Stevenson saw the difficulty and responded, not by rejecting emotivism but by refining it (and at the same time, coining the term). Stevenson argued that a moral judgment is not just a manifestation of a subjective attitude, but also a subtle form of manipulation. Perhaps moral judgments don't truly *mean* anything, but we can give a more compelling explanation of how they are *used*. Their declarative, fact-like mode of expression pressures listeners to conform to the speaker's attitude (because we find it uncomfortable to contradict others). To say that we should incarcerate fewer people, then, is not simply to cheer for criminal-justice reform. It conveys something like, "I approve of this; *do so as well* [emphasis mine]."[33] Stevenson added that it makes perfect sense for people to highlight what they like about, for example, lowering the incarceration rate, the way someone might highlight what they like about key-lime pie, in hopes of prodding someone to try it ("it's the contrast between the creamy tartness of the filling and the sweetness and flake of the crust"). But this doesn't mean there are facts about good and bad, in either case. Stevenson saw no philosophically interesting difference between judgments about desert and judgments about dessert.

Stevenson's updated version of emotivism was an advance on Ayer's. But it faced equally grave difficulties. For one thing, it can only be a correct analysis of the discourse of people who don't understand it. Once people grasp that the surface character of moral discourse is deceptive, and useful only to manipulate, they can't interact the way they did before their eyes were opened. For one thing, they will arm themselves against moral talk.[34] If you know that the power of moral language lies in a misleading resemblance to factual discourse, you won't be taken in. Faced with someone who won't let you say you don't like baked-fruit pies, but keeps insisting that *baked fruit is delicious* (perhaps counting the ways), you're likelier to laugh in their face than fall into doubt. The plausibility of the emotivist analysis of moral discussion depends on the truth being concealed from the people involved. A person who knows they're being manipulated won't fall for it.[35]

There's also another, more important problem with Stevenson's version of emotivism. The practice of moral reasoning is more intricate than people simply expressing their likes or dislikes. We also try to work out the implications of our commitments, and press one another on perceived inconsistencies ("if you're really pro-life, shouldn't you oppose the death penalty?"; "if you object to killing animals, shouldn't you oppose late-term abortions?"). There is nothing equivalent to this in the realm of dessert. If I like apple pie but dislike peach cobbler, so what? Wouldn't it be absurd, someone urging me to be more consistent in my attitudes toward baked-fruit desserts?

Hare's new idea, which he began developing almost as soon as he took his degree, was that moral language is *universally prescriptive*. Any sincere moral judgment implies a command (a *prescription*), to anyone in similar circumstances (*universally*) to act in accordance with that judgment. Like Immanuel Kant, whom he studied closely when he returned to Oxford (with MacKinnon, like the Somervillians before him), Hare concentrated not on words like "good" or "bad" but on the word "ought." So, to say that I *ought* to look in on an elderly neighbor implies a command to anyone in circumstances like mine, with a neighbor like this, to look in on them.

Not all prescriptions are universal. (I can perfectly well tell someone to shut a gate and not imply anything more than that I want *this* person to shut *this* gate, here and now.) But some *are* universal. And these prescriptions—these "oughts"—have logical implications. If I say that professors ought to evaluate student work anonymously,

I can be criticized for inconsistency if I don't do so myself. And if I derived this "ought" from a more general principle, about evaluating others' qualifications without prejudice, I can be pressed too to accept further implications of this principle: in hiring practices, say. Hare saw this universal prescriptivity as the key to what he would call, in the title of his first book, "the language of morals."

Hare's theory neatly solved the problems of earlier forms of emotivism. Above all, it explained the possibility of moral reasoning: why we feel rational pressure to adjust or clarify our ethical views in response to criticism, as no one feels rational pressure to adjust or clarify their tastes. ("Goodness, you're right; I liked that strawberry-rhubarb pie. I retract what I said earlier about the apple. It wouldn't be consistent.") On Hare's theory, moral discourse is not only meaningful; it has an internal logic. So moral argument makes sense.

But Hare retained the picture of a value-free universe, which Foot found entrapping. There are no ethical facts, Hare thought. There are just people living out different sets of ethical commitments. The kind of reasoning that people do, according to Hare, is reasoning about the implications of various possible commitments. We make "decisions of principle," as Hare called them, and then try to live by them.[36]

RICHARD MERVYN (I)

Hare was a difficult man, short-tempered and impatient with disagreement. His Balliol students made up a rhyme about him:

> My pupils I have always taught
> You cannot get from "is" to "ought."
> This is the burden of my song:
> "It's in my book, or else it's wrong."[37]

Hare had suffered, and not only in the war. As already mentioned, he was an orphan. His father died of a heart attack in 1929, when Hare was ten, as the first months of the global recession began tearing at the family business. Hare's mother took it over and tried to preserve it, but it continued to decline, and with it, their standard of living. The Hares moved from a large country house to a small one, and then to a flat. Five years later, in 1934, Hare's mother died, leaving him in the care of two uncles, her brothers.

The stream of bad news must have reached young Hare mostly by letter. From age eight, two years before his father's death, he was at boarding schools, initially at Copthorne in Sussex (which he later described as "a cruel place"), then from 1932 at Rugby, where he had won a large scholarship.[38] A school report survives from a few months after his mother's death. Hare was distinguishing himself in most subjects, especially in his studies of Demosthenes and Lucretius. His housemaster remarked that he wished he "could be of more help" to the boy, describing the young Hare as "very self-contained."[39] Doubtless he was. And then came the war.

How did these experiences form Hare? Already forced in late adolescence to rely on himself, Hare was "pushed onto his back leg" (as a student of his later remarked) by his wartime experiences. On the Burma-Thailand railway, "[m]oral principles could not be argued about with one's captors, only affirmed in the face of them by an act of will."[40] It is a short step from there to the doctrine of *The Language of Morals*, that each individual must "make up his own mind which way he ought to live; for in the end everything rests on such a decision of principle."[41]

Interestingly, his experiences did not lead Hare to embrace the billiard-ball picture—or not at first. In the book he wrote as a prisoner, *An Essay in Monism*, he sought to rise above his sufferings by discerning a deeper, more important reality behind or beneath what we experience. The book's central notion is "rhythm" or "harmony." The particular "things" about which we talk and think—people, their actions, objects in the world—are defined by ordering principles which Hare calls "rhythms." In the end, everything is connected to everything else by a larger, encompassing rhythm within which everything finds its place. The book concludes with some reflections on worship, which draws together all the diverse ways that we achieve harmony with ourselves and the world. "It is thus," Hare writes, "that the partial Rhythm of the Person finds its rest in the perfect Rhythm of the Whole."

That closing sentence is representative of the elevated and elevating tone of the book, quite unlike Hare's published works. Under the influence of the kind of professionalized, analytic philosophy he encountered on his return to Oxford, Hare quickly came to regard his wartime efforts as "worthless." He turned to more respected topics and a more reserved tone. But as A.W. Price notes, there are traces in the *Essay* of Hare's later views, notably in the connection he draws between the meaning of life and *will*: "if we are to find order and unity in the world," Hare writes in the *Essay*, "we must make our own contribution to it."[42]

Despite his brilliance and the awe with which many of his students regarded him, Hare never fit comfortably into the scene Ryle was shaping. He was not a collaborative thinker. Wounded and touchy, he inspired his students with his absolute integrity and his admonitions to face up to one's responsibilities, make one's own decisions of principle, and live them out. This was Hare's connection to the Dawkins sublime. Without trying to pass off your responsibility on anyone else, you have to choose a set of principles and live by them. It is the only way to be grown up.

But Hare was nearly as much an outsider to the Oxford mainstream as Anscombe, Foot, Murdoch, and Scrutton would become.

People who knew him well attest that he was rescued by his 1947 marriage to Catherine Verney. Her brother Stephen, one of Hare's earliest pupils, admired him greatly, and arranged an introduction between Hare and his sister. Hare was, Stephen told her, "one of the coming philosophers."[43] Catherine certainly noticed his intelligence, but was equally impressed with how practically skillful he was: growing vegetables, designing and making sandals (a pair of which she was still wearing, years after his death). Did she, like Desdemona, love Richard too "for the dangers [he] had passed"?[44] They were swiftly engaged, and Catherine spent the ensuing half-century soothing and softening Richard in his frequently combative relations to his peers. She maintained a bridge to the wider world. Richard later described his life from 1934, when his mother died, until 1947 as "a night of mostly bad dreams between two extremely happy days."[45]

A WORLD OF WOMEN

In late summer 1948, Murdoch moved back to Oxford, rejoining her friends and taking up the appointment she had won (over Scrutton) at St. Anne's College.* Foot, who had informed Murdoch about the opening, then offered Murdoch lodgings with her and Michael at number 16 Park Town. Murdoch stayed with the Foots for over a year before moving just around the corner into a house, number 43, where she had lived briefly as an undergraduate. Since 1945, Scrutton had been living in the attic of a building (number 55) a short way uphill, in an adjoining crescent. Living frugally, but reveling in her

---

* Scrutton indulged her frustration by beheading a bed of irises, but she and Murdoch were quickly reconciled. Murdoch for her part felt wretched about competing with her friend and told herself (and Foot) that Scrutton was sure to get the position, though she applied all the same. See Iris Murdoch to Philippa Foot, April 24, 1948, in *Living on Paper*, ed. Avril Horner and Anne Rowe (London: Chatto & Windus, 2015), 107.

independence after too long at home or in institutional housing, Scrutton livened up her room with "a huge Chinese flag . . . displaying a big purple dragon with bulging black-and-white eyes on a sulphur-yellow background."[46] And now finally, after years of Foot and Murdoch and Scrutton seeing one another seldom and separately, "the sweeping view from [Scrutton's] attic window included them all."[47]

Number 16 Park Town is the last in a curving terrace of graceful, mid-Victorian houses facing a shared garden space. Clad with honey-colored Bath limestone, and built in the same Greek-revival style as so much of that famous resort town, the Park Town crescents stand in sharp contrast to the Gothic and neo-Gothic architecture of most of Oxford's colleges and some of its grander residences. To help with their mortgage, the Foots routinely took in lodgers. The ground floor was the Foots' living space and where the three Somervillians began to meet regularly—often joined by Anscombe, living most of the time on her own and now a Somervillian too.

Foot hosted her friends, even when she had little energy to participate in their conversations. Newly appointed to her lectureship at Somerville, she was cramming Greek so she could tutor Greats students and secure her long-term future. But Foot never did anything at the expense of her students. Averaging 12 hours of tutorials per week, not the 10 for which Somerville had contracted her, overpreparing for every tutorial (she later advised a junior colleague at Somerville, "never ask a student a question to which you do not know the answer"),[48] Foot's work/life balance resembled MacKinnon's during the war. Michael had now finished his B.A. and was working on a graduate thesis about Gladstone. When he got a chance, he would regale visitors with his working hypotheses and with the latest things he'd learned in the archives. Philippa would fall asleep in her chair as he talked. She was on sick leave through most of Michaelmas term, 1948.[49]

The friends went on meeting, though: they met at the Foots'; they met in tea shops; they went together to lectures and classes, including to Anscombe's debut lectures that fall, on "Some Ground Problems in the Theory of Knowledge." And they began, finally, to talk seriously about Ayer and Stevenson and Hare. They had one year together, before Scrutton secured a job at the University of Reading and left Oxford for good. Not knowing it was the end, they laid hold of it as fiercely as if they did.

Murdoch's journals from this year give a picture of what their life together was like. They are littered with shorthand references to her friends: Mary or M (though M could also be "Michael"), Pip or P, Elizabeth or E, often in combination. After visiting Oxford to interview for the position at St. Anne's, she wrote, "A world of women. I reflected, talking with Mary, Pip & Elizabeth, how much I love them."[50]

What did they talk about? They talked about an idea that Hare too was exploring. In 1950, Hare won the T.H. Green Moral Philosophy Prize, for a thesis in two parts. The first part would become *The Language of Morals*. The second part, which Ryle and the other judges dissuaded Hare from pursuing, was that "thick" concepts—concepts that seem to involve both description and evaluation, fact and value—might be a foundation for moral judgment. In his thesis, Hare recalled, one of his examples was "friend."[51]

In their tea shop and parlor conversations, the four friends were talking about a similarly thick concept, inspired by Foot's patrician upbringing: rudeness. "Rude" is plainly a descriptive term, and one can gather evidence to support a judgment that an action is rude. These judgments can be correct or incorrect. But rudeness is also an inherently evaluative concept, a concept one could not understand without recognizing that to call an action "rude" is to judge it as *bad* behavior.

Like so much else that the four women were thinking about together that year, the idea of thick concepts came to them from Wittgenstein, through Anscombe. But it began to suggest a possibility to Foot—to all of them. If judgments of rudeness could be objectively correct or incorrect, what other judgments might be? What about judgments of cruelty or compassion? Justice or injustice? What about evil, like the scenes Foot had seen in the Pathé newsreels? What about good?

Hare could be terribly stubborn, but like nearly everyone, he was susceptible to others' judgments about intellectual respectability. Did he come to *perceive* that there is no *kosmos* (as the Stoics called it)—no harmony or "rhythm"—underlying the things of this world? Or was that simply a view that no "coming philosopher" could defend in postwar Oxford without provoking a smirk? Did he regretfully recognize some insuperable objection to the idea that friendship could be one among many foundations for objective moral judgments? Or was the near-universal acceptance of the billiard-ball picture by his Oxford peers simply too difficult to resist?

There is a sad irony in the fact that Hare would become the *bête noir* of Foot and her friends, the person whose views they targeted and worked to overthrow. They were so alike, Foot and Hare especially: recoiling from the inequalities they had known, traumatized by the horrors of the war and inspired to think about ethics by those horrors, earnestly committed to doing good in the world, disciplined to a fault.

But Hare was committed to a metaphysical picture on which the things the Nazis did were not objectively *wrong*.[52] And that was the thought that Foot and her friends were determined to resist. The first thing they had to do, though, before they could clarify their contrasting thoughts, was to get clear on the picture they needed to smash. And that it was a picture. The best person for the job was an aspiring novelist.

Chapter 5

Murdoch's Diagnosis

"HARD & LUCID & INVIGORATING"

Wednesday, October 24, 1945. Iris Murdoch locked her hotel room on Rue Neuve and set off at a brisk pace toward the eastern edge of the old town. She had an appointment to keep, for a change.[1]

Murdoch had been biding her time in Brussels for about eight weeks, resorting to sightseeing as she waited for someone to put her to work. Her employer, the United Nations Relief and Rehabilitation Administration (UNRRA), had an ambitious and inspiring mission—coordinating dozens of far-flung aid organizations to address the needs of war victims. But precisely because it involved fusions of cultures, national and institutional, the UNRRA was in a perpetual state of disarray, reflecting the postwar disarray of Europe itself. When Murdoch first left the Treasury in mid-1944 to work for the UNRRA, she wrote to a friend, "I wander, amidst . . . what may one day be an organisation, trying to persuade myself and others that I am doing a job."[2] To another, she described her coworkers: a mixture of "inept British civil servants (whom their departments could well spare; me for instance), uncoordinated foreigners with Special Ideas and an imperfect command of English and go-getting Americans and Canadians. The result is pretty fair chaos."[3] Now finally on the continent after over a year of waiting and hoping—wanting to do something concrete for the good of the world—Murdoch found herself cooling her heels again. Almost as soon as she arrived, an administrative reorganization left her with few responsibilities.

Brussels was the European capital least damaged by the war, and Murdoch spent day after day wandering the streets. She took pleasure in "masquerading as a British officer"[4] at the servicemen's clubs, but above all in getting the richest experience of high culture she could. She was on the continent for the first time since her school days. Murdoch brought to Brussels her whole Oxford and post-Oxford education plus the restive energy of someone who hasn't been anywhere new for years. She walked around in reverie, taking in the eclectic mix of architecture—gothic, baroque, art nouveau—and all the incidental textures of the city: "the French voices, ridiculous little dogs, the little clanging trams, and the way everyone rides on the running boards and never pays their fare . . . ."[5] Best of all, she spent hours in the Musée des Beaux Arts, gravitating again and again to Brueghel's *Landscape with the Fall of Icarus.**

Murdoch surely knew W.H. Auden's famous pre-war meditation on Brueghel's painting—or, really, on human suffering and how easily we turn from it. In both the poem and the painting, wingless Icarus

---

* Murdoch's joy was partly—but only partly—explained by her love for the painting itself. It was also joy at the restoration of something loved and long withheld. Direct encounters with art were, like travel, one of the sacrifices of war while it lasted. In June, Murdoch wrote to a friend, in ecstasies about the first few dozen pictures that had returned to the National Gallery in London: "Oh heavenly bliss! . . . The Van Eyck man and pregnant wife. Bellini and Mantegna Agonies. Titian *Noli me tangere*. Rubens' *Bacchus and Ariadne*. El Greco *Agony*, Rembrandt portraits of self and of an old lady. His small *Woman Bathing* (lovely!). A delicious Claude fading into blue blue blue—blue lake, mountains, sky. Incredible distances to breathe. Two Vermeers, so blue and lemon, honey stuff, girls at the Virginals. And then oh more Bellini and Rubens, and then the Ruisdaels, the Hobbemas, and chaps like Cuyp that one had forgotten about. I still feel delirious with the first shock. It felt *really* like peace. And all the people wandering around looked dazed." (Iris Murdoch to David Hicks, June 1, 1945, in *Living on Paper*, 43–44).

drowns offshore as everyone else—the plowman in the foreground, a fisherman by the shore—sticks to his routine. She had been an appreciative reader of Auden's poetry since late adolescence; when he visited Badminton School, she was picked to sit beside him. Both the poem and the painting ("one of the most poetic of great pictures")[6] would have had special resonance for an earnest young woman who had come to the continent to help:

> ... the sun shone
> As it had to on the white legs disappearing into the green
> Water, and the expensive delicate ship that must have seen
> Something amazing, a boy falling out of the sky,
> Had somewhere to get to and sailed calmly on.[7]

She spent hundreds of francs on a reproduction of the Breughel, which she hung in her office, west of the canal.

Rivaling the joy of riding the trams or standing in front of the Brueghel was the joy she felt at getting her hands on new books—especially works belonging to the existentialist movement, just then becoming a craze in Paris and beyond. Two weeks after her arrival in Brussels, she related to a friend in London how, "[w]andering the city ... I came on a highbrow bookshop ... where to my delight the assistant adored all my favourite authors & was clearly expert on the genre of *roman existentialist....*"[8] Her instantaneous friend, Ernest Collet, let her borrow a recently published novel by Julien Gracq, "about a young man who, not content with a superb mastery of life, decides death must similarly be mastered & ... commits suicide."[9]

Murdoch's letters from this time are filled with effusive discussion of books that had not yet appeared in English, and had only just appeared in England. She tore through Camus's *The Stranger*, half a dozen of Sartre's books, and Simone de Beauvoir's debut works of fiction and philosophy. De Beauvoir particularly inspired Murdoch. Before leaving London, Murdoch had already written and set aside two novels (the second, which she submitted to Faber & Faber, was personally rejected by T.S. Eliot). But she knew she would be writing more. After reading de Beauvoir's *She Came to Stay*, Murdoch judged her "everything that the modern novelist should be," adding: "and a woman, bless her!"[10] She was certain that what these French intellectuals were producing was "just what English philosophy needs to have injected into its veins,"[11] and spent every franc she could spare on cheap postwar editions she would keep for the rest of her life. She also bought a sturdy notebook with grey cloth covers in which to take notes on her new acquisitions.

Murdoch didn't need her friend Collet to tell her that Sartre was coming to town that October. His upcoming lecture at the city's premier contemporary art gallery was advertised in the papers. More to the point, it was relentlessly discussed in the cafés Murdoch frequented in her (mostly) free time. Chico Marx was in Brussels at the same moment and generated far less excitement than the short, spectacled philosopher from Paris. Collet *was* probably the one who wangled Murdoch an invitation to a private gathering with Sartre after the talk.

But it was no good attending the after-party if she was crowded out of the talk itself. Murdoch set out early. Gathering her notebook and (hoping for an autograph) her copy of *Being and Nothingness*, she made her way down the cobbled streets of the old city, past the medieval cathedral, past the neo-classical city park, to hear a man she regarded as a prophet of late modernity.

The day was warm for October. Murdoch hurried down the Boulevard du Regents and ducked into the Galerie Georges Giroux, exulting as always in "the soft twitter of French" around her.[12] Her beautiful notebook was virtually new; she'd saved it for this. The only things she'd written yet were her name and address and a quote from de Beauvoir's *Pyrrhus and Cineas*. Before Sartre could speak, there was a long introduction by a professor from Louvain. Finally, Sartre stood up. Squinting at the crowd, he apologized for being underprepared, perhaps a joke at the expense of the man who had introduced him. It wasn't evident what he meant otherwise; he had a script. For over an hour, as Sartre read to the hot, tightly packed gallery, he awed Murdoch both with what he said and with his clarity and directness: "hard & lucid & invigorating. It's the real thing . . . ."[13]

She opened her notebook and began to write:

". . . Each man is a '*projet*.' . . .
. . . Man is defined from without by his acts & habits . . . .
. . . We can't <u>not</u> choose. We must <u>create</u> values . . . ."[14]

Sartre's position—to which we will return—was that we are abandoned and adrift in the universe, without horizon or charts. It is up to us to choose the guiding principles of our lives. But we are *condemned* to this freedom; it is our plight. With every deliberate act, we commit ourselves to the principles implicit in that act. There is no opting out of choice. ("We can only choose not to choose," Murdoch scribbled.) To act with good faith—authenticity—rather than bad faith is to make our choices in full recognition of their inescapability and our abandonment. It is to embrace "<u>Anguish. That is, solitude in the face of a universal decision</u> [emphasis Murdoch's]." But this was not all bad news, thought the 26-year-old Murdoch. It was also bracing, an invitation to take responsibility for the world in the aftermath of war. "It is a philosophy of vigour & action," Murdoch noted: "Denuding. Stimulating."[15]

She would later criticize almost everything Sartre said that day. But she would trace her determination to become a philosopher to the encounter.[16]

In December, Murdoch was finally sent to the first of a series of placements in Austria, where UNRRA aid was all that stood between the residents and starvation. In these placements, she finally came face-to-face with the desperation of the displaced persons she had gone to serve. With one married couple, the Jančars, she inaugurated a life-long friendship. Unlike the ship's captain in Brueghel's *The Fall of Icarus*, she would not look away. She had known grief and fear and had suffered vicariously with her friends during the war; she had written in generic terms in a string of wartime book reviews about the need for any adequate postwar creed to address "the cities and . . . the battlefields of the contemporary world."[17] But this was the first time she confronted, close up, "how irrevocably broken so many lives have been by this war. Nothing nothing nothing ahead for these people."[18] She thought any philosophy worth teaching had to speak to this. By the summer of 1946, UNRRA operations were beginning to wind down. Murdoch stayed until the end of June.

"A RATHER BITTER EXPERIENCE OF LIFE"

Compared with Anscombe, Foot, or Scrutton, Murdoch was notable not only for how early she found her philosophical voice and project, but also for how little confidence she had in herself as a philosopher. This juxtaposition takes us to the heart of who she was as an intellectual.

Elizabeth Anscombe, the subject of the next chapter, is an instructive contrast. In the first 10 years after her return to Oxford in 1946, Anscombe published only three pieces that were not translations of Wittgenstein: a comment on a paper by C.S. Lewis in the journal of a student-run debating society; an essay (dominated by Wittgenstein's voice) in an obscure volume by Cornell University Press; and a terse reply to a conference paper, published with the original in the annual conference proceedings. In careerist terms, she had done almost nothing. Only those close to her had any idea what she thought.

But this was not owing to any doubt about her *vocation*. Anscombe did not immediately know what she wanted to say, at least in print. But she was also the most single-minded and self-possessed of any of her Oxford friends, cranking out version after version of her thesis on "The Identity of Bodies." She was concerned only with satisfying herself—with getting things right.

Murdoch, by contrast, was a great experimenter and prone to recurring, terrible doubts about "her reality as a thinker."[19] She was always willing to put herself forward, to try things, whether poetry or acting or fiction or relief work or playwriting or Russian or religion. As soon as her thoughts began to take shape, she immediately wrote about them: in reviews, in letters, in radio broadcasts, at academic conferences, in a short book. But Murdoch also feared that she was a mere dilettante, or simply had little talent. And the philosophical agenda she began formulating during her stint with the UNRRA was difficult for her contemporaries to place and appreciate.

At first, she had no clear agenda, other than to attend both to her Anglophone peers and to the Parisians who excited her so much. She knew that most Oxford philosophers would scorn Sartre and de Beauvoir, finding their ambitions grandiose and their language undisciplined. And she was not prepared to reject Oxford philosophy. Oxford was home; its people were her people. MacKinnon had made her see the importance of engaging with the objections of thinkers like Ayer. But she was determined to attend to whatever spoke to her and her moment, and to figure out later how it could be defended from charges of meaninglessness.

Soon, though, she began trying to bring these divergent figures and traditions together in her mind. And she was the only one who could. Murdoch was at once familiar with and distant from both the French and the English thought-worlds. So she uniquely could see what the fact–value dichotomy *meant*. She perceived the unexamined background picture that gave this dichotomy so much power over the minds of her contemporaries on both sides of the Channel and beyond. Murdoch's agenda, from then on, was to interpret and criticize her age, to *diagnose* it—particularly its images of the human condition.

But her very familiarity with the philosophy and literature of the continent made her a liminal figure in the anthropologist's sense: a person who exists between established categories. Murdoch was unclassifiable. She wasn't French. And she would never be an "Oxford philosopher" herself. She would feel this more and more as time went on.

The winter after Murdoch left the UNRRA was famously brutal— one of the worst on record. For nearly two months, there was snowfall every day, somewhere in the UK, with daily high temperatures often staying below freezing. The snow piled up. It was a mirror of her soul.

Murdoch had been trying to find her way back into the academy, but instead she was back living with her parents. Over the previous two years, before and during her stint with the UNRRA, she had applied for lectureships or studentships in philosophy at half a dozen different universities, including the studentship Foot had secured at

Somerville. Nothing had worked out. She struck a casual "oh, well" tone, writing to another friend: "[Foot] has the . . . post at Somerville which I was after too, but she deserves it anyway, as she is much better at philosophy than I am . . . ."[20] But the thought of Foot was especially painful at that moment. It had been since the final year of the war.

Murdoch was feeling estranged from Foot, whom she loved like the sister she'd never had. The rift between them was mainly in Murdoch's head, but even one-sided misunderstandings divide. The former flatmates scarcely wrote during Murdoch's term with the UNRRA. The cause was a love quadrangle worthy of one of Murdoch's novels. It left her especially lonely and vulnerable in her first year back.

In the spring of 1944, Murdoch and Foot (then Bosanquet) exchanged lovers. First, Murdoch stole—or was stolen by—Bosanquet's boyfriend, the attractive but ruthless Thomas Balogh (Bosanquet later described Balogh as "an emotional fascist").[21] Murdoch had been seeing Michael Foot, feeling more pity than attraction but enjoying his puppyish admiration. Balogh would tolerate no rivals, though, and Murdoch obediently dropped Michael.

Bosanquet was initially jealous, but she had never been deeply in love with Balogh. He was attractive, and amusing to be around, but nothing more. She was taken aback by Murdoch's audacity, but had no deep stake in the outcome. She recovered rapidly. Then, one day in April, Michael stopped by Seaforth, hoping to find Murdoch. Instead, he met Bosanquet, whom he had seen before only at a distance. She later recalled how beautiful and forlorn he seemed, "this enchanting and slightly shy-looking character at the door." They "never looked back."[22] Michael felt far more aggrieved toward Murdoch than Bosanquet did; once or twice, out of consideration for his feelings, Bosanquet banished her flatmate for an evening so that she and Michael could be alone. When he left later that summer on the covert mission that would see him captured and nearly killed, life at Seaforth mostly returned to normal. But Murdoch continued to be harassed by her conscience, feeling she had done something unpardonable. Explaining the situation to a friend, Murdoch wrote, "I saw my relation to [Bosanquet] being gradually destroyed, by my own fault, yet I did nothing to save it. She behaved beautifully throughout."[23]

Bosanquet probably behaved so beautifully because she was unaware that her friend was in agonies of self-recrimination. It was months after Murdoch returned from Austria before Murdoch tentatively, plaintively reached out to her now-married friend, Philippa Foot: "When one has behaved as I then behaved to two people one loves the hurt and the sense of guilt go very deep . . . . My dear heart, I love you . . . . Be tolerant to this perhaps tiresome letter."[24] We do not have Foot's response to this naked cry, but it seems to have been at once baffled and affectionate, insisting that there was "no opposition between [her] love for Michael and for [Murdoch]." Murdoch's reply was as heart-on-sleeve as her initial plea: "Dear, there have been times when I felt lacerated and broken beyond repair. But . . . the fact that this precious, central thing in my life, my friendship with you, does remain, gives me such courage . . . ."[25] Murdoch began writing to Foot regularly, Foot responding when her health and heavy workload permitted.

Nonetheless, it would be years before Murdoch felt like there was no unwanted distance between her and Foot—certainly not until Foot helped bring her back to Oxford in 1948 and the Foots invited her to lodge with them, and not fully until after Michael walked out on Philippa in 1959. Even as her friend's letters helped to sustain Murdoch through the winter of 1947, the lingering sense that she had done irreversible damage, that things would never be the same, made that terrible winter much worse. Foot had moved on and married someone who might never forgive Murdoch—or so it seemed to her. And Foot was doing the thing Murdoch most wanted to do: think and talk and write about philosophy. Murdoch, by contrast, was in stasis.

When she resigned from the UNRRA, Murdoch had had a plan for 1946–47. As the impending dissolution of the UNRRA had come into view, she had applied for the Smithson studentship at Cambridge (the one Anscombe had held in the early 1940s), and also for a studentship at Vassar College, two hours' drive up the Hudson Valley from New York City. Vassar said yes.

What did she want to do? As she wrote in her application for the Smithson, she wanted to think about ethics. Through her encounters with Kierkegaard, Sartre, and others outside the Anglophone sphere, she began to think for the first time "that ethics could be seriously and profoundly treated from an academic point of view"—that it could deal with "the real moral problems that were distressing [her] and [her] contemporaries."

It was a matter of breaking out of the strictures imposed by Ayer and other logical positivists and finding a vocabulary in which to talk seriously about human nature and the human condition. What instruction about life could one expect from people who were skeptical of any talk that went beyond definitions, rules of logic, and observation reports? Murdoch wanted to find a philosophy with something to say about "man here and now . . . with definite social and emotional problems to face—the man who goes to the cinema, makes love, and fights for or against Hitler." She allowed that this agenda would probably "have to be narrowed down."[26]

In June, Murdoch learned that she had won the Durant Drake award at Vassar, and withdrew her candidacy for the Smithson. She began dreaming of another year of intense enrichment in a new environment, near another great city. It never came to pass.

Applying for a visa to the United States, Murdoch scrupulously acknowledged her former membership in the Communist Party. And that was that: her application was denied. She was not short of advocates. MacKinnon, Somerville Principal Janet Vaughan, the Vice-Chancellor of the University, even celebrities like Bertrand Russell lobbied on her behalf, to no avail. By the time the hopelessness of the situation became evident, the Smithson studentship had been awarded to someone else. Murdoch would spend the year at home in suburban Chiswick.[27] For the diversely talented, perpetually experimenting, and chronically self-doubting Murdoch, that winter—having no clear task—was among the most miserable seasons of her life.

It wasn't only Foot from whom Murdoch felt distant at this moment. It was MacKinnon, too. In the earlier loneliness of mid-1943, before Bosanquet joined her at Seaforth, Murdoch had become increasingly dependent on MacKinnon, traveling to Oxford at every opportunity to see him. She spent hours in his office, weeping over her spiritual uncertainties, her misdeeds, her loneliness, making him her confidant and confessor. Both Murdoch and MacKinnon described their interactions to others as a melodrama with Murdoch playing Mary Magdalene to MacKinnon's Jesus. Intensely conscientious, MacKinnon felt increasingly responsible for Murdoch and was drawn into an intellectual and emotional intimacy beside which his marriage looked remote. When Lois MacKinnon finally intervened in September 1943, her husband cut off both Murdoch's visits and their correspondence. Murdoch continued to speak adoringly of him in letters, though, writing things like "I think I'll always be a bit in love with Donald."[28] She got some news of him from Bosanquet, with whom MacKinnon remained close.

MacKinnon never ceased looking after Murdoch, during or after the war. He may have been responsible for the commissions she received in 1943 and 1944 to write book reviews for *The Adelphi*—one of which appeared a year after their break. All of the books Murdoch reviewed address the place of Christianity in the modern world— one of MacKinnon's leading preoccupations. And MacKinnon wrote on Murdoch's behalf both to Cambridge and Vassar—and then to the US Embassy.

When Murdoch returned to England from Austria in July 1946, MacKinnon initially declined her request to visit. By August, though, he had relented. MacKinnon agreed to give her informal guidance as she read Kant, Hegel, and Kierkegaard at home. This gave her some sense of forward motion in a time when she otherwise had none. Murdoch was delighted to discover that since they had last spoken, MacKinnon too had begun reading the French existentialists. He shared Murdoch's sense that they were speaking to the needs of the age. MacKinnon was surely pleased by Murdoch's increasing open-ness to Christianity.

Perhaps the outcome would not have been so grievous if they had resumed contact a year or two later, when Murdoch was less desolate. Or if Murdoch and Lois MacKinnon had been friends (Lois was only three years older). Donald tried to supply Murdoch with third-party support, so that they would not fall back into their old roles as Christ and penitent Magdalene. He directed her to an Anglo-Catholic abbey in Kent that welcomed retreatants.[29] (A priest he consulted recom-mended the Abbess as "good with difficult cases.")[30] But Murdoch's devotion and neediness were more intense than ever.

Their relationship came to a second crisis during Holy Week 1947. They met in London for a conversation that lasted all afternoon and into the evening. Afterward, either distrusting Murdoch or dis-trusting himself, MacKinnon again cut off contact. As before, he did what he could at a distance, occasionally sending Murdoch a book that he thought she would find instructive. He wrote her a glowing testimonial when she reapplied (successfully) for the Smithson studentship at Cambridge, adding that "She has had a rather bitter experience of life in the last few years, but has learnt from it a great deal that has made her disciplined and self critical."[31] He wrote to Foot of his determination to show "a true care for I[ris]."[*, 32]

That same spring, MacKinnon received an offer to take up a distinguished professorship at the University of Aberdeen, which he eagerly accepted. With MacKinnon leaving England and little prospect of repairing the breach, Murdoch wrote to Foot,

> I feel such misery at present, about D . . . . He matters to me so absolutely—Cambridge & my own 'future' are just nothing in comparison. But there's nothing to be done, except remember him & carry on. I'm sick at heart & can't work. Life's been disintegrated in a nightmarish way for so long now, one almost forgets what it would be like to feel normal & secure & loved.[33]

Murdoch and MacKinnon would see one another just once more, 15 years later, meeting by chance on a street in Cambridge. His name recurred in her journals to the end of her life.

---

* MacKinnon may have been responsible for securing Murdoch her position at St. Anne's the following year. At the request of Principal Eleanor Plumer, he wrote a joint reference for Murdoch and Scrutton. Scrutton, MacKinnon told Plumer, was "a very strong candidate": an excellent classicist, more experienced, more *reliable*. The Somerville authorities, he predicted, would recommend her over Murdoch. But Murdoch, he argued, had greater upside: she was "more engrossed by . . . the fundamental problems" of philosophy and was thus likelier to become a really inspiring tutor. (Murdoch, he perceived, was more like *him*.) The only hint of their history was this remark: "She is a person who makes a very strong impact on people, and can easily, without knowing it, influence them a great deal." Donald MacKinnon to Eleanor Plumer, June 1, 1948, St. Anne's College Archives.

Murdoch had the sense to plan a two-week holiday in France with Scrutton before going up to Cambridge in the fall of 1947: anything to take her mind off her misery. But it was nevertheless with this sense of disintegration—coming to terms with the loss of someone who had been her intellectual and spiritual mentor—that Murdoch began her graduate studies. Consciously or not, she was looking for new influences and new masters. She found them—in particular, in the person of her old undergraduate friend Elizabeth Anscombe.

Murdoch was also on the cusp of discovering one of the leading themes of her philosophical career. In August, just before going up, she wrote to Foot, "Did you hear Copleston . . . the other day on the [BBC's] 3rd prog[ram]? . . . .one word he used gave me a clue—'heroic.' . . . Close subterranean relation between . . . Sartre & the romantic movement."[34] Like the Romantics, Sartre glamorized feelings of alienation from the inauthentic herd. Could Sartre be an unwitting Romantic? Could one interpret his teaching as a Romantic re-presentation of something like . . . Ayer's picture?

"A WITTGENSTEINIAN NEO-PLATONIST"

MacKinnon was not wrong to testify to the selection committee at Cambridge that Murdoch had "matured considerably" and was "on the threshold of creative work of a high order."[35] Murdoch's 1947 research proposal was far more grounded and assured than the one she had submitted the year before from Austria. Her second proposal was twice as long as the first and studded with references to her previous year's reading under MacKinnon. It also greatly clarified her outlook and task:

> although I have a great admiration for its methods . . . I cannot regard logical positivism as the whole of philosophy.

A consideration of ethical problems first convinced me of this.... One cannot abolish a sphere of human thought by branding it as "imaginative literature." The unrest and the debate about the nature of human goodness and of "human reality" will continue whether or not it is permitted to call itself philosophy. The linguistic philosopher should be prepared to take this challenge seriously. But to do this would mean revising his conceptions of meaning.... It might also point the way to some sort of real contact and exchange of ideas and methods between the two seemingly irreconcilable schools of philosophy.[36]

It wasn't clear to her yet *how* to challenge the positivist account of meaning. But it was widely known that this was a central preoccupation of Anscombe's mentor, Ludwig Wittgenstein. Wittgenstein had just retired, so there was no question of Murdoch attending his lectures or classes anymore. That may have been for the best. For someone so given to unchecked devotion, with the wound of MacKinnon's rejection still open, this could have been dangerous. There was danger enough from Anscombe herself.

Almost as soon as she arrived in Cambridge, Murdoch approached Anscombe, angling for an introduction to Wittgenstein. Either Anscombe or Wittgenstein himself was initially resistant, devastating Murdoch. In late October, though, shortly before Wittgenstein left Cambridge to take up an itinerant life in Ireland, upstate New York, and elsewhere, Anscombe came through. Murdoch was ushered in for a brief interview with the reclusive genius. As Murdoch recalled later, "both he and his setting were very unnerving."[37] Wittgenstein's rooms were nearly empty: two chairs and a bed, no more. There were no pleasantries, either. Wittgenstein began the conversation by asking why Murdoch wanted to see him. Her journal entry on the encounter recalls Jesus' exchange with the Canaanite woman in *Matthew* chapter 15. Wittgenstein said, "It's as if I have an apple tree in my garden & everyone is carting away the apples & sending them all over the world. And you ask: may I have an apple from your tree." Murdoch replied, "Yes; but I'm never sure when I'm given an apple whether it really is from your tree." Wittgenstein seemed to like this, but morosely added, "What's the use of having one philosophical discussion? It's like having one piano lesson."[38] Reflecting back on the incident a dozen years later, she said, "with most people, you meet them in a framework, and there are certain conventions about how you talk to them .... There isn't a naked confrontation of personalities. . . . perhaps that's why I always thought of him . . . with awe and alarm."[39]

Murdoch got further with Anscombe herself. Anscombe took Murdoch into the small community of Wittgenstein disciples in Cambridge and shared with her Wittgenstein's unpublished lecture notes. She shared, too, her draft translations from Wittgenstein's late masterpiece, *Philosophical Investigations*.

Wittgenstein's influence on Murdoch isn't always appreciated; she wrote much more about Kant and Kierkegaard, Sartre and de Beauvoir, Plato and Simone Weil. But she described herself to an interviewer once as a "Wittgensteinian neo-Platonist." What were the principal lessons she took from her (mediated) encounter with perhaps the most influential philosopher of the twentieth century?

Like Richard Hare, Wittgenstein had worked out his earliest philosophical thoughts while trapped by war: in Wittgenstein's case, the Great War, in which he served with an Austrian artillery unit on the Russian front. There are interesting similarities between Wittgenstein's first book, *Tractatus Logico-Philosophicus*, and Hare's unpublished *An Essay in Monism*. Each sought an elevated vantage point on the horrors around them; each found this vantage point in the thought that the world has a hidden structure—crystalline, beautiful—beneath the blood and the stench. For the young Wittgenstein, the structure was one that made it possible for language to describe the world. At a deep level, he thought, the *world* and our *words* must be isomorphic. Our sentences and thoughts are pictures— schematic diagrams—of how objects are arranged in the world. (Wittgenstein began his career as an engineer and architect.) There was a more challenging implication, too: Wittgenstein famously took the view that the meaning of life is inexpressible, because this meaning is not a mere arrangement of objects: it can't be *pictured.*

Like Hare, Wittgenstein came to repudiate his early work.

Starting in the 1930s and continuing until his death in 1951, Wittgenstein worked out a sharply contrasting view, often exploring and defending it through an imagined dialogue with his earlier self ("the author of the *Tractatus*"). On Wittgenstein's later view, meaningful language refuses to conform itself to any single pattern. Two of Wittgenstein's students relate an incident that was clearly pivotal in Wittgenstein's own narrative of his changing views. A friend of Wittgenstein's made an obscene gesture and asked Wittgenstein, "what's the logical form of *that*?"[40] This broke the grip of Wittgenstein's earlier conception on his imagination. The older Wittgenstein compared language not to a blueprint but to a row of controls in a locomotive. At first glance, you might think: they're all the same, they're all knobs; you grab them.* But when you begin to use them, you find that they do very different things.[41] And so it is with words, which might seem superficially alike (they're all for speaking or writing) but serve a hundred purposes besides naming objects and picturing their relationships: joking, counting, crying out, calling someone's name. The author of the *Tractatus*, Wittgenstein came to think, was held captive by a too-tidy picture. The picture of *picturing.*

---

* Some interface design is more legible than this!

Anscombe was deeply invested in Wittgenstein's entire project. But here is what Murdoch, Foot, and Scrutton took away from their late-1940s conversations with her: language use is a complex, many-sided form of behavior—a "form of life," Wittgenstein called it—and any simple set of rules (like Ayer's) purporting to lay out the necessary conditions for language to have meaning is just wrong.[42] There can be no such rules. And this thought suggested another. As Scrutton later wrote, "language has to be rooted in the complexities of real life . . . . [B]ecause speech is a central human activity, reflecting our whole nature—because language is rooted . . . in the wider structure of our lives . . . it leads on to an investigation of our whole nature."[43] In real life, description and evaluation are not neatly separable. This was especially evident with words like "rude" or "friend," but it was more subtly true even of the words Ayer and Hare preferred to analyze, like "good" or "ought." The inseparability of description and evaluation in ordinary human discourse would be a major theme in a seminar Murdoch and Foot taught together in the early 1950s— "Analysis in Moral Philosophy"—though it would be Foot who went on to develop the idea most thoroughly.[44] The thought began with Anscombe teaching all of her friends what she had learned and found so liberating.

Anscombe had another effect on Murdoch, too. She became a new object of devotion. All through her early adulthood, Murdoch sought out master figures like MacKinnon, with whom her relationships were simultaneously intellectual and erotic.[45] Once she began interacting more extensively with Anscombe, Murdoch soon became infatuated with her. It was perhaps the first time she was infatuated with a woman—though by no means the last.

Like Wittgenstein—like MacKinnon before him—Anscombe represented a standard of intellectual and spiritual seriousness before which Murdoch felt herself hopelessly inadequate. As she confided to her journal already in the summer of 1947, "The ruthless authenticity of Elizabeth makes me feel more and more ashamed of the vague self indulgent way in which I have been philosophizing." In the same entry, she quotes her friend: "No second rate philosophy is any good."[46] In this state of awed self-abnegation, Murdoch spent much of the next two years tailing after Anscombe, devotedly attending her lectures and seeking out every opportunity for informal interaction. Many pages of her Cambridge-year journal are devoted to reflection on topics Anscombe was thinking through, like our relationship to the past. (One sign of a crush is that you can't stop talking about him or her.) A friend told her later that he had noticed her, "every week, waiting for E. outside schools, before he knew me, & how . . . I would flush for pleasure when she came out." "He's hellish observant," she conceded.[47]

Murdoch's half-conscious "courtship" of her friend came to a decisive turn sometime in late November or early December of 1948. Judging from Murdoch's journals that fall, Anscombe had come to regard Murdoch as an important friend too, going out with her evenings and stopping by her lodgings. Then some line was crossed, though we have only Murdoch's side of the story. Even there, seven pages are missing from her journal, between entries for November 23 and December 11. Shortly after the missing entries, Murdoch remarks, "I need a strong box to keep this damn diary in. Probably I ought to destroy all the entries of the last 3 weeks."[48] Seemingly, she did. What are preserved afterward are ten pages of tortured longing and self-criticism:

Intense desire to know what's really going on in E's mind.

Tried to pray, last night & this morning. All darkened with emotion.

Overwhelmed with a . . . wish that she may be well, that she may not be harmed by this. Yet this feeling is so utterly mixed with self regarding wishes. . . . There must be utter steel in my love, a willingness not to ask or get anything for myself. . . . Easy to write this—intensely hard to take even the next small step towards it.

I have always managed to work through my worst crises <u>with</u> someone—Pippa, D. Have yet to learn loneliness. . . . Must root out the weak desire for an audience.[49]

Murdoch recorded a decade later that "E and I never touched each other, except for my touching her arm . . . ."[50] Whatever happened, it alarmed Anscombe enough that on December 10 she fled to Ireland to see Wittgenstein. To Murdoch's chagrin, their mutual friend Yorick Smythies said to her that he regarded Anscombe's "getting away as she did" as "the result of prayer." Murdoch, for her part, tried to pray, as MacKinnon had prayed over her, "that I may really desire her well-being."[51]

Again, we have only Murdoch's side of the story. But Anscombe refers obliquely to the incident at the start of a notebook of reminiscences about Wittgenstein. She writes,

I visited [Wittgenstein] in Dublin in 1948 in need of . . . help and advice because of a matter that was troubling me. . . . I had certainly got into a queer state of mind, partly assisted by having employed a hypnotist to help me to give up smoking; this had been partly successful . . . but [I] was beset by a troublesome obsession and by insomnia.

More than one thing was eating at Anscombe; besides trying to quit smoking, she was also working feverishly on a late draft of her first original philosophical publication. Anscombe related to Wittgenstein some of the thoughts she'd had as she tried to hypnotize herself, "lying in [her] bed in Somerville," thoughts of being suspended above a deep well by an elastic cord, and of reaching up to cut the cord. Wittgenstein told her firmly, "don't do it again." Indeed, he told her to resume smoking.

This worked wonders. Some cigarettes, a few nights' sleep in the hotel where Wittgenstein had booked her a room, a series of outings together to the Botanical Gardens, to the cinema, and to the Dublin Zoo, and "the troubling images that were disturbing [her]" began to subside.[52] She recalled the episode later chiefly as an example of the generosity of spirit hidden beneath Wittgenstein's intimidating demeanor. It is ambiguous, in the end, what Anscombe experienced: a conflicted attraction? bewilderment at her friend coming on to her? Whatever it was, it was compounded by acute nicotine withdrawal and professional anxiety. The only clear thing is that the incident was never repeated.

When Anscombe returned to Oxford after Christmas, she and Murdoch gingerly worked on reestablishing normal relations. Murdoch was relieved. On February 3, she recorded, Anscombe visited her but seemed nervous. They talked philosophy for a while, relaxing into their old pattern. A few weeks on, Anscombe shared with Murdoch "a very disagreeable letter written by some woman who objected to her wearing <u>trousers at early mass</u>."[53] (Later, Anscombe reported back that an elderly and severe-seeming priest she had sought out for counsel had assured her that "<u>there was no objection</u> to her clothes!")[54] Murdoch and Anscombe would go on meeting occasionally over coffee, and Murdoch sent copies of her first five novels to Anscombe. But the friendship was never again what it had been in late 1948. Late in life, Anscombe mused, "I don't think we ever quite managed to work out what we meant to each other."[55]

Murdoch's "bitter experiences" of the 1940s grounded a career's worth of psychologically acute novels, the first of which, *Under the Net*, appeared in 1954. It seemed to Murdoch's friends to contain half-portraits of many people in her life, including Anscombe. *Under the Net*, like many of her later novels, centers on an alluring mage-figure who exerts conscious or unconscious power over others and on the conflicted interior lives of characters trying to free themselves from the mage's influence. Murdoch had been both subject and object of obsessive devotion and knew its dynamics well—how it exalts and grips and occludes.

The tribulations of her twenties were enough to convince Murdoch that Sartre's inspiring picture of human beings was flawed. We are not as solitary and self-possessed as his early writings suggested. Rather, we are (as she would put it later) "egocentric system[s] of quasi-mechanical energy, largely determined by [our] own individual history[ies], whose natural attachments are sexual, ambiguous, and hard for the subject to understand or control." Philosophical ethics, she thought, must theorize the "fat relentless ego" and determine what techniques might enable us to overcome it.[56] It would take her another decade to work out a vision for this, drawing inspiration from Plato. But already she knew that the way out of a controlling obsession is *not* to courageously assert your freedom. Changing your life is more like steering a ship or building a habit than like taking a single, fateful step. It is hard, but in a different way.

THE DIAGNOSIS

By 1950, Murdoch was sure of two things: first, there was a subcuta-
neous likeness between contemporary British thinking about ethics
and the existentialist ideas crossing the Channel from France; second, with respect to the ideas that bound them together, the British
and the French were both wrong. Because she was immersed in both
British and French thought, Murdoch saw before anyone else did the
massive and telling convergence, the yet-unnamed *Zeitgeist*. And perhaps because all her philosophical mentors had been contrarians, she
was primed to resist.

Murdoch had been back in Oxford less than a year, was barely
settled at the Foots' and at St. Anne's, when she began receiving high-
profile invitations to explain existentialism to a curious public. It is
unsurprising that once Murdoch had the prestige of an Oxford post,
she would begin to draw attention. She was as dramatic a figure in
Oxford in 1949 as she had been a decade before. Open-tempered and
personally attractive, Murdoch gave off an aura of both bohemianism
and spiritual rigor that always intrigued, even when it didn't impress.

As a tutor, she channeled MacKinnon. She was selfless with her
time, letting tutorials run long and meeting up with students outside
of lessons for worship or drinks. She also emulated MacKinnon's
devoted attention to his students' personal needs. She took one forlorn international student home with her for Christmas. She even
emulated MacKinnon's eccentricities, listening to student essays
from a prone position or curled in a ball, twirling her hair. She would
assign students to read and discuss whatever came to her mind during their conversations together: Lenin, Kierkegaard, Weil. First-year
students, anxious to cover the syllabus, were sometimes frustrated.
More advanced—or needier—students became devotees. She
attended a huge number of weddings, often giving lavish gifts.

And it took little time for her to develop a reputation among her peers as a leading expert on contemporary French thought. In 1949, she was commissioned by the Foots' friend and new lodger, BBC producer Prue Smith, to give a pair of talks about existentialism on the BBC's still-young highbrow channel, the Third Programme. The first of these, "The Novelist as Metaphysician," was about the philosophical significance of Sartre's, Camus', and de Beauvoir's fiction. But it ranged well beyond that. Murdoch spent much of the talk linking the doctrines of Sartre and his friends with those of Ayer and Stevenson that she and her friends were routinely discussing at tea shops in Cornmarket Street.

Recall Sartre's view: we are condemned to be free, forced to invent values in a world where none can be found. This sounds grim, but it is also an invitation to heroism—to face the hard truth that others will not. In taking up this challenge, we ennoble ourselves or at least dispense with illusions. We also create ourselves; our identities are the sum of our choices. Making no excuses, but living authentically—in the root sense, as *authors* of ourselves—we acknowledge that we are whatever we summon the will to do.

In her talk, Murdoch quotes a paradigmatic statement of this outlook:

> There is nothing to be done . . . except look at the facts, look at them harder . . . and then come to a moral decision. Then asking whether the attitude that one has adopted is the right attitude comes down to asking whether one is prepared to stand by it. There can be no guarantee of its correctness, because nothing counts as a guarantee. Or . . . something may count for someone as a guarantee, but counting something as a guarantee is itself taking up a moral standpoint.[57]

Murdoch adds: "This is not Sartre but Professor A.J. Ayer writing in a recent number of *Horizon.*" But with small adjustments in vocabulary, it could easily have been Sartre. All the elements are there: criterionless choice, the inescapability of decisions of principle despite the impossibility of getting them "right," the sober challenge to live out these anguished decisions.

We have here both elements of the modern outlook sketched in the opening chapter: the billiard-ball universe, the Dawkins sublime. Values are human projections onto a value-free reality. They cannot be right or wrong. In her radio address, Murdoch speaks of "the free and lonely self" in a world without "objective values." She begins by summarizing Sartre's thought, but notes that "by dissimilar paths the existentialists and [Ayer] have reached positions which are . . . strikingly alike."[58]

She notes, too, the implicit or explicit admonitions to courage or strength or adult responsibility that often accompany such positions. These admonitions, she remarks, are undercut by the positions themselves: "We are told that we are lonely individuals in a valueless and meaningless world. Yet it is also hinted that . . . certain moves are preferable to certain others."[59] Consistent or not, these are the aspects of the picture that inspire.

Around the time of her BBC debut, Murdoch signed a contract to write the first study in English of Sartre's thought. She titled it *Sartre: Romantic Rationalist*, sounding a theme to which she would return repeatedly. Calling Sartre's views "Romantic," she highlights his subtle and likely unconscious invocation of two Romantic tropes: the sublime and the Romantic hero. The two go together. The existentialist hero, she notes, rises above his sense of the absurdity of life by confronting it courageously. Like the figure in Caspar David Friedrich's *Wanderer above the Sea of Fog*, he stares down the abyss, finding sublimity both in the unfathomable drop and in the spectacle of himself standing above it. Because the absurdity of life, not the obscurity of the land below, is the source of the sublime, the existentialist hero isn't a mountain climber but one of the alienated rebels who have been part of the Western canon since the Romantic era: Goethe's Werther, Byron's Manfred, Charlotte Brontë's Mr. Rochester. Murdoch notes that the invitation to identify with this type involves more than a little self-aggrandizement: "It is patent that what many readers of Sartre find in his writings is a portrait of themselves. A likeness is always pleasing, even if one is not handsome; and to be told that one's personal despair is a universal human characteristic may be consoling."[60] As Murdoch would write later, the gloom characteristic of existentialist writing "is superficial and conceals elation": "the reader feels himself to be a member of the élite, addressed by another . . . ."[61]

The point was more tartly expressed in the title of a French-language broadcast to which she contributed a few months after her BBC debut: "L'Angoisse, snobisme moderne," "Anguish: modern snobbery."[62]

Pictures matter. This is one of Murdoch's enduring insights. Pictures matter, and some pictures are better than others. At a time when her contemporaries didn't think they were inside a picture at all, Murdoch borrowed the idea of an imprisoning picture from Wittgenstein and wrote, "Man is a creature who makes pictures of himself and then comes to resemble the picture."[63] Murdoch came to find the "existentialist" picture of human nature and the human condition comically distorted. She had immersed herself in Christian devotional practices and tried with painful difficulty to overcome a string of obsessional attachments. She knew what moral and spiritual striving was like. And tough-sounding admonitions to pull yourself together and choose were false to her experience of change and growth. Indeed, they made nonsense of the goal-oriented idea *of* growth—of the upward or outward yearning that is inseparable from the moral life. At around the same time as she was diagnosing both Sartre and her fellow British philosophers, she was devouring the writings of twentieth-century French mystic Simone Weil. Her third broadcast for the Third Programme, in 1951, was a discussion of Weil's *Waiting for God*. She gravitated especially to Weil's idea that the human task is to decenter ourselves and give full and un-self-interested attention to the reality of others—to *really look* at them without trying to possess or control, the way one looks at a work of art when thoroughly absorbed by it. This un-selfing is what she had prayed the strength to do with regard to her friend Elizabeth Anscombe.

"AUSTIN"

Murdoch left Oxford in 1963, after 15 years on the faculty of St. Anne's. She had more than one reason. The work of an Oxford tutorial fellow is demanding; by the early 1960s, Foot, too, was eyeing the possibility of escape to an American university. And Murdoch wasn't just teaching. Following the publication of *Under the Net* in 1954, she had written almost a novel a year.[64] But she had written them all during the summers, over the long vacation. She judged, plausibly, that if she was going to progress as a writer, she had to commit more exclusively to the work.

She wasn't in the same place professionally as she had been 15 years earlier. Neither was she in the same place personally. In 1956, she had married literary critic John Bayley—a man she loved deeply but in a quieter, less worshipful way than she had loved MacKinnon or Anscombe or the dominating, destructive Nobel laureate Elias Canetti.* "Puss," she called Bayley in her journals, the way she called her father "Doodle." Bayley, and their overgrown property outside Oxford, Cedar Lodge, had become sources of serenity.

Now, in 1963, that quiet, separated world was under threat. Murdoch had become embroiled in an affair with a St. Anne's colleague, Margaret Hubbard, a situation that threatened to become a scandal.[65] But Murdoch had grown. She now had the fortitude to walk away from such an obsession, where before she had not. For the good of the College and to preserve her seven-year-old marriage to Bayley, she cut ties both with Hubbard and with St. Anne's. From 1963, she and Bayley were in but not of Oxford, and Murdoch in particular had less and less to do with the University.

She had a further reason to quit the University, though. Murdoch had concluded that in a deeper sense she didn't belong. She had concluded that she wasn't really a philosopher. She had diagnosed her contemporaries, describing the picture they unconsciously inhabited; she had broken the illusion of inevitability by naming what held them captive. But offering this diagnosis served to marginalize her further.

Gilbert Ryle had achieved his postwar aims. Under Ryle's leadership, the rigorous but narrow conception of philosophy as linguistic analysis had come to dominate in Oxford and beyond. The new

---

* It is unclear exactly when Murdoch withdrew from Christianity, but it seems to have coincided with the period of the atheist Canetti's greatest influence over her. In 1951, she described herself to a BBC staffer as Anglican, and she was an active participant from 1948–1953 in a group of High Anglican philosophers and theologians calling themselves "The Metaphysicals." Hare, too, attended sporadically. In 1953, the year she first came powerfully under Canetti's influence, she withdrew, remarking to Basil Mitchell that she felt like "more of a fellow-traveller than a Party member." See Kelly James Clark, *Philosophers Who Believe*, (Downers Grove: IVP, 1993), 47. The change outlasted Canetti, though. And A.N. Wilson reports Murdoch saying to him that Bayley, not Canetti, "got rid of God." See Wilson, *Iris Murdoch as I Knew Her* (London: Hutchinson, 2003), 145.

ideal was this: philosophers could illumine and refine our thinking by attending to the nuances of ordinary language, the intricate but underappreciated apparatus shared by intellectuals and plain persons alike.

Ryle did more than anyone to promote the new Oxford approach, which came to be known as "ordinary-language philosophy." But J.L. Austin was its leading theorist and practitioner. Austin's methods had roots both in the patient textual scholarship he practiced as a Greats tutor and in his wartime experiences sifting military intelligence. Working collaboratively with his (male) junior colleagues at Oxford, whom he convened informally each Saturday morning during term-time, Austin tried to get as clear as possible about subtle differences among clusters of topically related words: "hounding down the minutiae," as he put it.[66] Austin was determined to make *progress* in philosophy. And surveying the wreckage of philosophical history—all the grand systems constructed, then abandoned—he renounced system-building. Or at any rate, he determined that the only way to build something worthwhile was extremely slowly, piece by piece, scrutinizing our words and, through them, our concepts. Under Austin's influence, a whole generation of Oxford philosophers came to share his impatience with generalization and synthesis, his intellectual aesthetic of clarity and cleanliness. "Words are our tools," Austin wrote, "and . . . we should use clean tools."[67]

It is not difficult to see the attractions of Austin's approach: the painstaking carefulness, the submission to the ideal of getting something right, even if it is nothing grand. But in a context obsessed with that ideal, Murdoch's eclectic, allusive essays, concerned with big, competing visions of the world and the human condition, were bound to appear merely sloppy. Murdoch inspired those close to her and some outsiders with her range and insight, but her philosophical writing was less and less appreciated in Oxford as the 1950s wore on. Colleagues regarded her as a helpful expert on a minor—and not especially highly regarded—subject, contemporary French thought. Hare's remark on French existentialism is telling: "the thing wrong with the Existentialists and the other Continental philosophers is that they haven't had their noses rubbed in the necessity of saying exactly what they mean."[68]

In the milieu Ryle and Austin had created, Murdoch's work didn't register as properly disciplined, properly *philosophical*. Isaiah Berlin, who adulated Austin, quipped about Murdoch that she was "a lady not known for the clarity of her views."[69] It is a sad remark, as Berlin himself was full of self-doubt on account of the similarly allusive and visionary qualities of his own best work in the history of ideas. He didn't think what he did was real philosophy either, because real philosophy, in that time and place, meant "what Austin did." Berlin had on his desk, like a *memento mori*, a sign he'd picked up from an auto repair shop, which read simply "Austin." Even friends like Mary Warnock, who liked Murdoch and cribbed from her work on existentialism, mocked her invocations of Simone Weil on loving attention to others. If she or her husband mislaid their keys, the other would say in a grave tone, "have you *really looked*?"[70,*]

Well before she resigned, Murdoch withdrew from philosophy rather than try to fill the "void" she saw "in present-day moral philosophy": the lack of a "working philosophical psychology . . . ."[71] For most of a decade, from her increasingly marginal position, she had been calling for a recovery of the detailed, nuanced vocabulary and

---

* One wonders too whether Murdoch's curious but vigorous insistence in interviews that there is little connection between her novels and her philosophy reflects the internalization of a communal judgment that the kind of reflection on human motivation and the human condition embodied in her books doesn't merit the name "philosophy." She could simply have been insisting that her fiction isn't didactic. But readers of both her novels and her philosophy typically find preposterous the suggestion that there is no link.

psychology of the virtues and vices. But she had novels to write. She had neither the furious passion nor the fearsome debating skill to go on trying to change her colleagues' minds, to make her complaints against Oxford moral philosophy impossible to ignore.

Her "old friend-foe" Anscombe did, though.[72] She only needed provocation.

Chapter 6

Elizabeth Anscombe
versus the World

PROSPERO AND ARIEL

Sunday, January 27, 1957. The light was failing and a daylong gale beginning to die down as Elizabeth Anscombe closed the door of the cab, gathered her brown duffel coat around her, and set her face toward Broadcasting House.

The BBC's art deco headquarters has suggested a battleship to passersby since it was built, the curved bow of the great, grey edifice cutting through the asphalt channel of Langham Place. It features a stylized waterline, a signal deck, an aerial mast. Gazing down on Anscombe as she walked to the entrance was the ship's figurehead: Eric Gill's monumental *Prospero and Ariel*. There could have been no more fitting welcome.

Gill, an ardent Catholic convert, was commissioned in 1929 to make sculptures for both the interior and exterior of the new building. The cantankerous, earthy Gill, estranged from his increasingly secular fellow Britons, fashioned a set of works that nod to the Shakespearean material specified in his commission. But they convey a good deal more of the Christian gospel—particularly *Prospero and Ariel*. From his alcove above the entrance, Prospero towers above the globe like God the Father. He offers the childlike Ariel to the world. Ariel descends with an ecstatic look, but he is also naked and vulnerable; his hands, spread in benediction or surrender, bear stigmata.

Gill seems to have wanted a confrontation. His letters, and later his autobiography, contain derisive remarks about the BBC and the concept they had proposed.* (He seems not to have known *The Tempest* well.) Perhaps worrying that his work would be gently admired by the Corporation or the public—and determined not to be gently admired—Gill did something gratuitously provocative. He made Ariel's genitalia conspicuously large. Sir John Reith, Director of the BBC, was notified of the problem before the piece was unveiled and called a special meeting of the Board of Governors up on the scaffolding. One of the Governors, a former public-school headmaster, is supposed to have offered the decisive judgment: "I can only say, from personal observation, that the lad is uncommonly well hung." Gill made the required adjustments.[1]

Gill died in 1940. But he and Anscombe would have understood each other. Like Gill, Anscombe was a zealous Catholic convert in anti-Catholic, twentieth-century England.[2] Like Gill, she had accepted a commission from the BBC, an institution they both distrusted. Like Gill, her idea was to use her platform to promote some truths of the faith to a society controlled by its enemies. Like Gill, she was going to conjure a tempest. She was in London to record, in her soft, sweet voice, a work of biting irony, titled "Oxford Moral Philosophy: Does it 'corrupt the youth'?"

---

* In his autobiography, Gill writes: "Very clever of the BBC to hit on the idea, Ariel and aerial. Ha! Ha! And the BBC kidding itself, in the approved manner of all big organizations (British or foreign, public or private), that it represents all that is good and noble and disinterested— like the British Empire or Selfridges . . . ." See Eric Gill, *Autobiography*, (New York: Biblo and Tannen, 1968), 261.

TWICE A CONVERT

Who was Elizabeth Anscombe? We do not have her journal; nor did she ever write as autobiographically as Scrutton (later Midgley) did. She was the subject of a hundred anecdotes—some better corroborated than others—concerning her abrasiveness, her brilliance, her unconventionality. Legend holds (for example) that Anscombe was once stopped at the entrance to a restaurant and told women weren't allowed to wear trousers inside. She promptly stripped them off. Who was the *person* behind these stories?[3]

People who knew Anscombe often remark on the musical quality of her speaking voice: a quiet alto, sometimes faintly tremulous, but with utterly precise enunciation.[4] Her student Rosalind Hursthouse reminisced that it "made [her] want to curl up in her lap and be told stories in it forever."[5] Not that Anscombe's speech was always gentle. Even as a young woman, she sometimes spoke in a dreamy, musing tone, sometimes in a scolding, quietly furious one; each drew dramatic power from the contrast. The mesmeric force of Anscombe's voice was heightened too by the cadence of her speech: slow, deliberate, in perfectly crafted sentences, separated sometimes by long, reflective pauses.* Her husband Peter Geach claimed that he heard Anscombe before he saw her. She was seated behind him at a philosophy talk and offered some comment or question. Impressed both by the voice and by what it said, Geach said to himself, "The girl with that voice I mean to marry."[6]

The story of Anscombe's development through the 1940s and 1950s is one of discovering or rediscovering her voice. In doing so,

---

* An anecdote, retold by many sources: Anscombe is supposed to have said to Ayer once, "if you didn't talk so quickly, people wouldn't think you were so clever." To which Ayer is supposed to have replied, "if you didn't talk so slowly, people wouldn't think you were so profound." See, among others, John Haldane, "Elizabeth Anscombe," *The Herald*, January 9, 2001, 28.

she imitated the English Catholic martyrs whose stories first awakened her imagination to Catholicism. She wasn't killed for her faith. But a martyr, in the Catholic understanding, doesn't seek death. A martyr is a witness: one who testifies. Context determines the cost—how much one must endure for one's testimony. The mark of a martyr is not death, but readiness to die. This was Anscombe's stance: she would testify to the truth, whatever anyone said or did—whatever the consequences. And like Thomas Aquinas, she came to see the philosopher's devotion to truth as entwined with her devotion to God. God *is* truth, Aquinas wrote: the source and explanation of all that is.[7] Anscombe eventually came to see service to God and service to the truth as a single pursuit.

Indeed, Anscombe's whole outlook on ethics was shaped by Richard Challoner's stories of recusant Catholics in sixteenth- and seventeenth-century England: tales of priests shuttled up and down the Thames like passengers on America's Underground Railroad, celebrating furtive masses by candlelight, hiding behind false panels while the houses of the faithful were searched, everyone facing imprisonment or worse. The inspiration Anscombe took from these stories appears again and again in her later writings. The ideal of fidelity to the truth, *ruat caelum* ("though the heavens fall"), turns up repeatedly, in her discussions of subjects as diverse as nuclear warfare and contraception. "We have to fear God and keep his commandments," she wrote in 1961, "and calculate what is for the best only within the limits of that obedience, knowing that the future is in God's power . . . ."[8] In these passages, she can sound very like Sir Thomas More, for whom she and Peter Geach named one of their sons.

Not long after the teenaged Anscombe discovered the Catholic martyrs, she discovered philosophy. She picked up Bernard Boedder's

Natural Theology and found she could not stop thinking about the questions it raised. Throughout her undergraduate years, and even beyond, this was her experience of philosophy: as a source of questions she could neither answer nor dismiss. Philosophy was gripping, tormenting. (Mary Warnock recalled Anscombe asking her, in the mid-1940s, "Do you stay awake worrying about the existence of the external world?"[9]) Anscombe was seized not only by Boedder's argument that everything that happens must have a cause, but by worries about perception and knowledge. Can we can say we *experience* objects like doorknobs or matchboxes—or only brute sensations like colors, sounds, smells? The latter view, known as "phenomenalism," was popular in the late 1930s and early 1940s, in part because of how well it accorded with Ayer's ideas. "I always hated phenomenalism," Anscombe wrote, but "felt trapped by it." She couldn't "see [her] way out . . . ."[10] This sense she had of being "trapped" explains the equally powerful sense of liberation— and devotion—that Anscombe felt when she began working with Wittgenstein in the early 1940s.

Wittgenstein had spent much of the war as a hospital orderly in London and a laboratory technician in Newcastle, returning to Cambridge on weekends to lecture. Anscombe began attending these lectures almost as soon as she took up the Sarah Smithson studentship in 1942. In 1944, when Wittgenstein moved back to Cambridge, Anscombe attached herself to him. Wittgenstein's aspiration, in the final phase of his career, was therapeutic. He saw himself as having been imprisoned by a tidy-minded but ultimately false picture of language and its relationship to the world. The metaphor is his: "a picture held us captive."[11] Wittgenstein sought release from his captivity; his primary audience was himself. His aim was to escape his own imprisoning pictures by making them explicit, breaking their sense of inevitability. "What is your aim in philosophy?" he asks himself. His reply: "To shew the fly the way out of the fly-bottle."[12] But

Wittgenstein understood that others were similarly imprisoned. He and Anscombe were perfectly matched.

Anscombe recorded, in print and in notebooks of reminiscences, how skilled Wittgenstein was at perceiving the pictures that held others captive. "Let me think what medicine you need . . . " he said to her one day as she articulated the theory of perception she hated so much. And the medicine worked: "I saw the nerve being extracted," she wrote.[13]

The result, initially, was that Anscombe became utterly, abjectly, Wittgenstein's votary. She described herself later as having entered a state of "besotted reverence" in which "almost anything that Wittgenstein said sounded true and important to me."[14] Not that they never argued: on the contrary. It was part of the trust Anscombe placed in Wittgenstein that she told him exactly what she thought, even when—especially when—her thoughts appalled her. As we expose our bodies and recount our histories to physicians, placing a terrible, delicate trust in them, Anscombe exposed her mind to Wittgenstein. It was in the service of healing, of freedom.

Even before Wittgenstein's death, Anscombe began working against her early, uncritical adulation. She had never accepted his views on religion (she would later remark to a student that "[on] religion, Wittgenstein is sheer poison.").[15] But her concern was more general. "In philosophy," she observed, "overwhelming influence . . . is not good." Influence *could* be good: "influence which improves standards of argument and seriousness," especially. But not all: "not influence which makes something seem convincing because it is a part of X's teaching."[16]

It is unsurprising that Wittgenstein's influence on Anscombe was initially "overwhelming." Anscombe had come to Wittgenstein "trapped" and he set her free; Wittgenstein was her philosophical savior. Early in Anscombe's career, she developed the annoying foible of many devoted students: half-consciously impersonating her teacher.

Mary Warnock recalled how Anscombe echoed Wittgenstein's pained gestures, his long silences, even his Austrian accent. And not only these: she also adopted his superhuman standards for what was worth saying. Anscombe later recalled Wittgenstein dismissing his own epoch-making *Philosophical Investigations.* "It limps" he said: "If this were philosophy, you could learn it by heart."[17] What chance did she have of rising to that fearsome standard?

The short-term effects of Wittgenstein's influence on Anscombe were almost silencing. A less powerful personality would have been silenced for good. Her declaration to Murdoch that "no second-rate philosophy is any good" reflected a long and sometimes brutal apprenticeship in which nurturing remarks like "[l]et me think what medicine you need" alternated with descriptions of her works in progress like "bought for a farthing" and "not house-trained."[18] Small wonder Anscombe never finished her doctoral thesis. Or that the one original article she published before her translation of Wittgenstein's *Philosophical Investigations* contains this disclaimer: "Everywhere in this paper I have imitated [Wittgenstein's] ideas and methods of discussion. The best that I have written is a weak copy of some features of the original, and its value depends only on my capacity to understand and use Dr. Wittgenstein's work."[19]

Those who studied with Anscombe in her maturity, in the late 1950s and beyond—Foot, Michael Dummett, Anthony Kenny—insisted that "[n]othing could have been further from her character and mode of thought than discipleship."[20] Still, she would say to people for years, "I don't have a single idea in my head that wasn't put there by Wittgenstein."[21] The truth is, Wittgenstein had *converted* her. His example of self-criticism and devotion to truth influenced Anscombe as powerfully as anything he taught her about language or perception. Working with him, she came to see philosophy not as a source of nagging, unanswerable questions, but as service to a sacred cause. What she found in Wittgenstein was a paragon of self-critical devotion. Anscombe never quoted Kierkegaard's famous remark about seeking a truth for which he could live and die, but the sentiment would have resonated with her.

AUSTIN (II)

Even as she worked toward a purer, more constructive devotion, Anscombe remained implacably hostile to anyone who failed to acknowledge Wittgenstein's genius—especially if that "anyone" was a perceived competitor for her teacher's renown. She particularly detested J.L. Austin, who dominated the postwar philosophical scene at Oxford. She attended Austin's classes but made trouble, scarcely containing her disdain. "To think that Wittgenstein fathered that bastard!" she fumed to Warnock on her way out one evening.[22]

What was it about Austin—"wizened, tweedy, pipe-smoking, very precise"[23]—that Anscombe hated so much? Austin's project, recall, was the patient teasing out of nuances of ordinary language, with the idea that there are often interesting distinctions embedded in these nuances. We miss the distinctions and think crude thoughts if, like Ayer, we embrace grand theories of language and meaning.

Many readers of both Wittgenstein and Austin have observed that they share some key convictions. Each opposes simplistic theories of language. Each is thus "anti-theoretical" in outlook, though each tentatively advances some constructive generalizations about language and thought. In their constructive modes, each emphasizes the importance of attending closely to how language is used: "don't think, but look!" as Wittgenstein wrote.[24] Warnock certainly saw a likeness between them, and said so to Anscombe: "had [Wittgenstein] not said that he was concerned to destroy houses of cards?" Wasn't that exactly what Austin was doing to Ayer's positivism? It was a mistake: "Elizabeth . . . turned white with rage. She said that if I thought there was anything whatever in common between Austin and Wittgenstein, then I had totally misunderstood everything she had taught me . . . ."[25] Anscombe's hostility to Austin was reciprocated. He referred to her as "that ninny."[26] Austin was as cool and genteel as Anscombe was earnest and blunt; he abhorred her unrefined manner and hot outbursts.

The division between Austin and Wittgenstein, and by extension between Austin and Anscombe, Warnock concluded, was not one of conflicting claims about language but of conflicting styles of philosophizing: "but matters of style can go very deep," she notes.[27] Wittgenstein was deadly earnest, aiming at healing or liberation from tormenting, entrapping thoughts. Austin, by contrast, was urbane and witty, dismissive both of grand ambitions and of dour sobriety. A later commentator remarked that Austin wanted "to exist as a dry crackle."[28] Mary Warnock's husband (and Austin disciple) Geoffrey once recalled to an interviewer how Austin would occasionally read out a passage from Wittgenstein in a lecture, "to show how incomprehensible and obscure [he] was, and how easily he could be parodied and dismissed." Puzzled by Geoffrey's admiration of Austin's behavior, the interviewer asked: "Were there some things about him that were human?" "Oh, yes," Geoffrey replied. "He taught us all absolute accuracy."[29]

Though Austin inspired some by his high standards and was lavishly generous to (certain) colleagues, he was also domineering. Even his most enthusiastic followers acknowledged it. At the Saturday morning gatherings he organized, Austin was always the most senior person present. (The gatherings were popularly called "Austin's kindergarten.") The criteria for invitation seemed calculated to exclude people he didn't want, like Anscombe and Murdoch. And although the conversations were freewheeling and intensely stimulating for

Austin's colleagues, Geoffrey Warnock reported that they always felt "just a little as if the headmaster were present."[30]

This was at a select gathering of friendly, admiring younger faces. In public venues, Austin crushed dissent. He was a brilliant lecturer, but also "negative," "frightening," "captious," "dismissive."[31] A colleague recalled how, in the course of a discussion about different kinds of excuses, a student asked what Austin thought about the larger philosophical question of free will. Austin "was withering, looking down his nose at him, as if he had made a bad smell."[32] On another occasion, Austin was asked about Gabriel Marcel, a Catholic existentialist Murdoch admired. Austin retorted: "A complete fraud. Next question?"[33] Austin's hostility to grand theories like Ayer's may have been born of a determination to check hubris. But in combination with his competitive, intimidating personality, it effectively suppressed large-scale reflection of any kind. Murdoch's judgment on Ryle could be applied equally to Austin: his world was one, she wrote, "in which people play cricket, cook cakes, make simple decisions, remember their childhood or go to the circus; not the world in which they commit sins, fall in love, say prayers, or join the Communist Party."[34]

For Wittgenstein and Anscombe both, philosophy was a spiritual activity. Anscombe was maddened by Austin's lightness, his unseriousness. As Mary Warnock noted, "Elizabeth . . . longed to wipe the grin off his face."[35] Anscombe's character and eccentricities would probably have alienated her from many of her Oxford colleagues regardless; the animosity between her and such an adulated figure alienated her further.

It was not natural to her anyway to adhere to a movement, like linguistic analysis. Her instinct, formed during her years studying under Wittgenstein, was to criticize her own tribe. Tribalism was antithetical to truth-seeking.

THE LEWIS DEBATE

Anscombe's 1948 Socratic Club debate with literary scholar and Christian apologist C.S. Lewis is profoundly illustrative of who Anscombe was, and was becoming, in the opening years of her career.[36]

The Socratic Club was founded in 1941, Bosanquet's, Murdoch's, and Scrutton's last year as undergraduates. A Somervillian, Monica Shorten, approached an evangelical chaplain, Stella Aldwinckle, complaining that there was no venue at Oxford for serious discussion of hard questions about faith. After a couple of loosely organized but heavily attended gatherings at Somerville, Aldwinckle approached Lewis to ask if he would serve as President of a new, University-wide club. Lewis agreed, and began inviting intellectuals within and beyond the University to debate with him and one another. Aldwinckle was Lewis's ambassador among women students. A South African transplant, she shared Murdoch's tendency toward easy intimacy (they formed an enduring friendship). Aldwinckle immediately struck Murdoch as "a thoroughly serious pure-hearted person."[37,] * But it was the Socratic itself that drew Murdoch and her friends. "Philosophy was then at its driest," Murdoch recalled. The Socratic was an oasis. Upon her return to Oxford, Murdoch began giving occasional talks there. And in Anscombe's second year back at Oxford, she agreed to debate Lewis.

Lewis was a philosopher as well as a literary scholar: he had read Greats back in the 1920s and taught philosophy for a year at

---

* Scrutton, less free-spirited, found Aldwinckle intrusive. Anscombe for her part was scornful of Aldwinckle's evangelical piety. Bernard Williams recalled an occasion when Aldwinckle declared that she had a "personal relationship with God"—to which Anscombe replied, "what bloody cheek!" (Letter from Bernard Williams to Peter Conradi, KUAS6/3/166, Kingston University Archives. Used by permission of Mrs. Patricia Williams.)

University College before receiving his appointment in English literature at Magdalen. His 1947 book, *Miracles*, was a work of popular philosophy, responding to David Hume and other critics of the idea that God acts in the world. In his third chapter, Lewis attacks what he calls "naturalism"—by which he means a picture of the world as a self-contained system of cause and effect. He has in mind the common late-modern idea that physics explains everything: roughly, the billiard-ball picture. Lewis argues that belief in naturalism undermines itself. The causes physicists study are non-rational: the mindless operation of physical forces. Lewis scents trouble for the naturalist in this belief. If everything is fully explained by non-rational causes, like chemical processes, magnetic attraction, or one piece of matter colliding with another, then so is the naturalist's belief in naturalism. And can anyone trust a belief that is fully explained by non-rational causes? Like Scrooge, who dismisses his experience of Marley's ghost on the grounds that "there's more of gravy than of grave" about the apparition, Lewis asks: would you trust a belief if you knew it was fully explained by what you'd eaten for dinner? In the first edition of *Miracles*, he called this "The Self-Contradiction of the Naturalist."[38]

Anscombe liked the Socratic as much as Murdoch and the others did. She appreciated how wide-ranging its topics were and how the Socratic carried over conversations from meeting to meeting. The Socratic was serious. But her first impression of Lewis was that he wasn't. A letter survives from Anscombe to Wittgenstein, recounting the debate. In it, she relates how provoked she was by Lewis's argument. She initially wrote, she says, a "rotten" draft of her response full of "pompous indignation at Lewis . . . ." But her friend and fellow Wittgenstein disciple Yorick Smythies called her out: "writing 'Shit!' against my remarks."[39]

In the end, Anscombe was faultlessly professional. "I am going to argue that your whole thesis is . . . specious," she said, "because of the ambiguity of the words 'why', 'because', and 'explanation.'"[40]

Briefly, she argued that there is no such thing as the "full explanation" of a belief. Think of a criminal investigation. We work to establish not only *who* committed the crime, but also *how* and *why*. These are different questions, with different answers. None of them is "the full explanation" of what happened. So too with beliefs, Anscombe said. There is no reason they can't have both physical explanations and rational explanations. But then "the self-contradiction of the naturalist" dissolves.

The consensus of those in attendance was that Anscombe won—that Lewis could not effectively answer her criticisms. Anscombe told Wittgenstein she was pleasantly surprised by Lewis's behavior: "He was much more decent in discussion than I expected," she wrote, "though he was glib."[41] As several of Lewis's friends reported, he found the experience devastating; legends have grown up around it.[42] But as Anscombe remarked later to someone asking about the encounter, a philosopher has a responsibility to criticize bad arguments, even when they are arguments on the side of her own convictions.[43] Anscombe and Lewis were both Christians, and neither of them was a naturalist by Lewis's definition. But Anscombe could never assess a philosophical issue in terms of team loyalty or victory. She had no interest in displays of dominance—another thing that divided her from Austin. Near the end of his life, Bernard Williams recalled about her:

she impressed upon [me] that being clever wasn't enough. Oxford philosophy ... had a great tendency to be clever ... there was a lot of competitive dialectical exchange, and showing that other people were wrong. I was quite good at all that. But Elizabeth conveyed a strong sense of the seriousness of the subject, and how the subject was difficult in ways that simply being clever wasn't going to get round.[44]

It is noteworthy that the question Lewis raised remained with Anscombe. It was the question that first drew her into philosophy: must everything that happens have a cause? It returned in the inaugural lecture she gave upon acceding to Wittgenstein's Chair at Cambridge in 1971.[45] And recalling the debate in 1981, in the introduction to a volume of her collected papers, Anscombe wrote: "rereading . . . my criticisms [of Lewis] . . . it seems to me that they are just. At the same time, I find them lacking in any recognition of the depth of the problem." She went on to contrast her own remarks unfavorably with the revised argument in the 1960 edition of *Miracles*, which corresponded "more to the actual depth and difficulty of the questions being discussed." She concluded, "I think we haven't an answer yet to [Lewis's] question . . . ."[46] Glibness, for Anscombe, was the great intellectual vice; recognition that a problem is *hard*, the great virtue.

"DIRT DOESN'T MATTER"

Anscombe was a research fellow at Somerville, not a regular tutorial fellow, from her return to Oxford in 1946 until 1958. The first six years, until 1952, she was supported by the Mary Somerville Research Fellowship. After that, she was supported by a series of grants from the Rockefeller Foundation, with a commission to produce translations of Wittgenstein's late works. But except for the first six months of 1950, when she was in Vienna working on her German, Anscombe always did some teaching. Particularly in the early years, the family needed the money.

After Peter Geach was hired at the University of Birmingham in 1951, their finances finally improved. The children moved to Oxford, and 27 St. John Street became the family home—though Anscombe and Geach continued to practice "telegamy" for decades.[47] Now Anscombe had to balance childcare and teaching.

Anscombe held tutorials in an upstairs room. The house was narrow and dimly lit, and her two—then three, four . . . seven—children's things were scattered everywhere, including in the tutorial room.[48] The room would not have been tidy, regardless. Some of Anscombe's papers found their way into a green filing cabinet, but others were piled about, together with unwashed dishes. On the floor next to the low armchair where Anscombe sat was a wooden bowl, at least a foot across, filled with water. Stub ends of cigarettes bobbed on the surface.

Philosophy was serious business, and the older children were given strict instructions not to interrupt tutorials for anything short of a fire. (Once a car caught fire in the street outside; one of Anscombe's children duly notified her.) But the younger ones would sometimes wander in and climb into their mother's lap. Anscombe was capable of maintaining concentration in circumstances that others would have found unworkable. A washing machine in the upstairs bathroom was bolted to the floor and made the whole building shake. A section of plaster collapsed during one tutorial. Anscombe carried on.

Committed to philosophy the way a nun or monk is committed to prayer, Anscombe's tutorials would sometimes run over by an hour, even two, as she gave students the experience, not of a discrete lesson, but of *doing philosophy* together, as Wittgenstein had done philosophy with her. One student recalled that "after a session with her my brain was usually so exhausted I would . . . go to sleep for a couple of hours, regardless of the time of day."[49] Anscombe liked nothing better than when one of her students challenged her own or Wittgenstein's ideas: "You mean you're *fighting* him?" she exclaimed to an undergraduate she had assigned to comment on a passage in the *Investigations*. They spent the rest of the tutorial developing the student's attack.

When Philippa Foot finally began warming to Wittgenstein's ideas—
much later than Murdoch or Scrutton—Anscombe commended her
for how long it had taken: "it is important to have one's resistances."[50]
On the other hand, a graduate-student-turned-colleague wrote,
"if I wrote . . . anything with which I thought she would agree, she
attacked me more vigorously than ever."[51]

The family had a devoted charwoman who kept entropy in check,
washing the windows and doing the laundry each weekday morning. But outsiders found the state of the house shocking. (Murdoch,
hardly a tidy person herself, remarked in her journal on the "terrible
untidiness" of Anscombe's house.)[52] Anscombe routinely spent long
afternoons in the Somerville Senior Common Room, talking philosophy with Philippa Foot. Once, a social worker inquired about
the welfare of the children and Anscombe (backed by Geach) fended
her off. (An Oxford legend, recounted by Christopher Coope, had
it that the younger children were sent outdoors with labels on their
clothing: "If found wandering please return to 27 St. John Street.")
A student recalled one of Anscombe's children approaching her and
asking "Can I go out in St. Giles [a major thoroughfare] and play?"
"No dear," Anscombe replied, "the police just don't understand."[53]
Literary critic John Carey lived on St. John Street for a time and
wrote an incendiary description of some neighbors who Mary Geach
Gormally says were her family:

> [T]he house was regularly left in the children's sole charge. The
> result was bedlam. The din of recorded music resounded from
> the place at all hours, and it never seemed to occur to anyone
> to shut a window or moderate the volume. One summer after-
> noon . . . my patience gave out, and I crossed the street to protest.
> As usual, every gaping window blared: it was like knocking at the
> door of a reverberating three-storey transistor set. . . . Eventually

a teenage girl, one of the daughters, answered, and . . . I asked if she would mind playing the music a little more quietly. . . . "Oh," she said, "it's no good your complaining about that. The whole street got up a petition about us once, but it didn't have any effect." And with that she shut the door.[54]

In 1959, the *Manchester Guardian* ran a profile on Anscombe, one of a series on successful women professionals. It celebrates Anscombe's disregard for convention and her devotion to the central causes of her life. Though the piece gives a vivid sense of life at 27 St. John Street and of Anscombe's dress sense (citing her "disreputable shirt and trousers") it leaves out a telling remark she made to the writer. To the question, "How do you manage a household with a husband and six children while carrying on your full-time career?," Anscombe replied, "You just have to realize that dirt doesn't matter."[55]

This is the key to all the most colorful stories about Anscombe: she drew a firm distinction between what mattered and what didn't. She then devoted herself unreservedly to what mattered. And she spent as little energy as possible on what didn't.

What didn't matter?

The rule at Oxford that women were supposed to wear skirts when lecturing didn't matter. But wearing trousers didn't matter either—she just liked them—and neither did how she looked, except when it was a question of honoring someone or something that mattered. So she would bring along a skirt and pull it on—over her trousers—outside the lecture-room door. "I am a great stickler for convention and propriety," she remarked to one bystander, as she stepped into the required uniform.[56] On similar occasions at Cambridge, later in her career, she used Wittgenstein's old academic gown as a makeshift skirt, wrapping it around her waist.[57]

Self-care (beyond the most basic) didn't matter, so she smoked like an engine until the day one of her sons suffered a near-fatal accident. In desperation, she promised God that she would give up cigarettes if the boy lived. He did—and she did. (She later took up cigars.)[58] And in 1954 she shocked Michael Dummett when he showed up to her house to congratulate her, a day after she'd given birth. There had been a group discussion planned for that day, but Dummett had heard that Anscombe's labor had been difficult; he assumed the discussion was off. It wasn't. "I found Elizabeth in a dressing gown and the discussion in full swing," Dummett recalled; "she merely glanced at me, remarking that I was late."*, [59]

Delicacy didn't matter, not in comparison with saying what you meant. So Anscombe salted her conversation with obscenities, and not only in private. Reading a paper distinguishing several types of pleasure, Anscombe offered as one of her examples "shitting," carefully pronouncing the double "t".[60] She cultivated an atmosphere in which very little was off-limits. Anthony Kenny recalled a time when he was an overnight guest of "the Geachcombes" (as some called them). Anscombe walked into the bathroom while he was in the tub and sat down on the edge, continuing a conversation they'd been having.

Her name *did* matter, and she routinely ignored mail addressed to Mrs. Peter Geach. But other sorts of deference did not, and Anscombe was often brusque in discussion, dismissing peers whose remarks seemed to her to show insufficient reflection.[61] She did not

---

* Another story—possibly legendary—recounts her trying to schedule a tutorial: "I have a meeting on Monday; I'm giving a lecture in London on Tuesday; I'm having a baby on Wednesday; Thursday would work." (Nicholas Denyer, conversation with author, June 29, 2012).

hold back even when anyone could perceive that a relationship was at stake. Anscombe vilified Mary Warnock's future husband to her face, referring to him as "that shit, Warnock." And she berated her undergraduate friend Jean Coutts over her marriage to John Austin.[62] Coutts, gentle and self-effacing, had been a close friend of Anscombe's when they were undergraduates. They had gone on long bicycle rides together as well as talking about Plato and doing their logic exercises for Martha Kneale. Recalling their break, Coutts would only say, sadly, "at first we saw a lot of one another; then we didn't."[63]

All this had consequences. As time went on, Anscombe was increasingly isolated from her colleagues, beyond a small circle of fellow Catholics, fellow Wittgensteinians, and appreciative students who proudly claimed her as their own. More magnanimous Oxonians outside these circles acknowledged her capacity and contribution and made peace with her as best they could. Others were less tolerant. Isaiah Berlin reviled Anscombe to BBC producer Anna Kallin:

[T]he Wittgenstein intimates—Miss Anscombe and her husband Geach and others—were thinking of founding a colony in order to live, think, eat and be like Ludwig. Originally it was intended to invite L. himself, but now that he is dead they propose to establish it anyhow. A great deal of violent artificial neurosis, not washing etc., anyhow you can imagine—hideous stammering in place of articulate speech, perverted Catholicism, and all the other delicious attributes.[64]

Did Anscombe feel her isolation? She must have known how conspicuous she was in her unbuttoned duffel coat and sandals, sometimes covering her extropic left eye with an eyepatch or a monacle. Her rages burned hot, then flamed out; she and Peter Geach even came to speak appreciatively about Austin. Whatever she thought he had stolen from Wittgenstein, Austin was at least committed to getting things right. They especially liked a thing he would say when someone airily asserted that there were "lots of examples" of some phenomenon: "name three."[65]

But many fellow Oxonians didn't know how to take Anscombe. She confronted people with the same disconcerting directness that her mentor Wittgenstein had. Her outbursts and eccentricities struck some (Bernard Williams, for example) as affectations. But in her journal, Murdoch records something Anscombe said to her in a moment of vulnerability: that "she felt a 'clod' beside the people she most cared for . . . surprised that they tolerated her."[66] This illuminates an episode from 1948–49 that Mary Scrutton recalled:

> She and Iris and I were having coffee together . . . in the Cornmarket and we were discussing the meaning of rudeness. . . . This discussion went on quite peacefully until Iris happened to say, "Of course, the . . . meaning of rudeness might not be all bad. For instance, Elizabeth, I should imagine that some people might sometimes describe you as 'rude'?"

Anscombe's rudeness was "proverbial," Scrutton said. Scrutton had assumed that it was a defiant choice. But Anscombe "froze and was wholly silent for a long time." Then she stood up, conveyed in a curt speech that she was deeply insulted, and walked out.[67] She had so few people she could rely on. The suggestion that one of them was *enduring* her was lacerating.[68]

Notwithstanding her earned reputation for abrasiveness, when Anscombe wasn't in the thick of philosophical argument—or a fight— she was quiet, even withdrawn. Through the early 1950s, Anscombe refused most invitations to speak. Two years after the Socratic Club debate, C.S. Lewis urged Aldwinckle to bring Anscombe back as a speaker: "having obliterated me as an Apologist," he wrote, "ought she not to succeed me?"[69] Anscombe declined.[70] Colleague Stuart Hampshire wrote to Anna Kallin at the BBC, encouraging her to put Anscombe on the air. But when another producer, Foot's friend Prudence Smith, reached out, Anscombe replied saying she doubted her own ability.

Scrutton later observed that Anscombe "was rather shy of talking to strangers, especially to those who were in any sort of authority. She tended to regard them as a dangerous alien tribe, and when they were friendly to her she didn't know quite how to take it. She was much more at ease in open warfare."[71] In a postscript to her letter to Wittgenstein after the Lewis debate, Anscombe wrote: "I find public discussion very difficult indeed. I am in a frightened hurry to reply to what is said to me; if I try to check this and pause to think about it, my mind goes blank. So I say a lot that is no use."[72] Nineteen-fifty arrived, then 1953, then 1956, and still Anscombe had published almost nothing besides her translation of Wittgenstein's *Investigations*.

But in the spring of 1956, the Oxford University administration announced its intention to bestow an honorary doctorate on former US President Harry Truman. Truman expressed gratitude, and joked about how he would look in a "floppy hat." Anscombe was not amused. Truman was known the world over for his decisions to bomb Hiroshima and Nagasaki. Those decisions, she judged, were wrong—profoundly wrong. Evil. What Truman had done mattered.

"THE WOMEN ARE UP TO SOMETHING"

Anscombe had published on the traditional Catholic doctrine of Just War once before, as an undergraduate. She and her friend Norman Daniel caused themselves and the head of Blackfriars Priory some trouble with their Archbishop when they wrote and published a short pamphlet opposing the war. Anscombe was no pacifist, but she and Daniel predicted—rightly—that, given the Allies' stated aims, they would eventually descend to intentional killing of civilians. This, she said, could not be squared with the traditional criteria of justice in warfare, which require that only just means be used to prosecute a war. Intentional killing of civilians, she wrote, is not a just means. Intentional killing of civilians is intentional killing of the innocent— that is, murder. Anscombe would press the same objection against Truman's degree a decade and a half later. Truman had authorized the incineration of two cities. These weren't raids on military targets with incidental civilian casualties. These were attempts to terrorize the Japanese into surrender by targeting civilians.

Anscombe's protest, in late spring 1956, became a minor international news item. The United Press coverage misidentified her as Gladys Anscombe, and headline writers on the far side of the Atlantic seemed most interested in the fact that she was a woman.* The protest failed. Alienated from most of her colleagues, Anscombe was the worst imaginable political organizer. She did not even canvass for support. She simply raised her voice and left the rest to God. On May 1, Anscombe stood to speak at the (usually sparsely attended) assembly that approved such degrees, and quietly but firmly denounced the nomination. One quote survives: "if you do this . . . what Nero, what Ghengis Khan, what Hitler or what Stalin will not be honored in the future?" But the University administration, forewarned when Anscombe inquired the day before about procedure, had solicited a crowd to show up and vote in support of Truman's degree. "The women are up to something," some were told. "We have to go and vote them down."[73] Only Anscombe, Philippa and Michael Foot

---

* Two headlines: "Woman Opposes Truman Degree" and "Oxford Honors Truman Over Woman's Protest."

(Michael from loyalty, not from conviction), and Murdoch's lover Margaret Hubbard voted "*non placet*" ("it does not please").

What infuriated Anscombe most was her colleagues' passivity. Did they believe it was all right to kill civilians? Or did they care more about institutional embarrassment than about the wrongness of murder? Surely they knew that Truman's actions were indefensible under international law; Anscombe advertised a reward of £100 (over £2000 today) for anyone who could prove otherwise.

The arguments her colleagues *did* make, she found contemptible. At the same assembly, Historian Alan Bullock was required *ex officio* to defend the nomination. In a pamphlet Anscombe circulated after the May 1 vote but before the awards ceremony, she remarked drily of Bullock that he had to "pretend to show that a couple of massacres to a man's credit are not exactly a reason for not showing him honour." "The defence," she concluded, "would not have been well received at Nuremberg."[74]

What did Anscombe want from Bullock and her other colleagues? She wanted them to take seriously the foundational precept of Just War theory that if the only way to win a battle, or even a war, is by committing an atrocity, then it is better not to win—better to die, even. Perhaps the heroism of the English Catholic martyrs is too much to *expect* of anyone. But if Anscombe's colleagues quietly agreed with her, she wanted them to have the courage to endure a little embarrassment for the truth.

Until 1956, Anscombe had not published anything on ethics except for the pamphlet she co-authored as an undergraduate. She had a secondhand awareness of recent developments in ethical theory from discussions with her Somerville colleague, Philippa Foot. But her scholarly energies had been almost entirely absorbed, for a decade, in the translation of Wittgenstein's later writings. As it happened, at the same time the University was preparing to honor Truman, and Anscombe was asking herself why "so many Oxford people should be willing to flatter such a man," Philippa Foot requested sabbatical leave. Anscombe agreed to take on some of her colleague's usual responsibilities, including tutorials in ethics. These two experiences—the Truman protest and the reading she was doing in preparation for her new tutorials—converged in Anscombe's mind. "I get some small light," she wrote, "when I consider the productions of Oxford moral philosophy since the First World War, which I have lately had occasion to read."[75] None of the prevailing theories, she found, ruled out the killing of the innocent—murder. None of them, indeed, ruled out anything. They spoke instead of the free adoption of principles in a world without values. None of them had room for Anscombe's own deepest ethical conviction: that "we have to fear God and keep his commandments, and calculate what is for the best only within the limits of that obedience."[76]

She included a paragraph about this at the end of her pamphlet on "Mr. Truman's Degree." The result was that in mid-July, a short note arrived from A.E. Harvey of the BBC Talks Department, asking if Anscombe might "develop the theme of the relevance of Oxford moral philosophy to situations such as the one which inspired your pamphlet."[77] Alight with sufficient indignation to overcome her shyness, she said yes. By the end of October, she had submitted a script, laced with irony: "Oxford Moral Philosophy: Does it 'corrupt the youth'?"

Anscombe's Truman protest had flared up, then died back into obscurity. Few outside Oxford saw her pamphlet, and—as the vote shows—polite Oxford society was mostly dismissive of Anscombe's objections. "[S]he was not someone whose doings signified," one colleague remarked later.[78] A national broadcast was another affair.

THE LISTENER

Anscombe began her talk disarmingly, saying that, in her view, Oxford moral philosophy does *not* "corrupt the youth." But not for any ennobling reason. No, "in order to show that a . . . teaching corrupts people, you must obviously show that they have (or would have come to have) better ideas without this teaching." In fact, Anscombe argued, "there is no difference at all" between the teaching of Oxford moral philosophers and the ideas the youth would absorb outside of the University: "It is . . . a dead level."

She implied more, though. She implied that the typical Oxford moral philosopher is a conformist, a "child of his time."[79] Or, at any rate, that he has no resources in his philosophy (or character?) to resist the worst ideas and practices around him. After relating a number of what she took to be fashionable moral opinions (including that "it was right to massacre the Japanese" at Hiroshima and Nagasaki), and setting them alongside views she had encountered in philosophical discussions in Oxford, Anscombe summed up: "this philosophy is conceived perfectly in the spirit of the time." Indeed, it is "the flattery of that spirit."[80]

What did she mean? What features of Oxford philosophy did she have in mind? Her talk is full of biting and memorable asides:

A . . . point of method which I would recommend to the corrupter would be this: concentrate on examples which are either banal: you have promised to return a book, but . . . and so on; or fantastic: what you ought to do if you had to move forward, and stepping with your right foot meant killing twenty-five fine young men while stepping with your left foot would kill fifty drooling old ones. (Obviously the right thing to do would be to jump and polish the lot.)

But the talk is also scattered. Whether due to nerves or outrage or simple limitations of time, Anscombe never lingers over a point. Nevertheless, it is possible to work out her central concerns.

By 1956, "up-to-date Oxford moral philosophy" meant Richard Hare's. And early on, Anscombe made her principal target plain. She anticipated and deflected the suggestion that Hare could not be a corrupter, "in view of his obvious moral earnestness." (Quite the contrary: anyone who wanted to corrupt people, Anscombe argued, would find earnestness "an important item of equipment.") And at the end, she mocked Hare's views about moral education: "Everybody knows that we have long since discarded the hideous conception of parental authority. . . . In a changing world, with changing conditions, standards must change; and you must cut your morals according to your purposes . . . ."[81]

Hare, recall, held that moral judgments are what he called "universal prescriptions": commands (of a sort) issued to oneself and everyone else to behave in certain ways. If one says that someone "ought" not to steal, then one is committed not to steal, oneself. But on Hare's view, our prescriptions cannot be judged against any criteria other than consistency. They cannot be judged, particularly, against factual criteria. There are no right or wrong answers in ethics, only consistent or inconsistent ones. As Hare wrote a few years later, "we are free to form our own moral opinions in a much stronger sense than we are free to form our own opinions as to what the facts are."[82]

The word "free" is important. It betrays the Romantic, existentialist element Murdoch identified in her contemporaries' world-picture. In her talk and in the debate that followed, Anscombe echoed her friend's critique. With no objective criteria for moral judgments, we human beings—reflective creatures that we are—can only evaluate our options and make decisions in a condition of lonely freedom. Hare and others like him exhorted their readers to be adults, to own up to their condition with its attendant responsibilities. "To become morally adult," Hare wrote, "is to learn to use 'ought'-sentences in the realization that they can only be verified by reference to a standard or set of principles which we have by our own decision accepted and made our own. This is what our present generation is so painfully trying to do."[83]

So we are free to form the opinion, like Anscombe, that we ought never to deliberately kill the innocent. But we are equally free to form the opinion that we ought to kill the innocent if it would serve our strategic aims. Not believing in any standards above themselves, all theorists like Hare are left with are "common standards . . . 'our' standards, shown by 'what we say' in judging others." And this, Anscombe suggested, makes them scarcely distinguishable from the kind of complacent chauvinist who judges institutions and practices by how well they fit with "our way of life."[84]

The irony of Anscombe's broadcast talk was subtle enough that T.S. Gregory, her producer, first took the manuscript for "a vigorous defence of Oxford morals and moralists" and urged that she quote someone who thought Oxford moral philosophy *was* corrupting, if she meant to argue the contrary.[85] But when the piece broadcast on February 5 and then appeared in the BBC weekly, *The Listener*, its targets understood it well enough.[86] Two of them, Hare and P.H. Nowell-Smith, wrote letters to the editor that appeared the next week, filling a tabloid column each. Anscombe, ready for a fight, replied: "I was glad to read [Hare's] letter and Mr. Nowell-Smith's. They show that what I want to go for is really there."[87]

The tone quickly devolved, though, with Hare, Peter Geach, and Anthony Flew arguing in subsequent issues about whether Hare had suggested that Anscombe's talk was obscene, and T.A. Burkill of Woodford Green writing in to speak for Ayer: "It would appear from the controversy on this topic that the teaching of ethics in . . . this country is in a chronic state of scientific impurity."[88] Anscombe's interlocutors—Hare especially—failed to grasp her complaint at its root because they were distracted by her rhetoric. In her talk, Anscombe made a number of throwaway remarks to the effect that Hare's (and his contemporaries') philosophy was "very much in line with" various forms of cruelty, like evicting widows from their homes (and social workers pushing people around, "not because they have done anything, but in case they do").[89] Hare replied that this was outrageous, that he had never defended any of these things. To which Anscombe replied: I didn't say you had. I said "that . . . no one believing [your] philosophy can hold that there is any solid certainty as to their badness."[90] This was harder to deny. Recall Hare's words: "we are free to form our moral opinions . . . ." But Anscombe's point was, as Hare complained, buried under "tortuous sarcasms."[91]

Meanwhile, Gregory was in busy private correspondences with both Hare and Anscombe. Hare had written to Gregory back in January, when he first learned of Anscombe's upcoming talk. He dismissed her criticisms of "Oxford moral philosophy" in the Truman pamphlet as "a complete travesty" and inquired about the possibility of a rebuttal if she should repeat them on the air.[92] Gregory sent Hare an advance copy of Anscombe's script so he could make an informed judgment. All along, Hare framed Anscombe to Gregory as unhinged. Writing just after the broadcast aired, he wrote, "After . . . taking a sample of the impressions of other listeners, lay and professional, I think a reply would be a mistake. The professionals found it unclear and inaccurate, and the laity did not understand it at all. . . . [N]othing should be done which would increase Miss Anscombe's resentment against mankind, which has begun to alarm those who know her."[93]

While Hare weighed his options, Anscombe rapidly composed a second script, titled "Principles," and submitted it for consideration.

Figure 1. Philippa Bosanquet (right) with her sister Marion and a pony.

Figure 2. Donald Mackenzie MacKinnon.

Figure 3. Elizabeth Anscombe (back row, right) with friends from St. Hugh's College in 1938.

Figure 4. Somerville College 1938 matriculation photo (Mary Scrutton first row, fourth from left; Iris Murdoch second row, fourth from right).

Figure 5. 5 Seaforth Place, aka "Seaforth." The entrance was through the first opening on the left.

Figure 6. Murdoch on Oxford Street, London, winter 1946-7.

Figure 7. Ludwig Wittgenstein.   Figure 8. R.M. Hare.

Figure 9. 16 Park Town, Philippa and Michael Foot's home from 1946-1959.

Figure 10. BBC Broadcasting House, with Eric Gill's statue of Prospero and Ariel.

Figure 11. Geoff and Mary Midgley with sons Martin, David, and Tom, at Runswick Bay, North Yorkshire, 1959.

Figure 12. J.O. Urmson and J.L. Austin (right).

Figure 13. Somerville Senior Common Room, from the perspective of someone standing in front of the fireplace.

Figure 14. Front quad, Somerville College. Murdoch's room was above the gatehouse. Visible on the right, a building of the Oxford Oratory Church of St. Aloysius Gonzaga (where Anscombe was received into the Catholic Church).

Figure 15. Postcard from Murdoch to Foot, 1959.

Figure 16. Iris Murdoch.

Figure 17. Elizabeth Anscombe.

Figure 18. Philippa Foot.

Figure 19. Mary Midgley.

Figure 20. Philippa Foot with Iris Murdoch in 1998.

Hare's and Nowell-Smith's first letters to the editor had not yet appeared. But Hare's private correspondence had done its work. The Talks Committee rejected Anscombe's script, plainly with Gregory's concurrence, on the grounds that it was too personal an attack. Gregory conveyed the news. Anscombe replied:

> is that the real reason for the rejection? I.e. would you accept it if the personalities were removed? This is an attack on something that is strong both in Oxford and in the world; and something that you never hear attacked on the BBC at all. It appears to me that you have some personal responsibility for the constant outpouring of solemn blasphemy and corrupt morality; at least if you do not do what you can to secure the acceptance of scripts which really do something lively to oppose it. Would you have accepted the first one if you had understood it?[94]

That stung; Gregory was a Catholic, and he and Anscombe were acquainted independently of the BBC. He drafted a heated reply that, after some internal discussion at the BBC, he was forbidden to send. Getting no reply from Gregory, Anscombe began dropping barbed remarks into her letters to the editor: "I feel confident that the linguistic analysis philosophers are a sufficiently strong pressure group . . . to ensure that such dreadful things will never again be allowed on the Third [Programme]."[95]

Gregory's unsent reply is interesting for a number of reasons, including its dishonest or misremembering insistence that he had never missed the point of Anscombe's "Oxford Moral Philosophy" script. But its greatest interest lies in an allusion Gregory makes to the content of the rejected script: "you say that anyone can do anything on principle, and if you have a large enough stock of principles you can select as you please the one to justify the particular wrong doing you favour."[96] That sentence resembles some things Anscombe says in an article she published the following year. And that article, "Modern Moral Philosophy," would become one of the most cited philosophical publications of the twentieth century. We may have the decision of Gregory and the BBC Talks Committee partly to thank for a major shift in Anglophone moral philosophy.[97]

"IS" AND "OUGHT"

Freed from the constraints of a broadcast script, Anscombe backed up and considered the characteristically Wittgensteinian question her friend Murdoch had been asking: what *picture* stood behind the moral theories of her time? Like Murdoch before her, Anscombe looked to modern intellectual history to explain how the dominant picture emerged. But she went beyond this to ask a different question: what could be put in its place? Here she made a decisive suggestion, one that most of her contemporaries were unprepared to consider yet: that they return to the ethical outlook people left behind at the beginning of the modern period, when people first adopted the billiard-ball picture. That they return to Aristotle.

Anscombe begins by attacking the only argument that any of her contemporaries ever gave for the fact–value dichotomy. This argument, adapted from David Hume's *Treatise of Human Nature*, had been reduced to a slogan: no "ought" from an "is."[98] The point is a logical one: you don't have a proper deduction if terms appear in your conclusion that do not appear in your premises. This, for instance, is not a valid deduction:

1. All human beings are mortal.
2. Socrates is a human being.
3. So, Socrates is an Athenian.

Where did the term "Athenian" come from? Not from either of the premises, 1 or 2.

So Hume wrote:

> In every system of morality, which I have hitherto met with, I have always remark'd, that the author proceeds for some time in the ordinary way of reasoning, and establishes the being of a God, or makes observations concerning human affairs; when of a sudden I am surpriz'd to find, that instead of the usual copulations of propositions, *is*, and *is not*, I meet with no proposition that is not connected with an *ought*, or an *ought not*. . . . [A]s this *ought*, or *ought not*, expresses some new relation or affirmation, 'tis necessary that . . . a reason should be given, for what seems altogether inconceivable, how this new relation can be a deduction from others, which are completely different from it.[99]

Hare called this principle "Hume's Law"; it was another way of articulating the fact–value dichotomy. Facts are properly expressed in descriptive language: "ises." Values are properly expressed in evaluative language: "oughts." Thus, to say, no "ought" from an "is," is the same as to say, no value from a fact. That NASA's readings of average global surface temperature have increased by one degree Celsius over the past 50 years is a fact. What (if anything) ought to be done about this cannot be deduced from the fact.

Anscombe's attack begins with an acknowledgment of the logical point: any inference from "is" to "ought" is not a strict deduction. But that doesn't mean that such an inference can't be rational; there are other kinds of rational inference besides deduction. Anscombe points out that *lots* of plainly rational inferences would be excluded if the only kind of rational inference were deduction. Consider inferences from "is" to "needs." Surely what an organism—a plant, say—*needs* is grounded in *facts*. But consider this argument:

1. Blueberries first rust, then die if there is insufficient iron in the soil.
2. So blueberries need soil with sufficient iron in it.

Someone making this argument could be charged with introducing a term in the conclusion ("need") that was not present in the premise. The inference involved is interesting, and merits philosophical exploration. It has roots in Aristotle, with his notion of the proper function of an organ or organism. (What an organ or organism must have in order to thrive, it needs.) But the inference isn't at all dubious, and it raises the question: why shouldn't we regard "ought" the same way we regard "needs?" (Indeed, mightn't one infer, after some soil testing, "I *ought* to amend the soil around these blueberries"?)

A second main thesis of "Modern Moral Philosophy" also points back to Aristotle. Anscombe suggests that unless Hare and others believe in a divine lawgiver, they should stop insisting on making ethics all about *principles*. The vocabulary of principles, she suggests—including words like "duty" and "obligation"—is the vocabulary of a legal system. It made sense in contexts where most people understood themselves to be governed by a divine law. But if one doesn't believe in a transcendent law and lawgiver—as she did, but as many of her contemporaries did not—then why go on making ethics about systems of principles?

Actually, she says, this secularized talk of principles is a source of corruption. If one doesn't believe in a legislator who has imposed particular obligations (like, "thou shalt not murder"), one is left to ask, in a completely unguided way, "what principles should we adopt?" And with no criteria to guide one's answer to this question, one can marry an atmosphere of moral seriousness to any sort of behavior. The sensible course for a secular thinker—and maybe, for anyone—would be to express one's moral judgments in a different vocabulary, one that offers real guidance. Anscombe recommends the traditional Aristotelian vocabulary of vice and virtue. The advantage of terms like "'unjust' over the terms 'morally right' and 'morally wrong,'" she argues, is that "unjust" has some guiding content. It *means* something. Suppose you're considering appeasing a mob by punishing someone for a crime he didn't commit. The terms "morally right" and "morally wrong" get you nowhere in thinking about the case—or not if you accept Hare's view. On Hare's view, you simply ask yourself what principles you are willing to accept. But the action is *clearly* unjust. This is a paradigm case of injustice. If "unjust" means *anything*, it means things like this. And thus your thought can find ground.*

If we can return to Aristotle. If we can make sense of the idea of a human being's proper function, of a characteristically human pattern of life. If so, then we could, with Aristotle, begin to work out a table of the traits that enable people to live vibrantly successful (Anscombe's word was "flourishing") human lives, and build an account of ethics on that footing. To do so would require that ethics draw seriously on biology, psychology, anthropology, and more. And before turning to those disciplines, it would require breaking out of the billiard-ball picture, with its overlay of the Dawkins sublime.

---

* Some readers will wonder how Anscombe harmonized her belief in God as a lawgiver with her recommendation of the Aristotelian vocabulary of virtues and vices. Did she recommend the Aristotelian vocabulary for others, but not for herself? Up to a point, yes. About belief in God as a lawgiver, she remarked, "you can do ethics without it, as is shown by the example of Aristotle." Aristotelian ethics was, she judged, the best that secular thought had to offer. But in her own thinking, Anscombe harmonized Aristotelian and Christian ideas, drawing on the earlier synthesis of medieval philosopher-theologian Thomas Aquinas. *Very* cursorily, Aquinas holds that God's law guides us toward the virtues we need to flourish as human beings.

WHAT CAME OF IT

As the correspondence in *The Listener* was winding down in late March 1957, a sympathetic reader, Hugh Heckstall-Smith, asked Anscombe if she would briefly articulate her "starting-point" in ethics. What would she say, in contrast to the subjectivism of Hare? Anscombe replied:

> Mr. Heckstall-Smith's demand is unreasonable. It is as if he were to say, "But what's your starting-point when you speak of cancer as really a disease?" If the world were full of doctors saying " 'disease' is really only an objection-expressing term" and acting accordingly, and someone objected to *them*, it would not be reasonable to say, "Just state your starting-point in a few words."[100]

She meant it. Through the late winter and early spring of 1957, as the correspondence columns in *The Listener* throbbed with rage, Anscombe was polishing up one of the few pieces of general ethical theory she would ever write, "Modern Moral Philosophy." But she was also giving the lectures that would become her slender but influential primer on the philosophy of action: *Intention*. *Intention* is not a work of ethics—though Anscombe hoped it would clarify some crucial background concepts. Anscombe's judgment was that any real, constructive work in moral philosophy was a long way off: as she wrote, "it is not profitable for us at present to do moral philosophy."[101] How do you talk medicine with people who think that "disease" is only an objection-expressing term? How do you even begin?* And so, in the coming years, apart from some explicitly Catholic reflections

---

* As she writes near the end of "Modern Moral Philosophy," "if someone really thinks, *in advance*, that it is open to question whether such an action as procuring the judicial execution of the innocent should be quite excluded from consideration—I do not want to argue with him; he shows a corrupt mind."

on topics like nuclear weapons and contraception, Anscombe walked away from ethics. Her next project after *Intention* was *An Introduction to Wittgenstein's Tractatus*. When fellow philosopher Mary Mothersill asked her to name a work for which she would like to be remembered, Anscombe replied, "My *Introduction to Wittgenstein's Tractatus*." She had no interest in debating with Hare or in replacing his theory with one of her own.

Her task, as she saw it, was to resist destructive madness. And her temperament would not have allowed her to engage in patient give-and-take over views she found abhorrent. In 1958, Anscombe was on the Third Programme once more (and for the last time) with Glanville Williams, a Cambridge law professor who had just written a book espousing permissive views on abortion and euthanasia. It was a profoundly awkward broadcast, in which Williams spoke genially with a doctor and an anthropologist while Anscombe listened silently. When the host finally turned to her, she denounced Williams' views as inhuman:

> We want to have everything pleasant about us and we shall see to it that it is . . . . Affliction is offensive to us, the solution is to prevent or stop the existence of the afflicted, not to mend their lot; if our comfort is threatened by the need to feed too many mouths, we're not going to put ourselves out, it's much simpler to use contraception, sterilization and abortion to cut out the superfluous mouths.[102]

The conversation then continued as if nothing had been said. What could they say? What meeting place could there be between them?

Reflecting back with dissatisfaction on one of her essays on the ethics of war, Anscombe wrote, "if I was torn by a *saeva indignatio* ["savage indignation"], I wish I had had the talent of a Swift in expressing it."[103] The comparison to Swift is apt. Like Anscombe, Swift was a person painfully out of step with the world around him but determined to seize its attention and make it think again. But she had done that much; she had smashed any sense that theories like Hare's were the only ones a modern person could responsibly hold. And she had suggested a way forward.

She was happy enough if someone else wanted to take it from there.

Chapter 7

The Somerville Senior Common Room

A DAY IN THE LIFE (I)

November 1956.[1] Philippa Foot looked haggard most days as she mounted the stairs up to Somerville Hall for lunch. When she wasn't delivering the meticulous lectures for which she was known around the University, she was giving tutorials, sometimes back-to-back-to-back. Anscombe could afford to give multi-hour tutorials to the carefully selected students assigned to her by Somerville—or occasionally, grudgingly, by colleagues.* She was principally supported by the Rockefeller Foundation. For Anscombe, every tutorial was an open-ended chance to do philosophy. The first- and second-year students who simply needed the basics—on whatever topic, from logic to ethics to Kant—fell to Foot. They got the best she could offer within the fixed hour, but then she had to move on. She routinely filled 11 or 12 hours a week just with her regular lessons. Ten was a full load. For her long-time colleague, Barbara Harvey, one enduring image of Foot was "her coming into lunch after a morning's tutorials,

---

* "If you must," A.J. Ayer said to Christopher Coope, who had heard Anscombe on the radio arguing with Glanville Williams, and wanted to study with her. Coope, correspondence with the author, January 4, 2013.

with a look of complete exhaustion on her face."[2] Foot desperately needed her upcoming sabbatical.

Students fearful of the philosophy portion of the syllabus found Foot encouraging. She invariably found something to praise even in the weakest essays. Her tactfulness could be comic. One student recalled Foot saying "I see you've thought about this," leaving the rest to be inferred: you didn't do the reading.[3] But she always offered criticism, too, pushing students toward the exactitude that was the highest virtue in Oxford philosophical circles. "More than anyone in Oxford," a student recalled, "Philippa . . . helped me to grow up. I was clever, but terribly opinionated. She wouldn't stand for it; she insisted I justify my wilder statements, but . . . so gently that I responded."[4] As Rosalind Hursthouse recalled, whenever she showed Foot her work, Foot "radiat[ed] support—*so* interesting, she particularly liked the point about such and such." "[H]appily reassured that I was not a fool," Hursthouse said, "I would enjoy every minute of the subsequent discussion, and leave eager to throw myself into the needed rewriting . . . [which] was usually total because, in our enjoyable discussion, she had incisively torn the original paper into shreds."[5]

Some students, of course, were intimidated by Foot, the way Mary Scrutton had been intimidated by her back in 1939: "her standards, I felt, would be very high, could I hope to meet them?"[6] All of Foot's surface attributes—her accent, her sharp but conservative dress sense—suggested primness. And most Somervillians were at least vaguely aware of Foot's grand origins. As they came to know her, though, they came to rely on her. What Donald MacKinnon had done for her and for Murdoch, Foot did for a new generation of young women: she never refused a request for counsel or support. The result was that students booked appointments with her at odd hours to talk about their extracurricular problems: lost love, unexpected pregnancy, harassment. She gave them time—and strength—beyond what she could spare. If she had a few minutes between tutorials, she would lie down. She would lie down *during* tutorials if she could, in an adjustable armchair that snapped into its reclined position with a crack like a gunshot. That was when she didn't need to spend the hour doing demonstration logic exercises in her spidery hand.

Foot arrived at lunch most days, wrung out. And though she needed to eat, the experience of lunch in Hall was seldom rejuvenating. Thanks to the kitchen-table operation she'd undergone as a child, Foot was deaf in one ear. The din of the undergraduates, resounding off the oak-paneled walls of the large, round-vaulted room, made it hard to converse even up at high table. Each day she retreated, as soon as seemed decent, down to the Senior Common Room. That was where she truly came back to life.

The Senior Common Room (SCR) at Somerville College is a grand Victorian parlor with papered walls, white wooden trim, and a worn rug over dark wood floors; large, 16-paned windows look out over the College lawn.[7,] * A miscellany of armchairs and tea tables is scattered along its length, from the entrance opposite the fellows' private dining room to the fireplace at the far end. Flanking the fireplace is a pair of fireside stools, upholstered in a floral pattern of red and blue over dull gold.

Afternoon by afternoon, term by term, from the late 1940s through the late 1960s, Elizabeth Anscombe and Philippa Foot made for these stools, sat down, and started talking philosophy.[8] Anscombe generally proposed the topic. It was conversation between colleagues and friends. It was an uncompensated tutorial. Over time, Foot realized

---

* Like "cabinet," "Senior Common Room" names both a place and, metonymically, the group with privileged access to that place—the fellows of a college.

that they were probably discussing the same topics Anscombe had once discussed with Wittgenstein. In Foot, Anscombe found the kind of interlocutor she prized: someone who took philosophical discussion as seriously as she did, someone hostile to the "affected frivolity" that characterized many of their male colleagues,[9] someone who would never yield just to please her, someone she could mentor in the same, sustained way that Wittgenstein had mentored her.

In Anscombe, Foot found someone to keep her from stagnating under the burden of her teaching. There was little pressure to publish in mid-century Oxford. But the corollary was that there was little time for junior fellows to write—or even to think about anything besides their upcoming tutorials or lectures. In effect, Anscombe did for Foot day after day what Austin did for his (male) junior colleagues in their famous Saturday morning meetings.[10] Anscombe provoked and befuddled Foot, led her into perplexities, made her think and rethink. For a few hours each afternoon, Foot's tutorial burden and everything else vanished. Colleagues came and went from the SCR, making no impression. For Barbara Harvey, this image stayed with her as vividly as the image of Foot dragging herself into Hall at lunchtime: Foot revived, absolutely alert, perched on her stool as she and Anscombe sat "tearing up Wittgenstein" together.[11] They were usually still at it in the late afternoon when the tea tray arrived.

In mid-century Oxford, afternoons were seldom used for formal instruction. The latest start time for lectures was noon. But late-afternoon/early-evening instruction and discussion groups were common (a survival from a time when Oxford dons were unmarried and had no domestic life outside their colleges). Off and on, through the late 1950s, Anscombe held once-a-week graduate classes or informal discussions of Wittgenstein's *Investigations* in Bedford House, a dilapidated, drafty little building enmeshed in nettles, lying at the southwest corner of the College grounds. The building was known as "the shed behind Somerville," and Anscombe's discussions as the "Bible Reading Fellowship."[12] But most philosophy graduate students attended, and many of Anscombe's colleagues, including Austin. And Foot. She had apprenticed herself to Anscombe and was going to miss nothing that her Somerville colleague said.

It was late one evening in November 1956, then—surprisingly late—when Harvey, in her second year on staff, heard a great clanking begin below her bedroom. She lived above the office of the treasurer, and she thought she had better investigate. She found Foot, bleary but determined, running off copies of an appeal for refugees from the crushed Hungarian Uprising of the month before. Between teaching and lunch and discussion with Anscombe, there had been no time earlier in the day. The *ad hoc* relief group which Foot served as treasurer would soon raise the contemporary equivalent of a million pounds and bring dozens of Hungarian students to Oxford, like the Jewish refugees of the 1930s and 1940s. Several of them stayed with the Foots at 16 Park Town.[13]

Did Philippa and Michael even see one another during term-time? In passing, at least. They shared a bed and occasional meals. And they looked forward each year to their summers in a primitive cottage at Connemarra, on the Irish coast. But it was hard to find time for much more.

NOBLESSE OBLIGE?

Foot spent her whole adult life in flight from her upbringing. Her decision to go to university at all was a rebellion. And her parents were taken aback by the company she kept afterward. Murdoch visited the Old Hall at Kirkleatham during the war and shocked Esther Cleveland Bosanquet one evening by laying her head on the table after dinner—and another time by going into the kitchen and making herself a sandwich.[14] Foot reveled in the freedom of her Seaforth days, and in the modest life she and Michael began to make afterward—even if other women couldn't help noticing that her clothes were always better than theirs: "conspicuously not home-made."[15] When she finally left Somerville in 1969 and began spending most of her time in the United States (chiefly California), she exulted in an environment in which none of the distinctions she had internalized as a child existed: in which students put their bare feet on the desks in front of them and colleagues smoked joints at parties.

But we seldom entirely shed the dominant influences of our childhoods. Often, instead, we transmute them, like ex-evangelicals who go on seeing the world in terms of the saved and the damned—only reversing the labels. Foot chose Somerville over Lady Margaret Hall, she said, because it had a reputation as "intellectually but not socially snobby."[16] Foot yearned for distinction—but in things that mattered. She certainly couldn't unlearn the way she talked or the fact that, like an experienced birder, she perceived details that many around her did not. In a late interview about her long-running involvement with Oxfam, she mentioned in passing an early supporter, "Lady Mary Murray." She then paused, noticing what she'd noticed: "If you're called 'Lady Mary' somebody, you've got to be terribly grand, much grander than being called 'Lady Murray.' It's the kind of thing I knew. I hated it, this sort of knowledge: I can't help it, I know this."[17] Unable to unlearn these things, she eventually began using them as comic illustrations in her philosophical writings (e.g., "It is rude to wear flannels at a formal dinner party, but merely not done to wear a dinner jacket for tennis").[18] The effect was always an ironic reminder to her audience that she descended from a different stratum.

Perhaps as significant as any of these vestiges of her upbringing was the drivenness Foot shared with her mentor, MacKinnon. She was never physically robust. More than once during her Somerville career she was forced to take extended sick leave.[19] But like MacKinnon, she worked herself to exhaustion, worked as if to atone for something. She taught more students than her colleagues did. She taught herself Greek. After her undergraduate roommate and best friend, Anne Cobbe, joined the Somerville SCR in 1955, the two of them became a force in College governance. They discussed everything together. And they made themselves into Somerville Principal Janet Vaughan's right and left hands. All along, Foot gave herself to other causes, like the students fleeing the aftermath of the Hungarian Uprising. And Oxfam.

The Oxford Committee for Famine Relief was formed in 1942 by a cluster of activist Quakers and prominent Oxford citizens, including furniture and real-estate magnate Cecil Jackson-Cole. The initial purpose of the Committee was ambitious but narrow: to get food to starving people in occupied and blockaded Greece. After the war ended and continental Europe began to get back on its feet, it was a question whether the Committee should dissolve, like the UNRRA. The Committee decided instead to broaden its mission. Jackson-Cole in particular helped bring an entrepreneurial approach to Oxfam. His own business ventures were always built to support charitable activities as well as turn a profit. He did more than anyone to turn Oxfam into one of the world's largest anti-poverty organizations, funded by an experimental new model: a chain of second-hand clothing stores. Charity shops, like the ones you find on every British High Street today.

Foot began working for Oxfam shortly after she and Michael returned to Oxford.[20] Jackson-Cole had put an ad in the newspaper, soliciting volunteers to help sort and pack donated clothes to send to

Germany. Foot hardly needed more to do, but she was always moved to offer herself. And sorting clothes made an oddly refreshing break from Greek and from teaching. She began working regular shifts in a commercial building off Oxford's Gloucester Green (the market square adjacent to the bus station), sorting ready-to-wear items from "shabby, unmended."

More refreshing than the work itself were the people. Foot had never known Quakers, the original core of Oxfam. They were a revelation. If Foot had had any worry when she volunteered—other than how she would find the time—it was whether charity work would re-immerse her in the social world of her childhood. After all, *Lady Mary Murray* was involved. "[M]ost charities in those days," as she told an interviewer in the 1990s, "were . . . dominated by titled ladies and county people opening fairs. You know, the local landowners, Lady so-and-so, would open the bazaar. . . . I hated that background," Foot said, "and escaped from it."[21] But Oxfam was the antithesis of all that. Letters from Oxfam were (and are) addressed, "Dear Friend," and Foot quickly discovered that the organization was pointedly egalitarian, giving no special authority or honor to people on account of worldly prestige: "the only colonel who sat on the committee was Colonel Widdowson . . . but where was Colonel Widdowson a colonel? In the Salvation Army."[22] The committee met in the front window of their building at 17 Broad Street: a literal interpretation of transparency.

In 1948, Foot herself was noticed. Not because she was President Cleveland's granddaughter or because she was an Oxford alumna. Rather, because of what she did one lunchtime when a van showed up unexpectedly to collect boxes of clothes. Foot had lingered after her shift to do a little more sorting and was the only one in the building. She knew where the packed boxes were stored and figured out how to work the lift to bring them down to the loading area. She was asked if she'd like to join the Committee. She said yes, and was an early supporter of Jackson-Cole's controversial proposal to raise funds by selling donated clothing, rather than trying to give everything away—high-heels and all.

Did Foot leave behind the social world of her childhood? Yes and no. She admired organizations like Oxfam and Somerville that were practical and unfussy, where no one cared about "your people" or whether you said "napkin" or "serviette." It is small wonder that she and Anscombe gravitated to one another; each drew sharp—and partly overlapping—distinctions between what mattered and what didn't. But Foot's organizational leadership and charity work was also a transmutation of *noblesse oblige*. This was what privileged people did. As Harvey observed: Foot didn't leave behind her background; she enlarged it.

There was one thing that mattered to Foot, though—one form of self-giving—that she couldn't simply choose. She and Michael wanted a child. Writing to Principal Janet Vaughan in early 1947, she requested a contract adjustment.[23] She noted how much time she was putting into learning Greek (at Somerville's request) and into her teaching. She wasn't going to ask Michael to take over the household; he had already lost half a decade (and nearly his life) as a soldier. If Foot was going to be able to look after a baby or pay for help, she needed less teaching or more pay. Though she sometimes ignored them, she had limits.

She got the adjustment. She and Michael started trying.

"IT IS IMPORTANT TO HAVE ONE'S RESISTANCES"

With hindsight, it is easy to think of Foot's philosophical trajectory as inevitable. She apprenticed herself to Anscombe. Anscombe taught her Wittgenstein's methods and argued that modern moral philosophers should recover some of Aristotle's ideas—in particular, his concepts of virtue and vice and of a flourishing human life. Foot took her colleague's suggestion and developed it. And Anglophone moral philosophy was never the same.

It is half true.

The fuller truth is messier. The sketch above leaves out MacKinnon and Murdoch and Scrutton, Locke and Kant and Nietzsche—even Ryle and Hare and Austin. And it leaves out how slow and juddering Foot's development was. Foot was the most protean of her friends, undergoing more dramatic shifts of outlook than any of the others. She published her only monograph in 2001, at age 80, and only committed to the central theses of that book in the 1990s. And *Natural Goodness* was not the most influential thing she wrote. It was an earlier metamorphosis that led to her making her most decisive contribution, one she was seemingly born to make. And even the route to that point was tortuous.

How did Foot appear to her professional peers in the late 1940s? In 1948, Vaughan asked Gilbert Ryle for some comparative observations about Anscombe and Foot.[24] After observing that "Miss Anscombe has real philosophical power" (citing the Lewis debate), Ryle wrote,

> Mrs. Foot strikes me as being a much more normal Oxford product—sensible, studious, careful, open-minded but tame. I should be surprised to hear of her making a new sort of philosophical move. If I & some of my colleagues heard that Miss Anscombe & Mrs. Foot had made contributions to a discussion, I think we should at once ask "What line did Miss Anscombe take?"[25]

Ryle allowed that this prejudice might not be entirely fair, that Foot might have unsuspected abilities. But he also said: if he hadn't seen it by now....

Whatever disquiet Foot felt about logical positivism and its implications, and whatever lively conversations she was having with her friends about "rudeness" (when she wasn't too exhausted to stay awake), in the late 1940s Foot didn't see yet how to resist the outlook of emotivists like Ayer and Stevenson. Not knowing what to say about ethics, she immersed herself instead in the figures and topics that had first drawn her into philosophy: Kant and Locke, and the relationship between mind and world.[26] She threw herself into these studies the way she threw herself into everything.

But Kant and Locke were also evasions: "sensible . . . tame" topics, not what really troubled her. At a Christmas party, shortly after her return to Somerville, Austrian émigré Friedrich Waismann struck up a conversation with Foot and asked about her work. She explained that she was trying to understand Kant's Transcendental Deduction. Waismann wished her every success. The following year, at another party, they found themselves in conversation again, and he asked again about her work. Nothing had changed, and she gave him the same answer. "Mrs. Foot," he shouted, "you are a lost woman!"[27] The encounter shook her; she recounted it later to a student. Was she wasting her time? What was she supposed to be doing?

What did she even think? She wasn't sure. Her friendship with Murdoch had turned her into a more eclectic reader than most of her colleagues: all her life, she would be reflecting on Turgenev, Nietzsche, Proust, Gide. (Hare by contrast read no fiction at all, deputizing his wife to read Murdoch's novels, so he would have some idea what was in them.)* But unlike Murdoch, who tried to

---

* A widely attested anecdote about Gilbert Ryle exhibits a similar attitude: he was once asked whether he ever read novels. To which he replied, "Oh, yes. All six, every year"—meaning the novels of Jane Austen.

bring Kierkegaard and Marx, Freud and Sartre into fruitful conversation with her contemporaries, Foot saw no way to do this. She compartmentalized.

To the extent that she thought about ethics at all, her thoughts were conventional. It was perfectly possible to take a philosophical interest in concepts like "rudeness" and yet not shake loose from the billiard-ball picture and the fact–value dichotomy. Foot was living proof.[28] Years later, she remembered a moment when she said to Anscombe that some statement must involve a mixture "of descriptive and evaluative meaning." She experienced a familiar feeling of befuddlement when Anscombe retorted, "Of what? *What?*" And Foot thought, "my God, so one doesn't have to accept that distinction! One can say *what*?!"[29] Anscombe could have had no more ideal protégé, none who better understood what philosophical discussion is *for*.

Foot resisted Anscombe and yet turned to her in exactly the way Anscombe had resisted and turned to Wittgenstein. Foot recalled that, in their afternoon conversations, and in Anscombe's classes, she "opposed nearly everything [Anscombe] said." "Naturally," she said, "I was regularly defeated. But I would be there, objecting away, the next week. It was like in those old children's comics where a steamroller runs over a character who becomes flattened—an outline on the ground—but is there all right in the next episode."[30] This went on for half a decade. Then, without Anscombe ever urging it on her, Foot picked up Wittgenstein's *Investigations* and began reading it. Prepared by the stimulus and frustration of her years-long exchange with Anscombe, Foot had something like a conversion experience. "Why didn't you tell me?" she asked Anscombe. "Because it is very important to have one's resistances," Anscombe replied.[31] The best way to understand Wittgenstein, Anscombe thought, is to argue against him until you see what he is getting at.

The first effects of Anscombe's mentorship on Foot, then, were twofold. First, Foot abandoned the notion that she needed to have a fully worked-out, polished view in order to enter discussion. She adopted as a maxim something she had heard Wittgenstein say, the one time he had spoken publicly at Oxford:

> Wittgenstein interrupted a speaker who had realized that he was about to say something that, although it seemed compelling, was clearly ridiculous, and was trying (as we all do in such circumstances) to say something sensible instead. "No," said Wittgenstein. "Say what you *want* to say. Be *crude* and then we shall get on."[32]

Anscombe freed Foot to think out loud. Second, and relatedly, Foot finally began to do sustained and distinctive work on the topic that she'd known since the mid-1940s she wanted to address: ethics.

Foot's first professional publication, in 1952, appeared on the cusp of her conversion. It is titled "The Philosopher's Defence of Morality." Gathering essays in the mid-1970s for her first published collection, Foot omitted almost nothing. But she did omit "The Philosopher's Defence." It is not hard to see why. The article stands on the other side of a chasm from the work she began to do after she finally read Wittgenstein.

"Defence" is a strange piece. It shows none of the tendencies for which Foot would later be known: loving attention to subtleties and nuances of language, engagement with the richly descriptive pre-modern vocabulary of virtues and vices—even (or especially) an insistence on the objectivity of ethics. In "Defence," Foot argues that philosophers who attack "subjectivism" are mostly troubling themselves over nothing. She insists that what she calls "the logical thesis"—that "ethical terms are not property terms," that there is nothing for ethical judgments to get right—does not imply that we should not take our ethical judgments seriously. "Why not both?" she asks. She sounds much like Hare, whose *The Language of Morals* came out the same year. In his book, Hare argued that "in the end everything rests upon . . . a decision of principle. [A person] has to decide whether to accept [some proposed] way of life or not . . . if he does not accept it, then let him accept some other, and try to live by it."[33] In 1952, Foot seemed to agree. Why not let everything rest on subjective commitment?

Between 1952 and 1954, though, Foot's views began to evolve. In Trinity term 1954, Foot, Murdoch, and Basil Mitchell offered a graduate class, "Analysis in Moral Philosophy." Bernard Williams recalled this as the first place he encountered the ideas about rudeness that Foot and her friends had been discussing since the late 1940s and that would figure centrally in Foot's first influential article, "Moral Arguments," three years later. Later in 1954, at the Joint Session of the Aristotelian Society and the Mind Association, Foot contributed to a symposium titled, "When is a Principle a Moral Principle?" Her contribution fell into two parts. In the first, she criticized Hare's analyses of moral judgment as abstract and artificial: "*some* of our philosophical problems," she wrote, "arise because we keep before our eyes something general instead of something specific."[34] Hare had argued that all moral judgments take the form of a universalized prescription: "always do X" or "never do Y." Foot suggested that people's deepest commitments take all sorts of forms. It is a Wittgensteinian thought. (Wittgenstein considered as an epigraph to his *Investigations* Kent's line from *King Lear*: "I'll teach you differences!") In the second part of her symposium contribution, Foot broached another central theme of her upcoming work: the idea that not just anything could count as a moral principle, even if it were a universalized prescription—that moral principles presuppose "a certain background."[35] She was only a few steps from the positions that would make her reputation and reorient her career.

Foot became a philosopher because of MacKinnon. He introduced her to Kant. And he transmitted to her his sense of the seriousness of philosophical inquiry. That same sense bound Foot and Anscombe together. But Foot's apprenticeship with Anscombe drew something out of her that Ryle and others had not seen coming. Anscombe provoked Foot to make "a new sort of philosophical move."

HEDGEHOGS IN THE LIGHT OF THE MOON

In the 1950s, fellows of Somerville College were entitled to one term off from College responsibilities (with pay) after five years' service. After bringing her Greek up to par, Foot became a tutorial fellow of Somerville in 1950—Somerville's first ever fellow in philosophy. So she was eligible for leave by 1955. No one could take a leave, though, without first laying the groundwork for others to assume her usual responsibilities. Foot broached the subject with Anscombe by 1956, and finally took her sabbatical in 1957.[36]

That sabbatical was a catalyst for Anscombe and Foot, both. We have already seen how Anscombe's preparations to take over ethics tutorials prompted and informed her attack on Oxford moral philosophy. Just as consequential, though, was a quiet, private remark Anscombe made to Foot during her leave. Their whole history together had prepared Foot for the moment. Anscombe never told Foot to read Wittgenstein, but once she read him, she thought: why didn't you tell me sooner? So when Anscombe said to Foot in the autumn of 1957, "I think you ought to read Aquinas," Foot immediately went to work.[37]

Anscombe had studied Aquinas closely since her teenage years and looked to him for instruction on any and every topic. Her doctoral thesis was originally meant to be on Aquinas. She concluded over time, though, that referencing Aquinas made people "silly." Some Catholics were uncritically deferential to Aquinas as a Doctor of the Church. Citing Aquinas made these people stop thinking—an offense against philosophy. Some non-Catholics on the other hand, like Bertrand Russell in his *A History of Western Philosophy*, were ignorantly dismissive of Aquinas, so allergic to theology in general or Catholicism in particular that they were incapable of consciously learning from a medieval Catholic theologian. Anscombe generally chose, then, to absorb and rearticulate Aquinas's insights without mentioning him by name.[38] In the Truman pamphlet, she alludes to the Western tradition of reflection on the ethics of war. She does not mention Aquinas—though he is the most important figure in that tradition, and the originator of the distinction Anscombe invokes between intended and merely foreseen outcomes. And she says nothing about Aquinas in "Modern Moral Philosophy" either, choosing instead to direct her contemporaries to Aristotle—whom all Greats students read. By 1957, though, Anscombe knew Foot well enough to know that she could trust Foot not to be silly. And she knew that Aquinas was a richer source for reimagining ethics than Aristotle himself.[39]

Aquinas's *magnum opus*, the *Summa Theologiae*, is divided into three parts (encompassing five thick volumes in the most popular English translation). At Anscombe's recommendation, Foot turned particularly to the *Secunda Secundae*—the second part of the second part of the *Summa*. In the *Secunda Secundae*, Aquinas creates a taxonomy of virtues and vices much more intricate and expansive than Aristotle's. Aquinas starts from the four "cardinal" virtues acknowledged by the whole Greek tradition back to Plato: practical wisdom, justice, courage, and moderation. Under each of these, though, he identifies a cluster of subordinate virtues, all related to the central, cardinal virtue in question. For example, Aquinas links leniency in punishment to moderation about food, drink, and sex. Both leniency and this more familiar sort of moderation, he thinks, involve a similar capacity to say "no" to potentially destructive impulses.

Those are just the virtues. Under each of the *virtues*—the subordinate as well as the cardinal ones—Aquinas identifies various bad tendencies people can develop (vices) that stop them from developing the good one. There was a pragmatic—indeed, professional— reason for Aquinas to go into so much more detail. The mission of the Dominican order, to which Aquinas belonged, included listening to confessions. One sees in the *Secunda Secundae* a finely textured, carefully elaborated sense of the myriad ways a human life can go right or go wrong—exactly what a friar would need to help penitents think about how to amend their lives. It is exactly the kind of ethics, too, that a newly converted Wittgensteinian would love—full of differences!

What Aquinas taught Foot was how ethics could be a matter of objective truths: the result she had been seeking since 1945. In the *Secunda Secundae*, each virtue is praised because of how it helps rational, social animals like us succeed in a wide range of our characteristic activities. Each vice is condemned because of how it impedes or thwarts us. Human beings need courage because our individual and collective activities sometimes involve danger. Cowardice is a problem because of how it prevents us from standing up for ourselves and our loved ones, and from pursuing our goals. The example that brought this home to Foot, and most delighted her, was "loquaciousness":

> it struck me that there were always good reasons for saying of something that it was a virtue or a vice.... [So] [t]here must be a reason why this is a vice, if indeed it is a vice. I put this question to a pupil of mine: "Why on earth should loquacity be a vice?" And she said, "well if one is always talking, one doesn't have time to think." I was very interested in this, which wasn't Aquinas's reason but seemed to me to be right.[40]

Reading Aquinas, Foot finally knew what she wanted to say: not only to Ayer and Hare, but also to Nietzsche, with his jaded skepticism about all late-modern talk of "good" and "evil." One could summarize Foot's new position thus: Hare can't reply to Nietzsche; Aquinas can. If Nietzsche were to ask Hare, "why should I issue any 'universal prescriptions'? Why do they matter so much?", Hare would have to admit that there is no objective answer. People can offer *subjective* answers, reflecting their personal decisions of principle. But any *objective* answer would conflict with the billiard-ball picture. On that picture, nothing matters objectively.* But just as Foot had been freed to say "what? *what?*" about the dichotomy between facts and values, she had been freed to ask why we have to go on accepting the billiard-ball picture, instead of the older one discernible in the thought of Aristotle and Aquinas. As Foot

---

* Hare wrote an affecting essay about this, titled "Nothing Matters." In it, he relates how a young houseguest from Switzerland fell into despondency after reading Camus's *The Stranger*. "Nothing matters," the young man said. Hare's response is revealing: he told his guest that the only way anything ever matters is by mattering to somebody. So if something mattered to his guest—if he cared about anything—then that thing mattered in the only way it ever could: subjectively. To think that something could matter objectively is a confusion. See R.M. Hare, "Nothing Matters," in *Applications of Moral Philosophy* (London: Palgrave, 1972), https://doi.org/10.1007/978-1-349-00955-8_4.

concluded a BBC broadcast in 1957: "We should be able to turn to the analytic moral philosopher for an account of the basis of the different kinds of virtues and vices, for their necessary connexion with human harm and good. This is just the sort of work that he should be able to do: but usually we are fobbed off with talk about the favorable attitude which anyone who calls anything a virtue must take up—as if this was enough."[41] Foot delivered a talk about this to the Philosophical Society at Oxford. Then she published a pair of papers: "Moral Arguments" and "Moral Beliefs." They turned her, overnight, into Hare's foremost opponent.

The papers don't *feel* revolutionary. They are intelligent, funny, painstaking, but *limited*. Unlike Murdoch's early work, they are not— on the surface—about big, contending pictures of reality. Like most 1950s Oxford philosophy, they are about language. But this is what made them important. Hare claimed to have analyzed "the language of morals." Foot objected to his linguistic analysis. It was the only way to dislodge his view.

Foot asks, first, about the word "rude." "Rude," like "good" or "bad," "right" or "wrong," is plainly an evaluative word. Yet there are factual criteria governing its use. We do not have to—we do not *get* to—decide in anguished freedom what behaviors count as rude. Rather, to say that some behavior is rude means that it offends by showing disrespect. But suppose someone argues that there is an unbridgeable logical chasm between "is" and "is rude" (like the alleged chasm between "is" and "ought") so that *any* sort of behavior might be "thought rude," without explanation. Foot contends that a person making this argument has lost his grip on the concept of rudeness. If the factual criteria of rudeness are set aside, there is nothing left of the concept. If someone were to say " 'a man is rude when he walks slowly up to a front door', and . . . not because he believes that such behavior causes offence . . . [i]t is evident that with the usual criteria of rudeness he leaves behind the concept itself."[42]

In her second article, Foot presses closer to ethics. She turns to the word (and concept) "dangerous":

> There may seem to be a "warning function" connected with the word "dangerous" as there is supposed to be a "commending function" connected with the word "good." [But] suppose that philosophers, puzzled about the property of dangerousness, decided that the word . . . was essentially a practical or action-guiding term, used for *warning* . . . and this meant that anyone using it . . . committed himself to avoiding the things he called dangerous, to preventing other people from going near them, and perhaps to running in the opposite direction.[43]

This would be analogous to what Hare and others said about moral terms. Such terms, they maintained, express no facts—only attitudes or (at most) prescriptions. But this is "nonsense," Foot says: "It is logically impossible to warn about anything not thought of as threatening evil, and for danger we need a particular kind of serious evil such as injury or death."[44] It makes no sense to "warn" of the "danger" of stepping outside if what one means is that it is a mild day with a light breeze. To insist that this makes sense is not linguistic analysis; it is dogma put forward as analysis.

Finally, Foot closes the loop. What about "good" and "bad," "right" and "wrong," as applied to human character and behavior? Are these judgments, too, "logically vulnerable to facts"? Or could any use of these words—so long as it's consistent—make sense? Consider, she asks: could we understand someone who says that someone is a good man "because he clasped and unclasped his hands" or refuses to "run round trees left handed, or look at hedgehogs in the light of the moon"?[45] Setting aside special explanations that would connect these strange behaviors with recognizable human concerns (like the man's being very ill, so that even clasping and unclasping his hands was progress and showed his determination to recover): the answer is, no. We cannot strip away recognizable human concerns altogether—brush aside the skeptical question, "what's the point?"—and still use the word "good" in an intelligible way. Several times in her article, Foot repeats a refrain: "just try." Just try, that is, to assess people's characters and behavior without tethering these assessments to natural human concerns—thus leaving them vulnerable to facts. *Just try* to talk about ethics while leaving behind considerations of what makes human lives go well or badly—the foundations on which Aristotle and Aquinas built their whole theories. It can't be done.

The impact of Foot's articles was immediate. Hare remained the preeminent moral philosopher in Oxford; his book remained the one that philosophy students read in preparation for their exams. A few years later, he was named the White's Professor of Moral Philosophy. But the debate now turned to Foot's criticisms. For the next decade, students (who love seeing their teachers argue) attended the lectures and seminars of each, trying out the objections of the other.[46] In time, Foot wearied of it. She remarked to Rosalind Hursthouse one day, "I've got to go have another of those ding-dong battles with Dick."[47] But she had done what Murdoch and Anscombe could not. She had put their shared critique—the possibility of an alternative to subjectivist ethics—onto the official agenda.

Foot thereby achieved something at once vital and gently ironic. In carrying forward Anscombe's attack on Oxford moral philosophy, Foot became: an Oxford moral philosopher. It was Foot, not Murdoch or Anscombe, whom Hare approached in 1958, with the idea of teaching a course together the following year. And in the light tone and precision of her breakthrough articles, Foot resembled no one so much as J.L. Austin. Austin, recall, was known for his wit, his love of detail and nuance. "That man would find a difference between 'enough' and 'sufficient'," Anscombe once complained.[48] But there was more than a resemblance between Austin's criticisms of Ayer and Foot's criticisms of Hare. Foot, like Austin, was "hounding down the minutiae," attending to the subtleties of language, while Hare insisted on a grand, unified theory: *the* language of morals. As Foot remarked in her BBC talk: "Those who accuse the present-day philosophers of fiddling their time away may be surprised at the suggestion that what we need is therefore more detail, and more attention to the meaning of moral terms. But this may well be the case."[49]

Hare and Foot had, in a way, changed places. Hare had never been any more at home in Austin's Kindergarten than he had in Basil Mitchell's group of religiously serious outsiders, The Metaphysicals. Hare's metaphysical perspective—after the war—was essentially that of his contemporaries; so he wasn't willing to join Murdoch and others in alienated opposition. But he was also deadly earnest, in a way that most of his colleagues were not. He did not *hate* their frivolity, as Anscombe did. But neither did he share it. And his pained sternness set him apart. One term, Austin's Saturday morning group was discussing moral problems. Austin asked the group how they would respond if someone offered them a bribe. Hare spoke up: "I would say I have a principle against taking bribes." Austin remarked, "really? I'd just say, 'no, thank you.'"[50] Whatever Hare thought of Anscombe's character, he had more in common with her and her friends than he did with Austin, at least in his attitude toward philosophy.

But Foot had the light touch Hare lacked. She was serious, but she was also *clever*—a term of high praise in 1950s Oxford.* And no one

---

* Cleverness, in the mid-century Oxford imagination, was a debater's virtue. It encompassed facility with concepts, dialectical skill, and wit. Recall Williams' remark about Anscombe: "she impressed upon [me] that being clever wasn't enough."

could be more graceful, more *au courant* even in rebellion. Warnock recalled the delight with which Foot's papers were received at the Philosophical Society—without much regard to their merits. Their colleagues weren't invested either in the fact–value dichotomy or in its denial. Warnock said, "most of us . . . saw it simply as an elegant and enjoyable bit of Hare-bashing."[51] It did not help that Hare took criticism so badly, seldom budging in response. Hare engaged with Foot only in hopes that his own views might once more prevail—the views on which he had staked himself.

"OR ELSE I HAVE TO RESIGN"

In a late interview, Foot said of Anscombe, "I learnt everything from her."[52] But Foot did something vital for Anscombe, too: she was her friend.

It could have been otherwise.

As Foot remarked to many people, she and Anscombe were worlds apart, religiously. She routinely described herself as "a card-carrying atheist." MacKinnon had not converted her, though he came as close as anyone, it seems. She asked him once, in the 1940s, whether he thought she needed to become a Christian. For whatever reason— perceiving her unwillingness?—he replied, "no; it's not necessary."[53] It grieved Anscombe, though, that she lacked arguments that could bring her friend to faith. She wrote to Foot in the early 1960s, asking why she was an atheist. Foot barely engaged: "my thoughts are entirely conventional," she wrote. "I mean just what most atheists are inclined to think: 'how queer it all is, this theology, and what a strain.' "[54] Several friends noted how closed Foot was on spiritual matters. Foot remarked to Peter Conradi once that, whereas Murdoch had a spiritual life, she had a moral life. When Conradi asked her to say more, though, she showed "a semi-deliberate, semi-obstinate unwillingness to explore what she herself might mean."[55]

Despite this fundamental difference, Foot was Anscombe's friend—and the most important kind of friend Anscombe could have had in Oxford. However exhausted Foot routinely was, and however much she shared Anscombe's sense of standing against the world, no one fitted into Oxford society more easily. Foot belonged—effortlessly—wherever she went. Imagine Anscombe without Foot: with her suspect beliefs, her coarse and cantankerous self-presentation, her seven children helping raise one another under the disapproving stares of the St. John Street neighbors. Or simply consider how Anscombe appeared to the eyes of conventional prejudice: trousered and sandaled, wall-eyed and chain-smoking. Murdoch recorded in her journal a story Anscombe told her about being arrested by the Oxford police one night "for wandering about with her hair down"; she refused to give her name.[56] But Foot venerated Anscombe, and everyone admired Foot.

Foot quietly did something else for Anscombe, too—though she also did it for her own sake. She secured Anscombe's position at Somerville.

As 1957 turned to 1958, Anscombe was coming to the end of her Rockefeller Foundation support and beginning to explore options beyond Somerville. Somerville certainly didn't have the money to pay full salaries to *two* philosophers. There were no promising openings elsewhere in Oxford, though; anyway, no other college would hire Anscombe as a tutorial fellow. She had just published her first book, and would soon start to receive invitations to come teach in the United States. But at the end of 1957, those invitations were still several years away. What was to become of her, meanwhile? The likeliest thing seemed that she would pick up excess pupils here and there, from various colleges, but would have a proper home in none of them.

Foot perceived all of this. In November 1957, she wrote to Janet Vaughan,

> To my mind she is the best all round philosopher in the University . . . . I doubt if there is anyone better in the country . . . . There has never been a woman who could do philosophy as she can. . . . Now Somerville is obviously the place for her; the place where she would be happiest . . . . This seems to lead to only one conclusion; either we manage to split the job, or else I have to resign.[57]

She added "But I don't want to resign; I've never wanted to resign less than at the moment when I <u>think</u> I've got onto a fruitful line in moral philosophy." Foot proposed that she and Anscombe split the available pupils 50/50, and that most of the money go to Anscombe, without telling Anscombe or anyone else about the arrangement. Foot preempted the suggestion that this would pinch her and Michael: "Michael and I are not at all badly off. He earns just about as much as I do at the moment, and . . . we have no reason for having to live in any style." Foot reminded Vaughan of something Vaughan herself had once said: "no one is forced to take their salary."

Vaughan shared Foot's ambitions for the College. She needed little convincing to retain both her master teacher and perhaps the best philosopher in the country, at no added expense. The thing was done.

Foot passed 12 happy months, publishing some of her most important work, beginning to dream of a book, helping oversee Oxfam, talking every afternoon with Anscombe.

In late March 1959, Michael walked out. Philippa did not see it coming. She and Hare were scheduled to begin their class together in a few weeks. The lecture lists had just appeared. She wrote, "Dear Dick, I am so sorry but I am no use for next term. I don't want any commitments, don't even know where I shall be. . . . you will soon enough hear why & understand."[58]

In his memoir, years later, Michael said bluntly what he was thinking when he left: "I [was] passionately interested in having children; she turned out not to be able to have any."[59] Philippa was 38. Michael moved to London to be with his secretary, whom he married the following year. Philippa allowed herself some bitterness, remarking to a colleague that Michael had "run off with a bit of fluff."*,[60] Mostly, she was shattered.

Foot's friends sprang into action. She was invited to extra meals at 27 St. John Street, children clambering into her lap as usual. Her oldest friend and colleague, Anne Cobbe, insisted that Foot come live with her, a few doors down from where they'd roomed together as undergraduates. And Murdoch reached out as soon as she heard the news. She and Foot had fallen out of touch as Foot had attached herself to Anscombe. Murdoch wrote to her friend for the first time since 1948:

> I have just heard the news about M. It may be tactless and untimely to write to you, but I feel I must and at once. I simply wanted to send you all my old love. It's been a long time in store, but I think it's scarcely diminished, and that you knew then, and know now how much it is. My dear dear darling, I kiss you with very much love and all hopes for your absolute welfare. Ever I.[61]

Foot had never understood Murdoch's paralyzing sense of estrangement, but was never more grateful, either, for her self-doubting,

---

* On another occasion, in another mood, she mused bleakly to the same colleague, "so many of us were barren."

effusive friend. They quickly arranged to meet. Murdoch wrote to her afterward:

> I am still rather speechless after yesterday. It is strange and over-whelming so to recover a whole area of one's being which one thought was lost. But I still feel exceedingly shy & tentative where you are concerned. . . . I deeply hope that life is recover-ing in you, & each day is less sad; hard to speak of this too. Oh dear—just loving you very much indeed. I[62]

She then drew a picture of a woman walking a shaggy dog with a furi-ously wagging tail. The dog's tag reads "HAPPINESS."

But much of the experience of grief cannot be shared. Foot had lost her partner. How did it color her sense of loss that she too had wanted children—and that the person with whom she had shared that longing and that disappointment had abandoned her? Indeed, had abandoned her *because* of that disappointment? That July, in her journal, Foot wrote of the experience of returning to 16 Park Town: "In the big room physical desolation & neglect; a sense of the closeness of the old life, as if we had just moved the books from the shelves, & could put them back."[63] Foot taught that fall, but requested unpaid leave for the following spring.

A string had been cut. Foot was no longer tethered to Oxford. And like Anscombe, she had now done enough that invitations started to arrive from the United States. Foot taught at Cornell in 1961 and at MIT in 1964. As deeply as she loved Somerville, she felt more and more impatience with the tutorial and administrative bur-dens there. In 1969, when Anscombe was offered Wittgenstein's chair at Cambridge, Foot resigned, too.

Coincidentally or not, around 1960 Foot began another philosophical metamorphosis. In "Moral Beliefs," she had recommended a return to the conceptual vocabulary of virtue and vice, with its "internal connections" to natural human concerns. But even in that paper, she noted that there are times when the characteristic behaviors of virtuous people work against them, putting them in harm's way. A first responder jumping onto a subway track to rescue a man who has fallen, a prosecutor in a corrupt regime, arraigning a drug lord: these people risk death, risk leaving their families bereft.

In "Moral Beliefs," Foot appealed to the general tendency of virtues like courage and justice to benefit their possessors. She highlighted, too, the difficulty of being *selectively* just or brave:

> It is perfectly true that if a man is just it follows that he will be prepared, in the event of very evil circumstances, even to face death rather than to act unjustly . . . . For him it turns out that his justice brings disaster on him, and yet like anyone else he had good reason to be a just and not an unjust man.[64]

After 1960, Foot became dissatisfied with this response. Mightn't there be whole contexts—like Nazi-occupied Europe—in which virtue didn't pay? And while it might be *difficult* to be selectively virtuous, wouldn't it be more *rational*, if one could somehow pull it off? Or suppose someone rejected the standard of virtue altogether? Was that person *necessarily* making a mistake? Foot called this problem "the tight corner."

By 1972, in "Morality as a System of Hypothetical Imperatives," Foot had concluded that her earlier view—the Aristotle/Aquinas view—was propaganda, and might even provoke cynicism: "It is often felt," she wrote, "that there is an element of deception in the official line about morality."[65] Better, she thought, for those who would defend virtue to think of themselves like the citizens of besieged

Leningrad, who could not know they would prosper by standing together but who were determined to stand together anyway.

There was something ironic about this turn in Foot's thought. It was not a total rejection of her earlier work. She stood by her technical criticisms of Hare's theory. The subject-matter of ethics, she still insisted, was human good and harm. But she had seemingly come around to the very view she and her friends had hoped to counter: that ethical commitments are voluntary acts of self-definition. Unhappy with her conclusion but seeing no way around it, Foot turned for many years away from general questions in moral philosophy. She wrote about abortion and devised the first of the "runaway trolley" thought-experiments that have become a ubiquitous cultural reference.[66] She wrote about euthanasia and Nietzsche. She was as personally and intellectually unsettled as the 1960s culture swirling around her, a culture that was beginning to turn against the perceived elitism and detachment of the Oxbridge world.

Meanwhile, her old university friend Mary (Scrutton) Midgley had returned to philosophy after more than a decade, up in what Oxonians considered the hinterlands of the philosophical world: Newcastle. Midgley had never gone in for Oxford linguistic philosophy—though she admired Foot's interventions in that milieu. She had been raising her boys and reading everything *but* philosophy. But an idea was gathering inside her, one that spoke directly to the difficulties in which her friend now found herself.

Chapter 8

Slipping Out Over the Wall

A DAY IN THE LIFE (II)

3 Lyndhurst Gardens, Jesmond, greater Newcastle upon Tyne, Summer 1959. Mary and Geoff Midgley's youngest was down for his afternoon nap and the older boys were playing contentedly downstairs. The adults were glad to have an hour to themselves. Mary sat down to write. Before curling up with a book, Geoff switched on one of the radio receivers he'd placed throughout the house, tuning in to the transmitter in the kitchen. Happy voices. Mary and Geoff became absorbed in their work. Then: a sound of breaking glass. They looked at one another. Nothing for a moment. Now a seven-and-a-half-year-old voice, with the accent of a child who has listened to hours on hours of BBC English: "Ooh, you've broken it! Do it again!" And a six-year-old voice, answering: "Yes, I think I will!" Another crash. Mary and Geoff got up and went downstairs. Two large panes were missing from the window that looked out onto the back yard. Most of a set of building blocks was strewn on the floor. Their middle son clutched one block—an arch-shaped one—like a hammer. The boys looked up at their parents anxiously, like dogs that have messed on the rug.[1]

Mary and Geoff were both untidy people, and the Midgley home was typically in a state of barely controlled chaos. "Academic squalor," as one visitor described it. Two months before her wedding, Mary Scrutton wrote to Anna Kallin, her producer at the BBC; she said she thought her new name, Midgley, should be an adverb. Was this what it meant to live "midgley"? Geoff's radio projects—an outgrowth of his wartime service with the RAF—colonized the main living space until Mary insisted that they be relegated to a definite corner of the house.[2] By 1959, he had moved on to early computers. One of the boys woke from sleep one night and, wandering down the hall, came upon his father, entwined like Laocoön in programming tape, carefully punching holes as he held the tape up to the light.* Mary wasn't so different. She had tried the patience of her teachers as a child:

> If I reached where I was meant to be at all, I was late, without my books, covered in ink, and devoid of hair-ribbons. . . . Shoe-laces broke as soon as they realised they were on me, and I replaced them with bits of string, which came undone and tripped me up. One way or another, at the sight of me, right-thinking people always, at once, began to prepare a lecture.[3]

She was the same Mary at 39. And now there were three boys on the scene.

If there were a lot of *things* in the Midgley home—soft piles of multicolored computer tape and stray parts from disemboweled radios, stick insects from the local natural history museum and homemade stuffed animals like Wellington the Whale, recorders and oboes and associated paraphernalia—there was also lavish

---

* He was brilliant at this, and became a legend among the Newcastle computer-science faculty when he came in one day to collect the output of a program he had written. Normally, this would be garbage; something would be amiss in the code, and extensive debugging would be required before the program would run properly. Geoff's program was clean. He walked in, collected his printout, and walked out.

attention. Like Lesley and Tom Scrutton, Mary and Geoff welcomed their children to join in adult conversation as soon as they were able: about politics, about literature, about the foundations of logic, about what they'd heard on the BBC Third Programme the evening before. The boys *were* imitating broadcasting English. Mary wrote to Anna Kallin in the spring of 1955 that her older two were "both rather 3rd Prog. these days, & totter around saying 'Astonishing' & 'Fascinating.'"[4]

During the day, unless she was joining Geoff and his colleagues for lunch or raiding the biology section of the library, Mary was home with whichever boys weren't in school. They played word games, card games, and games like "heads, bodies, legs." One of them would draw a head on a piece of paper, then fold the paper to hide his work and pass it to the next person, who had to add a torso, and so on. They sat down together in the front room by the old coal fire (it *was* Newcastle) and read the Moomins books and others that showed up twice a year in great boxes. Mary reviewed children's literature for *The New Statesman and Nation*. Once, when the whole family was feeling terribly cooped up after a shared illness, Mary took the boys out into the back garden with a box of old china; they smashed it, piece by piece. She understood the deep, instinctual satisfaction of *breaking things*.

Especially during the school year, afternoons often included a stretch in which Mary could press ahead with the novel she was writing. She loved being with her sons, but the way she retained a wider sense of self was by cultivating side projects: writing, attending anti-racism and anti-war demonstrations, sewing "gonks" for the toy department at the local Fenwick's. If she had to sacrifice something, it was always sleep. Small wonder that her novel (never published) was a work of speculative fiction about hibernation.

She was no *Cordon Bleu* chef, but Mary was skillful enough at producing standard, middle-class English cuisine: meat, two veg, and a pudding, nightly. She particularly liked improvising, though: making stews or rice dishes out of whatever lay to hand. As she prepped what one of her boys in a spirit of youthful rebellion called "burning house potatoes," Mary would look out into the back yard. Outside, the boys liked to clamber over the old Anderson air-raid shelter—the eldest taking charge—or watch the passenger trains roll to and from the North Sea coast.

Mary wasn't good for much after the boys' bedtime—certainly not for anything that felt like work—but if she had a free hour in the evening, she might turn to one of the books she had checked out of the library. After discovering ethology—the study of animal behavior—in 1952, she had begun working through everything in the King's College collection: the works of field researchers like Tinbergen, those of evolutionary theorists like Dobzhansky, and everything the library had on "ants, red deer, lemmings, baboons or whatever."[5] She was fascinated with the animals themselves; she had loved watching and thinking about other creatures since childhood. But she had also begun asking herself what this body of anecdotes, field studies, and theories might have to say about the *human* animal—particularly in light of the work of her friends Anscombe, Foot, and Murdoch. And though she was not keeping up with philosophy in general, and she was living in what Oxbridge people thought of as an intellectual backwater, her life was feeding into her emerging reflections in unexpected ways. For she had "animal behaviour going on all around" her: "upstairs, in the garden . . . on the hearthrug."[6]

LATENCY

Until the past few years, it was easy to forget—or miss entirely—the link between Mary Midgley and her university friends. In his popular 2014 book about Foot's famous thought-experiment—in which a driver can throw a switch and steer a runaway tram from a track where it will probably kill multiple people onto a track where it will probably kill just one—David Edmonds includes a chapter on "the founding mothers": by which he means Anscombe, Foot, and Murdoch.[7] Murdoch's philosophical writings (unlike Foot's and Anscombe's) have little or no bearing on "trolleyology," but the connections among the three women were too interesting for Edmonds to ignore. But while Edmonds interviewed Midgley, he did not mention her in the text.

There are several reasons why Midgley hasn't registered as part of a group with the others, starting with the unusual shape of her career. Midgley was on the same trajectory as her friends—undergraduate degree, war work, graduate studies, first academic job—until 1950, when she resigned her post at the University of Reading, married, and followed her husband to Newcastle. She never ceased being a philosopher—and never ceased thinking of herself as one. In 1956, she was billed for one of her many BBC talks as "a writer and lecturer in philosophy."[8] But by 1951, Midgley had stepped away from the world of professional philosophy, as Murdoch would do a dozen years later.

Midgley remained an active cultural critic through the mid-1950s, broadcasting regularly on the BBC and writing reviews and thought pieces for major literary and cultural magazines. By that time, she had already begun to work unsystematically but steadily on the project that would occupy her for the rest of her life: understanding the continuities between human beings and the rest of the natural world. But it would be another 15–20 years before she would be ready to publish about it. She can thus seem like a writer of a different generation.

Consider: by 1960, Anscombe had not only said her piece about Oxford moral philosophy but had also published both of her monographs. Foot had established herself as Hare's preeminent critic, and Murdoch was already turning away from philosophy and toward fiction; but the first of Midgley's 16 books was 18 years away. It is easy, then, to miss the generational tie between Midgley and her friends.

Midgley's work has also not had the same impact in professional philosophical circles as that of her friends—though she is better known *outside* the academy than either Anscombe or Foot. Midgley was a deliberately multidisciplinary thinker. Early on—it is hard to say exactly when or how—she became convinced that moral philosophers must *relate* various bodies of knowledge to one another if they are to achieve an adequate understanding of human life, human motivation, and human success or failure. This unconfined tendency aligned Midgley more with Murdoch than with Anscombe and Foot, even during their postgraduate years. In a journal entry from 1948, Murdoch exults, "I talk philosophy with E. & P. & psychology with Mary!"[9]

There was precedent for the sort of integrative work Midgley wanted to do—and she knew it. This is how Aristotle approaches ethics: as a biologist studying an animal of particularly absorbing interest. Aristotle's "works" are widely thought to be student notes on the lectures he delivered at the Lyceum. His *Nicomachean Ethics* lectures pick up directly from his lectures *On the Soul*—the psyche— and continue from there to his lectures on *Politics*. Everything is connected to everything else, and biology and psychology and ethics and politics have to be considered in relation to one another. But this kind of integrative approach had become rare.

Relatedly, Midgley always shaped her writing with reference to an audience broader than any one disciplinary guild. "Because so many disciplines border [my] topic," she wrote in her breakthrough book, *Beast and Man*, "it must necessarily be discussed in plain language."[10] She would later liken philosophy to plumbing.[11] It is the unpretentious business of working out kinks and blockages in people's houses of thought. But again: plainness of purpose and speech does not always command respect. Nor do plumbers.

It was the integrative, multidisciplinary character of Midgley's work that made it important, though. Her friends' work was chiefly critical. Essays like Anscombe's "Modern Moral Philosophy" and Foot's "Moral Beliefs"—even many of Murdoch's philosophical writings—were attacks on a dominant way of conceiving ethics; at most, they gestured toward what might take its place. This is understandable, considering that the views they promoted were minority ones, unlikely to receive a hearing unless dominant, opposing views were not first undermined. It was also the predictable result of working within the genres of the professional society talk or the journal article. These genres are best suited to targeted attacks or incremental refinements, not the elaboration of large, visionary proposals.

Midgley, writing from the margins of the discipline, was the first to present a positive proposal for the kind of moral philosophy recommended but never developed by Anscombe, Foot, and Murdoch: a *naturalistic* moral philosophy, grounded in the character and needs of the human animal.[12] Indeed, she was the only one who could, the only one who knew both enough biology and enough moral philosophy to relate the two fields.

But philosophers have sometimes dismissed Midgley's work as insufficiently professional. Even old friends.

FROM OXFORD TO NEWCASTLE

Mary Scrutton and Geoffrey Midgley were engaged in the summer of 1950. They had met in the late 1940s. After completing his undergraduate degree in PPE, Geoff went on to the B.Phil., while Mary began her doctoral thesis. They attended the same graduate classes and talks, and sometimes found themselves in the same informal gatherings. Geoff recalled when he first noticed Mary. A mutual friend, Ann Martin, brought Geoff round to Mary's tiny flat, and the three of them talked from 11 to 5. Sometime in the middle of the afternoon, Mary slipped away to heat up spaghetti, which impressed Geoff more than it probably should have.

Conversations like these—with Anscombe, Foot, and Murdoch, with Geoff and Ann—were increasingly the point of being at Oxford for Mary. The more formal discussions that took place at the Jowett and Philosophical Societies were beginning to alienate her as much as they alienated Anscombe and Murdoch. One meeting of the Jowett stood out to her as emblematic:

> a disciple of . . . Austin's read a paper on a very small point of linguistic usage. Small though it was . . . that point hardly came up . . . in the subsequent discussion. As soon as the speaker had finished, his critics piled in to attack him—not on this supposedly main issue but on a crowd of even smaller linguistic points arising in the course of his argument, places where they thought his wording was mistaken. The game went on for the whole evening and obviously could have gone on forever.[13]

Mary walked away depressed. Was *this* what philosophy had become? If so, did she want any part of it? She was starting to have doubts, too, about her thesis, though she would keep working on it for another several years. She continued to be fascinated with her subject, Plotinus. But her advisor, Eric Dodds, was distant; she was starting to see the scope of her proposed project as unmanageable, and anyway she didn't need the D.Phil. to get a job. A generation-long expansion in British post-secondary education had begun, and there were "jobs for old rope."[14]

Foot tipped off Mary to the position at Reading in 1949, as she had tipped off Murdoch to the position at St. Anne's the year before. Mary applied, was offered the job, and took it. She might have made a career in Reading, succeeding the old Hegel scholar who hired her. She loved her colleagues in English and Classics, including distinguished literary critic Frank Kermode. They met regularly for lunch. But when she and Geoff both returned to Oxford for the summer of 1950, they fell in love and quickly decided to marry. He too was a year into his first appointment.

They thus faced a dilemma. Mary's chair at Reading had been thinking about bringing on a second lecturer and was willing to hire Geoff straightaway. But Geoff's chair at King's College, Newcastle, anticipated that he, too, would eventually have work for two Midgleys. But that wasn't certain, and it wasn't right away. Which direction should they go: southeast for the sure thing or (much further) north? Three considerations favored Newcastle. First, Mary's chair wasn't just a Hegel scholar. He was hostile to all schools of thought other than Hegelianism, while Geoff's chair had eclectic interests, both in a variety of often obscure older figures and in more recent ones. Then too, Mary and Geoff wanted children, and Mary wanted to be home when they were small, so the prospect of a delayed dual appointment was more appealing than an immediate one. Finally, Newcastle paid better. Indeed, it looked to Mary and Geoff as if salaries increased, the further one worked from the center of the philosophical universe at Oxford. Mary's lectureship at Reading paid £400 a year, while Geoff's at Newcastle paid £550. (Anthony Flew got £800 a year when he was hired at Aberdeen!)[15] It made them wonder what people were actually paid at Oxford.

So Mary resigned her appointment effective December 1950 (after Foot helped her find a replacement), and she and Geoff were married on the 18th in a blinding snowstorm. Some of the crowd who had planned to attend couldn't make it, but Murdoch was there as Mary's maid of honor. The couple stepped out of her father's Kingston church into sparkling, chaotic white. They had to spend their wedding night at Heathrow; their flight to Paris was canceled.

Newcastle sparkled, too, in its own way. Midgley noticed it as soon as they arrived. It sparkled *black*. There were crystals in the coal dust coating every building, and the street walls glistened in the sun. Midgley was under no illusions about the reason. The gleaming buildings were an effect of the grievous air pollution that the residents—especially miners—had endured for generations in this greatest industrial center of the north. The beauty of Newcastle was like the beauty of the sunsets of 1883 after the eruption of Krakatoa. But without forgetting any of this, Midgley was still taken with the loveliness of the place. She quickly became defensive on behalf of her new city's streets, its people, its institutions. When she left Oxford, she had to put up with several people—even friends—condoling her "on the dreadful prospect of [her] prospective exile from decent society." Midgley was offended by this "fairly awful piece of intellectual snobbery,"[16] and became over time an intensely patriotic, naturalized Geordie.

Late in the 1950s, she tried to think through the attitude she had encountered in some of her Oxford friends. "The magnetic idea," she wrote, "is that the real thing can only happen at a particular centre." She acknowledged that there are "many techniques which cannot be learned properly without the discipline of endless informed criticism." But, she added, "it will hardly do to maintain that most of human life is actually fictitious. Observation suggests that people in provincial towns are in general not . . . phantasmata or zombies . . . ."[17] This punchiness might seem odd in someone who later made a career out of resisting extreme positions, but as a colleague reminisced: "there is a bit of Mary that likes fighting."[18] If she saw a position as blinkered or extreme, she would attack it. She was good at this—a little better even than Anscombe, a little more *controlled*.

The Midgleys had a child on the way within months; their first son was born scarcely a year after the wedding. Midgley knew that when the baby came, she would be busy. During that year, then, she worked to ensure that she would not lose the niche she had carved out for herself as a public intellectual. She took the time freed up from teaching and put it into writing and broadcasting (still as Mary Scrutton). And she began branching out from reviews to original commentaries. She had to moderate her pace, in the end. She wrote to BBC producer P.H. Newby two days before her son was born, requesting a small extension: "I know it's the present fashion to type theses with one hand while having babies with the other, but I should feel happier with more margin."[19] (Was she thinking of Anscombe?) Still, she went on writing. She wrote about philosophy, but also (as her producers and editors got a sense of her range) about anything and everything. For the BBC alone, between 1949 and 1953, she reviewed books by Erich Fromm, Arthur Koestler, Margaret Mead, and Angus Wilson, plus biographies of Florence Nightingale and Robert Browning. Her original talks were equally wide-ranging. Soon she was also reviewing novels for Janet Adam Smith at *The New Statesman and Nation*. A new box arrived every three weeks.

Why was Midgley such a beloved freelancer? She had a rare virtue—one that would eventually allow her early reading and writing to feed back into her mature philosophical work. Midgley was not as intimidatingly brilliant as Anscombe, but she had a tremendous capacity to take in, retain, and synthesize. A colleague, Jane Heal, recalled how she could mention almost any significant "great" book to Midgley—a novel, a work in the history of science, a classic philosophical text—and Midgley would have read it. But that was not all. Anything Midgley had read was *there* for her, instantly available to be compared and connected with any of the rest.[20] At home, she would recite long stretches of poetry to the boys: by Arnold, Housman, Kipling, and classical authors.[21] This capacity to take in and hold onto things, and to hold them *together*, was not the most valorized trait in mid-century British philosophy. But it was essential for the work she was going to do.

"RINGS AND BOOKS"

Newcastle and domestic life *were* isolating. Though both were shaping her in far-reaching ways, and though she was impatient with their cultured despisers, there was no denying it: Midgley had less time for scholarship during the 1950s and early 1960s, and less conversation outside the home. She worked against it. Throughout these years, Midgley regularly joined her husband and his colleagues for lunch. The Midgleys made their home a hub of social interaction for the department. And she occasionally visited friends in Oxford. But she read less and less philosophy. Declining an invitation from BBC producer Roger Toulmin in 1961, she wrote, "I cannot talk about recent trends in philosophy, because I have taken very little notice of it in the last 10 years."[22] Her most philosophical writings of the 1950s came early in the decade and were not published in philosophy journals. They are interesting, though; they highlight two themes on which Midgley was reflecting as she went into a chrysalid state. The first theme is about philosophy itself; the second concerns human nature. When she returned to the discipline in the mid-1960s, she would return to these themes, informed by a wealth of extra-philosophical reading.

Both themes surface in an early piece on sexual difference. Midgley was the only one of her friends to publish about sex and gender, though these publications are obscure. (Her co-authored 1982 book *Women's Choices* is, she noted in 2005, "the only one of my books that is not in print.")[23] Her first reflections on these matters appeared in 1952, in a talk for the BBC Home Service: "A Letter to Posterity." Her assignment was to anticipate how the situation of women might change in the century ahead.

"My dear Posterity . . . ," Midgley began, and told Posterity straightaway that institutional discrimination, of the sort at stake in pre-1920 debates on women's rights, was finished. "I'm not saying that there is no injustice," she said. "But . . . it is not the profound difference in status that feels like a difference in species." In light of this, Midgley asked, what ought to be expected of women now that they had been "admitted to a thousand mysteries from classical scholarship to engineering"? For, she said, women as a group "still have their own peculiarities. They still defeat Plato and those other feminists who . . . think of them simply as men who have accidentally come out the wrong shape."[24] The androgynous ideal is a fantasy, Midgley thought. But what are women's peculiarities? More particularly, what are their characteristic strengths?

Midgley's (controversial) answer to her own question was that women as a group are more gifted at integrative thought—at bringing disparate types of information together—than at specialization. "Women by nature and habit are not specialists," she said. "They are more conscious of the complexity of their subject and less powerful at abstracting."* She wasn't merely generalizing from her own case, she insisted. She argued, for instance, that Virginia Woolf's great gift was for "holding together all the richness and complexity of experience":

> [Woolf] could catch and record the innumerable gleamings of
> its surface without distorting it; without forcing it to fit ready-
> made patterns and purposes. She attended to the shape of the

---

* Anscombe's daughter Mary Geach recalls her mother contrasting herself with her husband in similar terms: "she said that he had the more powerful intellect, but that she had the greater ability to see about and around a problem." "Introduction" in Geach and Gormally, eds., *From Plato to Wittgenstein* (Imprint Academic, 2011), xx.

whole, however subtle and baffling. She would never sacrifice that dazzling immediate vision for a diagram in black and white.

But Midgley acknowledged a personal—even confessional—element in her thesis. She testified how much she admired "thorough and methodical scholarship" of the kind Austin or Foot (or her husband) pursued. But it was not her destiny: "I treat it with that profound and remorseful veneration that all sinners feel for the virtue after which they perpetually struggle in vain."[25]

Whether right or wrong about group-level differences between women and men, Midgley was pursuing a point with wider application: specialist scholarship is neither the only intellectual virtue nor the supreme one. "Human thinking," she argued, "has two movements. There is the abstracting, critical process, which has always been recognised as thinking: and there is another process of imaginative comprehension, of comparing and balancing . . . ." This was not merely an observation, either. In the context of 1950s Oxbridge philosophy, it was a manifesto—a manifesto for the kind of philosophy Murdoch was already doing, and that Midgley herself would begin to produce in the 1970s. Hers would be a philosophy precisely of "imaginative comprehension," drawing on multiple bodies of thought, "comparing and balancing."[26]

This brings us to Midgley's second early theme: the diversity and several-sidedness of human nature. Apart from a few early reviews, all Midgley's philosophical writing from the early 1950s was about her philosophical heroes, thinkers of past centuries who had resisted over-simple pictures of our nature.[27]

Midgley's most interesting essay on this theme never saw daylight. It was a script she submitted to the BBC, which Anna Kallin rejected—the only proposal of Midgley's she ever turned down. Midgley's thesis was that not only one's sex but also the shape of one's household—whether one has a spouse and children—has consequences for one's thought. Midgley started pondering this soon after delivering her "Letter to Posterity." Three months after that talk aired, she wrote to Kallin, "I have an idea . . . nearly formed; i.e. I keep elaborating it when I do the potatoes . . . . It is roughly speaking about . . . how dons inevitably see their subjects as dons, and how much this matters."[28] As she said, the idea was almost whole already; she didn't think it would take long to write up.

When Midgley finally mailed the script two years later, it was much more pointed. It began, "Practically all the great European philosophers have been bachelors." After supporting this claim with parallel lists of famous ancient and early modern figures ("I do not cram the groaning scale with monks and friars"), Midgley went on to speculate on the differences this might have made in their theories of human nature. She focused particularly on the differences between Plato (unmarried) and Aristotle (married).[29] Aristotle, she noted, showed a tendency toward "married opinions," such as that humans are a species "that goes in pairs, not only for procreation, but for all the business of life." Moreover, Aristotle was alert to the many varieties of human lives: men and women, scholars, politicians, and tradespeople. True, he ranked men's pursuits above women's, and scholars' pursuits above the rest. "But, Midgley wrote, Aristotle "grasped the point that natures can *differ* . . . that there were other lives and other virtues besides those of the scholar; that perhaps it did really take all sorts to make a world." Plato, by contrast, "always kept the irritable sensibility of the adolescent in resisting the claims of temperaments alien to his own." Marriage, Midgley argued—a "willing acceptance of the genuinely and lastingly strange"—has the potential to shake people out of this sensibility, to awaken us to human diversity and complexity.

Kallin, a worldly Russian émigré, was taken aback by this intrusion of domestic matters into the serious business of culture: "I . . . think you lay yourself open to the accusation of narrow-mindedness. What about at least half of the philosophers you mention living in an illicit *menage* at least as heavy as legalized wedlock?"[30] Kallin's reasons for resisting Midgley's thesis may have been as personal as Midgley's reasons for proposing it. Kallin was unmarried, though she had been for several years the mistress of Austrian expressionist Oskar Kokoschka. But she also missed Midgley's point, which wasn't about sexual exclusivity but about the consequences for thought of certain *experiences*—specifically, the experience of sharing life with another person.

Both of Midgley's early themes sound once more in her most straightforwardly philosophical essay of the 1950s, an essay on one of MacKinnon's favorite figures: eighteenth-century Anglican bishop Joseph Butler. One of Butler's most famous arguments is an attack on monolithic and cynical interpretations of human behavior, like those of Thomas Hobbes. Hobbes famously interprets all human motivation as egocentric. (It is an interpretation with a long afterlife, down to the present.) Consider some apparently other-regarding concern: say you're hoping a friend gets her visa extended and can continue to live and work in a place she cherishes. The cynical interpretation is that this hope is somehow about yourself. After all, won't you be *pleased* if the visa comes through? Aha! says the Hobbesian: so you're only hoping for your own pleasure after all. But Butler argues that the Hobbesian interpretation is confused. Just because your concerns all *belong to you* doesn't mean that they're all *about you*. And the pleasure you'll get if things work out as you hope? It makes no sense except on the assumption that you care about something besides yourself. You can't rejoice over your friend's visa unless you care about *her*. Otherwise: some papers being stamped and mailed, someone receiving them—these are indifferent happenings.

It was this attention to the multiplicity of human concerns that Midgley admired in Butler. Butler, Midgley wrote, reveres "the infinitely rich and complex personality of man . . . that wealth of powers and impulses, which admits indeed of harmony and direction, but not of the mutilation prescribed by narrower moral systems . . . ."[31] Butler is delighted, not annoyed, to find that our impulses can't be reduced to a single type, that they "can never be understood by treating them all as acquisitive."

There is one more element in these remarks that is worth drawing out, because of its significance for Midgley's mature philosophy: her suggestion that the fundamental tasks both of moral theory and of human life are *integrative*. The task of moral theory is to understand our nature in its full complexity. It is to survey honestly the several sides of our nature, turning from none of them in disgust, but instead working out how far they permit "harmony and direction." The task of *living* is to enact this harmony.

"IT MAKES ONE SCREAM"

Midgley was falling farther and farther out of step with the philosophical mainstream of her time and place. The premier philosophical community in England—possibly in the whole world—was in Oxford, where her friends remained. And the dominant voice in Oxford was Austin's. Austin was the personification of specialist cleverness—"the cleverest thing on two legs," Foot later remarked—not of the comprehending intelligence Midgley possessed.[32]

The opposition was not total. Austin's thought bore resemblances to the later thought of Wittgenstein (however much Anscombe hated to admit it), and thus to the thought of Midgley and her friends. Wittgenstein had shown, as Midgley later put it, "how our thought about language has to be rooted in the complexities of real life, not imposed on it from outside."[33] This Wittgensteinian lesson was the most important thing Midgley learned from Anscombe, who rejected all "handy simplifications."

Midgley was impressed with Austin, but she was more like Murdoch than she was like the participants in Austin's Kindergarten—or even like Anscombe or (especially) Foot. What she was best at—"imaginative comprehension" of disparate bodies of knowledge—was not regarded as real philosophy by her contemporaries. Even if she had been keeping up with the journals, what she wanted to do had little standing among her peers.

Midgley more or less stopped publishing after her third son was born. She reviewed children's books and experimented with fiction, but dropped out of the public conversation. She didn't return until 1972. She was tired. And she was disillusioned with her own discipline. One of her last original essays before her quiet period was a piece in *The Twentieth Century,* comparing her experiences in Oxford, Reading, and Newcastle. She reflected on the large atmospheric differences between Oxford and these two "redbrick" universities, as they were informally known. But her comments had special application to the state of British philosophy in the 1950s. What struck her upon moving to Reading, Midgley wrote, "was that it was possible to talk freely. Dons openly admitted that they were interested in subjects other than their own." Moreover, "[t]he state of being unable to say or write anything for fear one might get it slightly wrong was not common, and where it existed, it was not held in honour. I cannot express how much I liked this."[34]

Midgley contrasted this with the Oxford atmosphere, in which each scholar

> forms part of a . . . system of mincing machines through which
> any new work [is] put . . . . [A]s Oxford is so sociable, there is no
> chance for a prospective author of forgetting for a moment how
> the mincing machines work. Before he can develop an idea, he
> has begun to think of answers to the criticisms that will be made
> of it. He would be a man of iron [who] did not spend more time

working out what will tell in argument than deciding what he really thinks.[35]

Among the bad effects of the Oxford atmosphere, Midgley wrote, is that it "narrows the subjects studied in an incredible manner." But her next remark was perhaps her most vulnerable. "It is so difficult," she wrote, "to insist that a thing is interesting when one's colleagues are bored with it; so embarrassing to be caught paying attention to what is supposed to be left for the amateurs."* Turning directly to philosophy, she noted how her contemporaries tended to neglect or misrepresent Aristotle—in particular, his richly integrated treatment of ethics and biology. Aristotle didn't limit himself to psychology, ethics, and politics. He wrote on octopi and chickens and mollusks. How would her contemporaries explain why Aristotle "took the trouble to write about four times as much on other subjects as on what they call philosophy?" It "makes one scream," she wrote.[36] Exasperated, and pregnant with her third son, Midgley absented herself from the professional conversation.

But she was still reading.

Soon after the birth of her first child—around the same time that she was writing about Butler's appreciation for the complexity of our nature—Midgley's parents recommended to her Konrad Lorenz's book, *King Solomon's Ring*. Lorenz was the co-founder, with Nikolaas

---

* Midgley would later connect her experience to one of Murdoch's great lines in "On 'God' and 'Good'": "It is always a significant question to ask about any philosopher: what is he afraid of?" Her peers, she concluded, were afraid of looking "*weak*—vague, credulous, sentimental, superstitious or simply too wide in their sympathies. . . . [T]hey were much more afraid of looking weak than they were of missing something unexpected and important." Midgley, *The Owl of Minerva*, 155–156.

Tinbergen, of the new field of animal behavior studies, and *King Solomon's Ring* was his attempt to make more widely available the ideas he and Tinbergen were developing.

Lorenz and Tinbergen's breakthrough insight was analogous to the one that led Darwin to his theory of natural selection. Darwin broke with naturalists before him by expanding his scope of vision and considering the sometimes-competitive, sometimes-supportive interactions among organisms. Earlier naturalists had devoted themselves to cataloguing species and arranging them in taxonomies. This taxonomic project required close attention to morphology, but little to behavior. Darwin, by contrast, was a field researcher—not just bringing home specimens but also observing how organisms live and die.

Lorenz and Tinbergen, for their part, insisted on studying animal behavior outside the artificial setting of the laboratory. Moreover, they *interpreted* this behavior, deploying not only their own innovative accounts of instinct, but also a controversial heuristic. They postulated that if Darwin was right—if humans and other animals are related—then our desires and emotions should not be incomprehensibly different from those of other animals. Our hypotheses about what other animals are thinking and feeling will often be correct. We have to be critical, of course, and consider alternative hypotheses. But we can also try to infer what other creatures are thinking and feeling.

This, as I say, was controversial. Critics accused the new ethologists—especially Lorenz, who kept lots of exotic pets—of "anthropomorphizing" their subjects. The aspiration of many mid-century scientists, including psychologists, was to eliminate the subjective perspectives of both researcher and subject. Thus, Jane Goodall was chided early in her career for assigning names to her chimpanzees instead of numbers. We can appreciate the ideal, which goes back to the modern scientific revolution: the more we eliminate peculiarities of individual perspective, the "cleaner" our results. But the attempt to study human and animal minds as if they were billiard balls—known as "behaviorism"—proved completely unfruitful in practice. We've learned far more about the lives of humans and other animals by following the lead of Lorenz and Goodall and David Attenborough than by studying them under the cleanest possible conditions and treating them like very complicated machines.

As soon as Midgley read Lorenz's book (which begins with a description of his own life of academic squalor, keeping company with rats, geese, and chimpanzees), she felt compelled to read more. Not only was Lorenz talking about a topic she loved, but she saw that his concepts "could be used, without distortion, to describe . . . the behaviour of humans . . . in terms that could be extraordinarily fertile for further thought."[37] Best of all, Lorenz—like Butler—reckoned fully with the complexity of his subject. Humans and other creatures, he acknowledged, have disparate types of motive that have to be integrated somehow, not imagined away. Even in his book *On Aggression* (in German, *Das sogenannte Böse*, "the so-called evil"), Lorenz was interested in *understanding* our impulses and their uses, seeking "harmony and direction," not "mutilation." Midgley knew she could bring Lorenz and Butler—Lorenz and moral philosophy generally—into dialogue.

Midgley began working through every study of animal life in the King's College library: the whole of section 591. She had never been so interested in anything. She didn't know yet where it might lead. She did know that anything she wrote about it wouldn't be considered philosophy by anyone else. She decided she didn't care. It was better to be damned with Aristotle than saved with Austin.

BEYOND THE FRINGE

Ironically, Midgley despaired of doing respectable, Oxford-style philosophy at the very moment when Oxford-style philosophy was coming under attack, and beginning to come undone.

As Anscombe's "Oxford Moral Philosophy" talk was about to air in early 1957, a young philosopher-sociologist, Ernest Gellner, wrote to T.S. Gregory, proposing a pair of talks attacking Oxford-style linguistic philosophy. Gellner, a Czech Jew whose family had fled to England in 1939, had been an embittered, troublesome student at Balliol after the war. Reading PPE and concentrating in philosophy, he was nonetheless scornful of what he was being taught and of those who were teaching him. He was passed from tutor to tutor as he belligerently refused to conform his work to the conventions of postwar Oxford philosophy. Finally, he was sent to MacKinnon. MacKinnon read Gellner's first essay and declared it fascinating, but not a contribution to the topic. He gave Gellner a different prompt and sent him away. This scene repeated itself for two weeks, until (as MacKinnon later recalled with delight) "he cracked, and produced a first class piece of work."[38]

Provoked by a great tutor, Gellner learned to *attend* to postwar Oxford philosophy (he got a first), but he never came to respect it. As a young lecturer at the London School of Economics—teaching philosophy, but housed in a department of sociology—Gellner set to work on a dismissive, outsider's critique of the whole enterprise of linguistic analysis as practiced at Oxford. A *sociological* critique. His BBC talks declared his thesis: that Oxford philosophers had made "a Koran" out of the *Oxford English Dictionary*, setting aside all great, enduring questions in favor of small questions of usage. Philosophy, he said, had been turned into "the higher lexicography."[39]

Gellner was aware of Anscombe's talk. He alluded to it in his second broadcast: "the usual objection made to this philosophy . . . is that it corrupts youth. My own objection is the opposite. Here is a philosophy . . . which could not corrupt a flea."[40] Gellner's complaint was that, in an effort to make philosophy rigorous in "a science-worshipping age," philosophers had banished all large ideas and large questions from discussion. Unlike Anscombe, Gellner had no alternative program to recommend, and lacking the sympathy or patience to interact closely with his targets, Gellner descended to mere insults: "the Higher Philistinism . . . the tranquiliser of the intellectuals . . . the constipated view."[41]

The book-length version of Gellner's attack, when it arrived in 1959, was more of the same. *Words and Things* might have made a small splash and quickly vanished. But then Gilbert Ryle refused to have it reviewed in *Mind,* and Bertrand Russell attacked Ryle's decision in *The Times.* The resulting fracas was louder than the one following Anscombe's talk. And since *Mind* would not review the book, numerous other publications rushed to do so. The book became a sensation, even as reviewers called it "tiresome," "bellicose," and "exasperating" (the last was Murdoch's assessment in *The Partisan Review*).[42] Editorials appeared, both about Ryle's treatment of the book and about the state of contemporary Oxbridge philosophy, and *Words and Things* became the biggest philosophical best-seller since *Language, Truth and Logic.* The controversy was dramatic enough to convince William Shawn of *The New Yorker* to commission a feature about it—which grew into a book of its own: *The Fly and the Fly-Bottle: Encounters with British Intellectuals* (1962).

The journalist Shawn commissioned, Indian novelist Ved Mehta, found his subject perplexing, and found Gellner of little help. Mehta concurred with the majority of reviewers about Gellner's book. *Words and Things* was "passionate, polemical, and disjointed, and grouped disparate thinkers indiscriminately—this much was apparent even to a novice like me."[43] Gellner mashed together Ayer, Austin, and Wittgenstein as if there were no differences between them. But Gellner, like Anscombe, had tapped into a growing sense among the public that there was something unsatisfactory—perhaps worse than unsatisfactory—about what went on at Oxford under the name of "philosophy." A significant number of Britons had some exposure to the Oxford style, as a result of how many Oxford degrees required philosophy, and as a result of how the BBC routinely featured philosophy talks and discussions on the Third Programme. The Third never drew many listeners; it struck many Britons as pretentious. But *The Listener* had a large subscriber base and gave the public some sense of what was under discussion, both on the air and at the great medieval universities.

It is possible for a bad book to raise a legitimate complaint—or at least a resonant one. Gellner had little insight into his sources; indeed, he prided himself on *not* engaging with the details of what Austin or Wittgenstein had to say. But he put his finger on the dismissiveness that was a signature of Austin's style. Gellner picked up especially on a cliché in mid-century philosophical discussions: not understanding. "Cleverness," he wrote, "is displayed not by understanding much, but by claiming *not* to understand."[44] Midgley observed the same phenomenon and linked it to Ayer's condemnation of large domains of ordinary discourse as meaningless: "a whole generation of undergraduates was excited to find that all they needed to do if they wanted to refute some . . . doctrine was to say . . . 'I simply don't understand that' or 'But what could that possibly mean?' "[45]

The public was now alive to these complaints. Indeed, for a few years in the early 1960s, Oxford philosophy became a punchline. In 1960, Oxford Revue alums Alan Bennett and Dudley Moore teamed up with Jonathan Miller and Peter Cook of the Cambridge Footlights and mounted a wildly successful revue, titled *Beyond the Fringe*. It became one of the most influential theatrical productions of the postwar era, breaking a path for other satirical, sometimes absurdist comedy like *Monty Python's Flying Circus*. One of the sketches in *Beyond the Fringe* was a send-up of Oxford linguistic philosophy.

The cast were clearly familiar with a lot of mid-century philosophical jargon, tossing off allusions to Ayer's "sense data," Ryle's "category mistakes," and Wittgenstein's "language games." They or their friends had been in lectures or tutorials with Austin, Hare, and others. Drawing on familiar caricatures of eccentric don behavior, Miller slouched and loped around the stage while Bennett twisted his arms over and behind his head in a picture of self-forgetfulness. But the cutting genius of the sketch is in its dialogue. The laugh lines reveal what a mixed audience in a West End theater in 1961 knew or thought it knew about Oxford philosophy. That it could work at all as West End comedy tells a great deal about the absorption of linguistic philosophy into the wider cultural consciousness.

Early in the sketch, Bennett raises the question of the role of philosophers in society: "I mean, other people have *jobs* to do, don't they?" Miller earnestly suggests that he will give an "example from real life" of the kind of statement that people fall into making if not chastened by philosophical analysis: "There's too much Tuesday in my beetroot salad." Bennett warmly calls this "a classic." (A bit later, he adds in a suspicious tone that Miller seems "very fond of *real life*.") Bennett dismisses Plato and Aristotle as mere "paraphilosophers" (like paratroops, because they have "their feet off the ground"). Why? Because they ask "entirely irrelevant" questions: "about life, about death."

The sketch concludes with an anecdote from Bennett, *proving* the relevance of philosophy for life. He was in a shop that morning, he says:

> BENNETT: And there was a shop assistant there who was having
> an argument with a customer. The shop assistant said "yes."
> And the customer said, "what do you mean, 'yes'?" And the
> shop assistant said, "I mean, 'yes.'"
>
> MILLER: Ah, this is very exciting indeed.

Bennett calls this "a splendid example" of "two very ordinary people . . . asking each other what are in *essence* philosophical questions . . . where *I* as a philosopher could help them." Miller asks,
"Did you?" To which Bennett replies sadly, "No. They were in rather
a hurry."[46]

In any case, it was now the 1960s, and with a host of egalitarian social
movements gathering, philosophers could no longer get away with
the old line that they had nothing to say about colonialism or racial or
sex discrimination or nuclear weapons—that it was their task simply
to clarify concepts. In 1955, Hare and Nowell-Smith had a discussion on the Third Programme, titled, "The Moral Philosopher's Job."
It would have sounded far away and strange a decade later:

> HARE: I want to ask you what you think we, as <u>moral</u>
> philosophers, are supposed to be doing. Here we are,
> supported partly out of public funds . . . and writing
> books which the general public as well as our professional
> colleagues buy; I should very much like to know . . . what
> you think the public is after for its money . . . .

> NOWELL-SMITH: This is a question that has often puzzled
> me; the answer must depend on the extent to which each
> individual purchaser is already familiar with philosophy. The
> most naïve may expect detailed practical guidance through
> life's problems; they certainly won't get it . . . . Philosophers
> nowadays are much less ambitious.[47]

The public *did* want help thinking about war and sexual liberation
and the distribution of scarce medical resources. By the end of
the 1960s, the first applied ethics center, the Hastings Center, was

created, followed quickly by the Kennedy Institute—both in the United States, far from Oxford and Cambridge. Freed partly by Foot's critique, partly by public derision toward linguistic philosophy, philosophers began to go beyond mere analysis and clarification, and to contribute to public conversations about euthanasia, abortion, and more.

The world was changing. And for the second time in her life, just as in 1939, Mary Midgley was in the right place at the right time.

"AN IMPOSSIBLE BUNDLE OF QUESTIONS"

In 1965, with her second son heading off to boarding school, Midgley finally accepted a long-standing offer to join the philosophy faculty at the University of Newcastle.* They had been in the North for 15 years. Midgley had never stopped loving the questions she first encountered at 16, when she pulled a dusty volume of Plato's dialogues off a library shelf at Downe House. She was as invested as ever in the conversations she'd had with her friends when she was a young woman in Oxford. And though she did not love the kind of philosophy that had taken over Oxford, she still loved talking about ideas with peers and students.

Newcastle was a place where cross-disciplinary conversation flourished. Though Geoff was a philosopher of language, he collaborated with the University's computer scientists and played in the orchestra. The Midgleys formed a friendship with psychologist David Russell, who shared Mary's love for ethology and suggested more books for her to read. And Mary had profited since 1961 from conversation with her next-door neighbors, Alan and Eva Ibbotson.

* As it now was. King's College became independent of the University of Durham in 1962.

Both were trained biologists, and their children were roughly the same ages as the Midgley boys. They went to one another's houses to watch the first seasons of *Doctor Who*. Eva would become a famous children's author at almost the same moment that Mary would begin to publish in philosophy. Alan was now Mary's colleague, and he had a wealth of insight on everything that interested her most.

Midgley's first years back in the classroom were exhausting, though she was officially part-time. Everything was new again, and she was also spending part of each day at home with her youngest. But within a few years, as the work at home eased and Midgley reacclimated, David Russell urged her to offer a course on animal behavior through the university's adult-education program. Russell shared Midgley's sense that a comparative approach, relating humans to other animals, would be of tremendous value for understanding human nature.

It was the pivot of her career. A few years later, she wrote that she would "vigorously recommend" teaching adults "to anyone who wants to get an impossible bundle of questions under control."[48] Adult-education courses in England in the mid-twentieth century were populated by adults seeking personal enrichment, not by professionals seeking advancement. Teaching these students of varying ages and backgrounds, all of whom were enrolled simply because they were interested in the topic, Midgley began to work out a biologically grounded framework for talking about human nature and human motivation, the thing she had been seeking since 1951. Back then, writing to Kallin, she had already anticipated her great theme: "the many-sidedness of human nature, and the inadequacy of *all* current official ways of regarding it."[49] Now, approaching 50, she published her first scholarly articles, culminating in "The Concept of Beastliness" in 1973.

"The Concept of Beastliness" begins with an attack on folk ideas about other animals, which infect our thinking about our own nature. The savagery of wolves, for example:

> I have read a chatty journalistic book on wolves, whose author described in detail how wolves trapped in medieval France used to be flayed alive, with various appalling refinements. "Perhaps this was rather cruel," he remarked, "but then the wolf is itself a cruel beast." The words sound so natural; it is quite difficult to ask oneself; do wolves in fact flay people alive?[50]

It isn't just wolves. Plenty of other examples could serve: think of the folk pictures of apes, snakes, sheep, lemmings, rats. Each is not only a folk picture of another kind of creature; it is a metaphor for a trait that humans are anxious to avoid. It's bad enough that these folk pictures lead us into unreasonable contempt or hostility toward other creatures. But they also lead us into unreasonable ideas about ourselves: either denying our animality or embracing fanciful pictures of it. Humans have long sought to understand themselves through comparisons with other animals but, Midgley wrote, we have "mapped [ourselves] by reference to a landmark which is largely mythical." We have aspired not to be "like wolves"—when not even wolves are like that. And when we find traits or behaviors in ourselves that correspond to our folk ideas about wolves, we have concluded that what we need to do is conquer our own animality. In the second half of the article, drawing on Lorenz and others, Midgley began to explore ways in which up-to-date pictures of our animal kin could give us more accurate instruction about our motivations and behaviors.

"The Concept of Beastliness" caught the attention of Max Black at Cornell University. By a delightful coincidence, Black had overseen Anscombe's first major publication in 1949, shortly after he arrived at

Cornell. Black was a linguistic philosopher, but unlike many of his contemporaries, he was interested in everything language was *about*. He invited Midgley to visit Cornell in early 1976 and lead a week of discussions with colleagues from across the University. The experience was overwhelming: preparing daily presentations for a group that included experts in every discipline touching her subject. But their responses were deeply confirming. And almost as soon as the visit was over, Cornell University Press offered Midgley a contract for a book.

By this time, Midgley had found a rhythm in her writing. The boys were all grown, and in the mild summer of 1976, thoughts she had been collecting for a quarter century came flowing out. She had experimented with a thesis and then with a novel. Now for the first time, she had a project she was determined to complete. She delivered the manuscript for *Beast and Man* that autumn. She had just turned 57. When it finally appeared, she would be almost 60.

BEASTLINESS

Midgley's working title for her book was *Beastliness*. In British English, this is a joke: "don't be beastly" means "don't be horrid"— don't be disagreeable. The title alluded to the thought that inspired her 1973 article: we frequently and disastrously misunderstand what beastliness—beast-likeness—is. Editors at Cornell doubted that American readers would get the joke and insisted on *Beast and Man*. Midgley suspected that the gender-exclusive "man" would eventually become more awkward than the Briticism, but she deferred to the Press's judgment. The original title would have been more apt, though. The impossible bundle of questions with which Midgley started—destined to become larger—centered not on a contrast between beast and human, but on our own beastliness.

Beast and Man was always going to be a substantial book, but it became larger in the writing. After Midgley submitted her first draft, the Press asked her to add a section addressing E.O. Wilson's controversial best-seller, *Sociobiology*. This set Midgley back a year. Cornell then sent the *resulting* draft for comment to experts in each of the major disciplines Midgley addressed. They should have known, Midgley reflected ruefully, that "no academic who is offered a chance to do this is going to miss the opportunity to think up some criticism or other."[51] The book grew and grew. It grew until it became hard to perceive its original shape. But the shape is still there, discernible under the accretions.

Like the article that preceded it, the book begins with an appeal to think more carefully about the likenesses and unlikenesses between humans and other animals, and to critically examine how we express these comparisons. The Western tradition has often been fearful or disgusted at our animality. But given that "[w]e are not just rather like animals; we *are* animals," this leaves us with a misleading and unhelpful sense of ourselves.[52] To think about our lives is to think about our nature, and our nature is an animal nature. Midgley then introduces some basic ethological concepts, in particular the distinction between "open" and "closed" instincts. Closed instincts, like a honeybee's dance, are behavioral patterns that are "fixed genetically in every detail." But for a wide range of animals, including humans, there is little in their behavioral repertoire that is "closed." Instead, we see "strong *general* tendencies" that express themselves in learned behaviors. Cats have an impulse to hunt, but their mothers show them how it is done, and adults go on refining their technique; they are "born with certain powers and a strong wish to use them, but . . . need time, practice, and (often) some example [to] develop them properly."[53] Open instincts.

With the aid of these and other key terms and concepts, Midgley turns to criticizing too-narrow conceptions of human nature and of ethics. As creatures with a wide repertoire of open instincts—of general motivational tendencies—we can develop this repertoire in various ways. But the repertoire itself is a given, and it is this repertoire from which we must begin when reflecting on how to live—that is, when doing ethics. As each of her friends—especially Murdoch and Foot—had argued back in the late 1950s, it is absurd to talk of "choosing" or "inventing" values, as if *just anything* could be important to us: never looking at hedgehogs in the light of the moon, say. Humans are capable of caring about very surprising things; the oddest things can become status symbols or conduits of religious longing. But these acquire significance for us *as* status symbols, or *as* sacred. They tether to some basic human concern.

It was a hallmark of *Beast and Man* and of Midgley's writing across her career to complicate extreme positions and easy oppositions. Not nature *or* nurture, instinct *or* learning, but invariably, both. Like her friends, she critiqued the existentialist picture of human beings as *deciding*, rather than *discovering* what matters. On the opposite side, she critiqued the behaviorist picture of animals and human beings as machines. In *Beast and Man*, working toward a biologically informed ethics, she criticizes particularly the timeworn opposition between reason and passion (including under that heading both emotion and desire). A central point—maybe the central point—of the book is to show how reason and passion form a system in which each plays a role. What a good ethologist does is think structurally and integratively about whatever species she is studying, asking how this or that aspect of an animal's nature fits into that animal's whole "form of life." She doesn't idealize anything. But she does insist that the animal has to deal with all of it somehow or other, that everything must find a place within the whole. What then are the roles of reason and passion in human life? How can we successfully integrate them?

As Midgley saw it, the heart of the book is its fourth part, and particularly its eleventh chapter, "On Being Animal as well as Rational."

There Midgley offers an account of the place of reason in human life. Again she argues, our evolutionary history has bequeathed to us a wide assortment of motives. It has also bequeathed to us conceptual and imaginative and social capacities that aggravate the conflicts between our motives. Unlike wolves, we anticipate these conflicts, fretting over them before we even face them. We even enter empathetically into the internal conflicts of others. We write novels and screenplays, dramatizing or inventing conflicts, and consume these stories for entertainment and instruction.

Any animal with conflicting motives requires some means of prioritizing and harmonizing them. For many animals, this is achieved by the operation of closed instincts. In her 1984 book, *Wickedness*, Midgley offers the example of migratory geese who hatch one nest of young after another all summer, until something—the temperature perhaps, or the angle of the light—triggers their migratory instinct, and they leave their last brood to perish. The difficulty in even *contemplating* this behavior is that we could not do it. Or, we could not do it the way the geese do. Some of the greatest novels of the past century—*Sophie's Choice, Beloved*—are about people who are driven to turn on their children in this way and cannot live with themselves afterward.

For humans, though, the same faculty that exacerbates internal conflicts by allowing us to anticipate or even manufacture them, also enables us to deal with them—to conceive, try out, and criticize various approaches to living as whole and integrated people. In several of her books, Midgley quotes the following passage from Darwin's *The Descent of Man*: "it is very probable that any animal whatever, endowed with well-marked social instincts, would inevitably acquire a moral sense or conscience, as soon as its intellectual powers had become as well-developed, or nearly as well-developed, as in man."[54] Our capacity to be destroyed by conflict—identical with our capacity to creatively *resolve* it—is what makes us moral beings. What then should we say about reason? " 'Reason' is not the name of a character in a drama," Midgley writes. "It is a name for organizing oneself."[55] Midgley's ethics is an ethics of self-integration, of thinking through how to do justice to our whole selves.

It is also an ethics that anticipates and addresses the difficulty Foot encountered in mid-career, though Foot never perceived this. Foot, recall, felt trapped by the thought that a virtuous person might end up worse off because of her virtue. In general, courage makes a human life go better. Think of all the important things you can do, for yourself and others, if you pay more attention to what is important than to danger. But sometimes courage leads a person to risk her life and there is no reward, or not on this side of death. The courageous person suffers and dies. In that case, Foot thought—in "the tight corner"—perhaps it would be more rational not to act courageously. She intensely admired an anonymous German farm boy whose last letter to his parents is preserved in a book of such letters by Nazi resisters:

> Dear parents: I must give you bad news—I have been condemned to death, I and Gustav G. We did not sign up for the SS, and so they condemned us to death. . . . Both of us would rather die than stain our consciences with such deeds of horror. I know what the SS has to do.[56]

Foot venerated this farm boy from the Sudetenland, whom no one could even name. He was a hero. But for years, she did not see how she could call him "rational."

She eventually came to see herself as having been once more captured by a picture—this time, a picture of rationality. Foot had not been able to see her way past the idea that to be rational is to serve one's own desires—whatever they might be. But is it? Starting in the 1990s, drawing on Anscombe and on the work of a later colleague, Warren Quinn, Foot asked: what "would be *so important* about practical rationality if it were rational to seek to fulfill any, even a despicable desire?"[57] Supposing you want something grotesque, or just trivial, and want it even at the cost of things that matter? Is that rational? Perhaps we need a richer conception of what it is to be rational—at least if it's supposed to be a good thing.

Midgley's integrative conception of rationality in *Beast and Man* generates the same insight. "What is it," Midgley writes, "that we so respect about rationality? What is so good about it? Why, for instance, does Kant sound convincing when he suggests that it is the only thing that can command respect? *We would not be likely to take this view of mere cleverness.* [emphasis mine]"[58] Midgley here brings back something like the distinction she developed in her earliest publications, between two movements of thought—the *abstractive* and the *comprehending*. The latter, she says, is what commands respect: not mere facility with concepts, but a person's capacity to hold disparate things together in her mind—the very capacity that guards her against disintegration.

Moreover, practical reasoning as Midgley represents it—a necessary response to our welter of available motives—"would be impossible if some preferences weren't 'more rational' than others."[59] In "The Concept of Beastliness," she expressed this in terms that even more plainly anticipate Foot's late views: "Rationality . . . is not an easy concept. It is not the same thing as Intelligence, since you could show great intelligence in the pursuit of something quite irrational. 'Rational' includes reference to aims as well as means; it is not far from 'sane.'"[60]

However important it is to have one's resistances, Foot needn't have waited 20 years to learn this. She could have learned it from one of her oldest friends.

OVER THE WALL

Why didn't Foot perceive what her friend had achieved: the solution to the problem of the tight corner? She maybe never read the book. A needless barrier had risen between Foot and Midgley. They never ceased being friends. Midgley would always visit Foot when she was in Oxford. But they were divided over philosophy in a way that they hadn't been in 1949. Foot bought into the conception of philosophy that Midgley rejected; in the early 1970s, she tried to revive Austin's Saturday mornings.[61] And she had Austinian ideas about what counted as philosophy and what didn't. Foot once told an interviewer, "[Midgley's] mind doesn't quite work like most straight Oxford analytic philosophers . . . I think she found her forte being witty and sane on television."[62] Midgley, for her part, returned the compliment in the Introduction to *Beast and Man*, where she described herself as having "slipp[ed] out over the wall of the tiny arid garden cultivated . . . under the name of British Moral Philosophy."[63]

Foot may have been one of the people who—however unintentionally—made Midgley feel like she didn't measure up. Foot reflexively classed and ranked philosophers, including her friends. Anscombe was first, she was next, followed by Murdoch and Midgley.[64] (Is anyone so alert to subtle differences in status as someone who feels herself to be in the middle?) *Beast and Man* appeared almost at the same time as Foot's first collection of papers. Foot dedicated her volume, *Virtues and Vices*, to Murdoch.* But Murdoch does not appear in the index. And when Foot settled in Los Angeles in the mid-1970s, she began to gather around her a group of colleagues and students whom she regarded, and sometimes spoke of, as "the right sort."[65] That language especially—and language she sometimes used,

---

* Midgley dedicated *Beast and Man* to her sons, "for making it so clear . . . that the human infant is not blank paper."

contrasting philosophers who could "take the fences" with those who "fell at the first ditch"—was one more vestige or displacement of her upper-class upbringing.

In 1956, in "Newcastle: Comments on a Case History," Midgley wrote, "Oxford philosophers perpetually . . . argue that philosophy which falls outside their own backyard is—not perhaps valueless, but *unprofessional*."[66] A sad episode may lie behind this remark. In the thrill of discovery, Midgley tried unsuccessfully to interest Foot in Lorenz and Tinbergen. Foot blew her off, more than once. "What has that got to do with philosophy?" Foot asked.[67] By rights, Foot should have been interested. In another mood, in another time, she might have been. But as we saw, Foot throughout the mid-1950s was barely treading water. It may have been mere self-protectiveness, then. Foot was always a slow reader. But her failure to connect with Midgley at that moment—to see what her friend was so excited about—made it less likely that they would talk later about Foot's philosophical worries. They remained friendly. In 2001, Midgley gave *Natural Goodness* a glowing review in *The Times Higher Education Supplement*. But after 1949, they never collaborated as they could have. Midgley learned from Foot, but not vice-versa.

Only Murdoch seems to have delved seriously into Midgley's book. The endorsement she wrote for Cornell shows a clear perception of its character and significance:

> This is a very important book. Mrs. Midgley, a professional philosopher with a considerable knowledge of biology, defends a philosophical conception of human nature enriched by biological study. . . . Her two-way exercise in relating facts to values is among other things a formidable contribution to contemporary debate in moral philosophy. . . . Mrs. Midgley has provided an urgently needed bridge between science and philosophy.[68]

But Murdoch was by then, like Midgley, an outsider. Murdoch wrote to Foot, recommending *Beast and Man* to her ("it's good, quite a large operation"); we do not have Foot's reply, but the topic does not resurface in their correspondence.[69] Of Midgley's university friends, only Murdoch saw, or half-saw, the significance of what Midgley had achieved: a culmination of conversations that had started between the four of them 30 years before.

Chapter 9

"Time, Like the Sea . . ."

What came of it all? The world never halts, waiting for philosophers' theories. These theories are self-interpretations of an endlessly self-interpreting species. As Murdoch wrote: "Man is a creature who makes pictures of himself, and then comes to resemble the picture."[1] But while some of our self-interpretations obscure, others enlighten. The four friends shone a new, old light on the human landscape. They let us see ourselves differently, and better.

Murdoch called the fact–value dichotomy into question. Anscombe and Foot undercut Hare's theory and urged a recovery of the concepts of vice and virtue, and what Aristotle called *eudaimonia*: a flourishing life. Midgley connected this idea of human flourishing to an updated account of the animals we are.

These ideas were then available, and philosophers began putting them to work—starting with Anscombe's and Foot's ideas, which were better framed for the guild. Especially significant was Alasdair MacIntyre's 1981 book, *After Virtue*. Drawing on Anscombe's "Modern Moral Philosophy," MacIntyre told a declinist history of modern Western ethics, arguing that the only options left to late-moderns are "Nietzsche or Aristotle."[2] *After Virtue* did more than any other book to press forward an Aristotelian revival within academic philosophy. Outside the academy, it generated debates about "the Enlightenment project," "the Benedict option," and the importance of virtue and vice in education and public life. A host of academic studies of "virtue ethics" followed, as well as popular books like William Bennett's *The Book of Virtues* and Linda Kavelin Popov's *The Family Virtues Guide*. The old orthodoxy was broken.

But what happened to the four friends?

MARY BEATRICE

It was ethics—ethics and animal behavior—that brought Midgley back into philosophy in the 1970s. Her books *Wickedness, Can't We Make Moral Judgments?*, and *The Ethical Primate* are all extensions of the project that began with "The Concept of Beastliness." But Midgley soon became better known for something else. Her reputation, throughout the 1980s and 1990s, was as a controversialist, "the foremost scourge of scientific pretension" in England.[3] She set herself consistently against all sorts of reductionism, arguing for the use of a plurality of metaphors and methods in understanding the world and (especially) ourselves. Ironically, the part of *Beast and Man* that launched Midgley's career as a public intellectual was the part she only wrote at the request of her publisher, critically assessing E.O. Wilson's *Sociobiology*.[4]

Wilson impressed Midgley, actually. His project was to show how evolutionary biology could help us understand social behavior—non-human and human. Drawing on his primary expertise about ants, Wilson argued convincingly that their self-sacrifices have a good evolutionary explanation: though self-sacrifice leads to the deaths of individual ants, the instinct to behave this way ultimately favors the survival and reproduction of ants with that instinct. Wilson then panned back, generalizing his conclusions to all social behavior in all animals.

The book was wildly controversial, denounced by Wilson's Harvard colleagues Richard Lewontin and Stephen Jay Gould for its genetic determinism. Midgley's take was more measured:

> People's difficulty about seeing themselves as members of the one creation has come from a crude, narrow, highly abstract notion of what the other members were like. Wilson . . . [conveys] that vastness and coherence. He shows how the tendencies that make social behavior possible have evolved separately in many very different kinds of animals, how they vary greatly . . . yet how their variations converge to certain patterns which, for intelligible reasons, must tend to favor species survival . . . .[5]

But Midgley noted, too, that Wilson's "thesis was couched in language . . . much cruder and more provocative than that of the ethologists." And Wilson was reductionist, insistent on one and only one mode of explanation. He dismissed the messy fieldwork of researchers like Lorenz and Goodall in favor of clean, quantitative studies of population genetics.

One of Midgley's purposes in *Beast and Man* was to persuade people that we cannot understand ourselves without understanding our animal nature. An evolutionary perspective is part of that. Certainly, no trait can spread *in* a population if it is incompatible with the spread *of* that population. But in *Sociobiology*, Wilson went further—describing evolved behavior as "selfish," involving "manipulation," even "spite." Midgley worried that such talk would distract people "from the serious enquiries into human and animal motivation that the ethologists had started."[6]

Wilson's talk of selfishness gave off an aura of tough realism, but it involved a conceptual confusion. Again: no trait can spread in a population if its tendency is to wither that population. But that doesn't mean that reproductive fitness is the only thing on an organism's mind—or that it's on that organism's mind at all. Notwithstanding occasional disclaimers to the contrary, Wilson regularly conflated the claim that a trait helps (or at least doesn't hurt) a population's stability with the claim that members of that population are *motivated* by this. Think of the ending of *Charlie and the Chocolate Factory*, when Willy Wonka selects Charlie to inherit his estate on account of Charlie's childlike innocence and wonder. Does this imply that Charlie had a factory-getting strategy? In a *sense* he did. Innocence and wonder *were*, in that odd context, factory-getting traits. A point worth noticing! But not one that illuminates how the world looked to Charlie or why. There is more to say.

While Midgley was working on *Beast and Man*, another book appeared that made an even bigger splash than Wilson's: Richard Dawkins' *The Selfish Gene* (1976). Midgley heard about *The Selfish Gene*, of course—anyone with her interests would have. In the middle of her 50-page discussion of Wilson, Midgley remarked in passing that she'd seen Dawkins promoting his book on television. She contrasted Dawkins with Wilson unfavorably. Where Wilson expressed "awe at the glory that outlives us," Dawkins gave off "the simple glee of the intellectual who has found a way to put down his public."[7] But Midgley was too preoccupied revising *Beast and Man* to delve into *The Selfish Gene* straightaway. In comparison with the "paving stone" Wilson had produced, she judged Dawkins' work sensationalist fluff. She didn't bother with it until 1978, when Australian philosopher J.L. Mackie published an article urging moral philosophers to adopt Dawkins as a guide.[8] That got Midgley's attention. *Her* purpose was to get philosophers to think again about the link between biology and ethics. It mattered to her greatly then, if philosophers turned to biologists who wrapped their biology in bad philosophy.[9] Midgley opened Dawkins' book and found the same ideas she had criticized in Wilson, expressed in even more inflammatory ways and without the compensation of Wilson's rich and detailed discussions of ants.

Midgley lashed out with the most intemperate thing she ever published. Was she worn down? She retired the following year to concentrate on writing and on the many speaking invitations she was beginning to receive. Did she despair at seeing a wildly popular book double down on Wilson's reductionism? Whatever the reason, Midgley let herself go. She had always been good at polemics; exasperated by Mackie's praise of a book she didn't admire, she opened with this: "Genes cannot be selfish or unselfish, any more than atoms can be jealous, elephants abstract or biscuits teleological." She was just getting started. "There is nothing empirical about Dawkins," she wrote.[10] "Dawkins's crude, cheap, blurred genetics," she added, "is the kingpin of his crude, cheap, blurred psychology."[11]

Dawkins was no less combative. He shot back:

> Some colleagues have advised me that such transparent spite is best ignored, but others warn that the venomous tone of [Midgley's] article may conceal the errors in its content. Indeed, we are in danger of assuming that nobody would dare to be so rude without taking the elementary precaution of being right in what she said. . . . She seems not to understand biology or the way biologists use language. No doubt *my* ignorance would be just as obvious if I rushed headlong into *her* field of expertise, but I would then adopt a more diffident tone. As it is we are both in my corner, and it is hard for me not to regard the gloves as off.[12]

Dawkins protested that he had said nothing about motivation. As employed by biologists, he wrote, "selfish" is a technical term, naming only the self-preserving or self-perpetuating tendencies of organisms or suborganisms (like genetic markers)—the ways in which their traits increase or at least stabilize their prevalence. If something about a species' behavior has a tendency to secure the survival of that species, that behavior is "selfish" in this sense. (If democratic institutions tend to secure their own acceptance, *they* are selfish in this sense.) Dawkins had included several disclaimers in *The Selfish Gene*, noting that "selfish" was being used in the technical sense; he was aggravated at what he saw as a perverse misreading of his work.[13]

The reality was complex. Dawkins was right; there is a technical, biologist's sense of "selfish," and it was the foundation of his book. Midgley had, moreover, ascribed to Dawkins views that he disavowed. In a reply to Dawkins, she apologized for writing "so crossly."[14] But her critique was not just a hasty, irritable misreading. Midgley commented in her initial article on the places where Dawkins said his talk of "selfishness" was metaphorical. She didn't miss them. The trouble was, Dawkins was inconsistent. In his quest for popularity—both accessibility and good sales—he cast off caution at crucial moments. He cast it off, indeed, at the most memorable and widely quoted moments in his book, writing of "ruthless selfishness" and "the tyranny of the selfish replicators." If you do not want people to misunderstand your technical usage, Midgley said, you should not mix it up with words (ruthless, tyranny) that scream the "unwanted" everyday associations. In fact, Midgley said, Dawkins was working a motte-and-bailey strategy: preaching psychological egoism until someone called him on it, then protesting that he'd only meant something dry and technical. Here, for instance, is Dawkins' summary statement about human nature: "if you wish, as I do, to build a society in which individuals co-operate generously and unselfishly towards a common good, you can expect little help from biological nature. . . . we are born selfish."[15]

Midgley, like her friend Murdoch, attended habitually to the ways background pictures structure and limit our thoughts. And in Wilson's and (especially) Dawkins' wilder remarks, Midgley saw unconscious captivity to Social Darwinism: the old, nineteenth-century idea that selfishness—ordinary, non-technical selfishness—is only natural. She called this "biological Thatcherism" and noted how badly it fits with "the widespread tendency of social creatures to help, favor, and delight in young that are *not* their own."[16]

People differed in their assessments of the controversy, unsurprisingly. Dawkins enthusiasts were scornful of Midgley. Konrad Lorenz, whose writings first drew Midgley to ethology, wrote to her in appreciation of what she'd said. The controversy certainly made her more visible as a public philosopher. She was soon asked to speak at a conference on "Evolution and Religion"; after reflection, she decided to speak about evolution *as* a religion. That became the title of the first of more than half-a-dozen books in the second stream of Midgley's authorship: writings about the late-modern tendency to look to scientific theories for sole or ultimate explanations, instead of crucial-but-partial ones. An invitation came a few years later to deliver the prestigious Gifford Lectures in Edinburgh. Midgley titled her lectures and the resulting book *Science as Salvation*.

The Dawkins debate was not the only fight Midgley picked in the years following publication of *Beast and Man*. Midgley was an activist, like her parents. The Scrutton view was that politics is part of life; Midgley was always puzzled by people who ignored it. Following her retirement, with more time on her hands and a growing reputation, Midgley invested herself in a cluster of causes loosely connected with her scholarship: animal welfare, environmental preservation, and above all, de-escalation of the international arms race. She was arrested in the early 1980s at a protest outside an American military base near Oxford (costing her a visit with Murdoch, whom she had planned to see that day). But her activism also took more constructive forms. Her school friend, Lady Anne Piper, had become involved with a newly founded organization, the Oxford Research Group (ORG). Midgley quickly joined, too. From that time on, the ORG would be the most important institution in Midgley's life. The ORG studied how government and military officials make decisions about nuclear weapons, with the aim of exerting a restraining influence on these decisions. In 1984, Midgley agreed to contribute to a regular column in *The Guardian*, "Body and Soul." The theme was wide open: non-technical reflections on topics of public interest. Of Midgley's dozens of columns over the next four years, some were about scientific reductionism, some about education, but the greatest number were about nuclear proliferation. It was the topic of her first column ("Who's afraid?") on October 31, 1984. Later titles included "Down to the last nuke?" and "No animal has horns which grow to six thousand times their length in forty years."

The ORG became the most important institution in Midgley's life in part because it was soon the only one left. In the mid-1980s, Margaret Thatcher's government pushed for the closure of a host of academic departments in universities around the United Kingdom, leaving just a few "centres of excellence" in each discipline. By the end of the decade, Newcastle—not being Oxford or Cambridge— had lost its philosophy program. Geoff Midgley, a quiet man, was despondent at the destruction of the little center of excellence he and his colleagues had built over the years. Mary recalled him sitting on the floor in their home, watching television westerns and playing solitaire. Mary turned to resistance, writing to her contacts at Oxford and elsewhere, asking them to speak up for Newcastle and other small departments.

A.J. Ayer wrote a forceful letter to the *Times*. But no one else of comparable significance was willing to commit themselves publicly. A couple of distinguished philosophers at Oxford wrote to tell Midgley that she was wrong; a friend of Anscombe's and Foot's suggested that worthwhile philosophy was so technically demanding that it could only be entrusted to a few top scholars. This was bitter, confirming everything Midgley suspected about the parochialism of the University that had formed her.

Midgley survived, though. She survived like few people do. She survived her husband by over 20 years. She outlived Murdoch, Anscombe, and Foot. In 2005, when Routledge published *The Essential Mary Midgley*, Foot attended a reception in Midgley's honor. They were the only two left. Midgley was 86, and had three books in her yet. Five years later, Midgley discovered a new venue for public philosophy, appearing several times at the "How the Light Gets In" festival at Hay-on-Wye. She turned up in her Wellington boots, giving informal talks under vinyl canopies on topics like immortalism. Midgley was not immortal and didn't want to be. Death, she said in her talk on immortalism, is the price we pay for membership in a species that evolves. But she only gave up the Hay festival at 95.

Midgley's last book, *What is Philosophy For?*, appeared just in time for her 99th birthday, and a month before her death on October 10, 2018.

JEAN IRIS

When she left St. Anne's College in June 1963, Murdoch didn't abandon teaching—only Oxford University.[17] That fall, she started a part-time gig teaching General Studies at the Royal College of Art (RCA) in London. Murdoch rented a flat near Earls Court in Kensington and spent every Wednesday with her new students. She had never been overly beholden to the Greats and PPE syllabi, but the RCA gave her complete autonomy. A postgraduate art college—the only one in the world, at the time—and not state-funded, the RCA was free from the regulations governing other art schools and universities. They could teach whatever and however they liked. A couple of years after joining the RCA faculty, Murdoch offered a series of lectures on "Moral and Political Pictures of Man." She had long been convinced that one of the central tasks of philosophers is to critically examine our background "pictures" of reality. In her lectures, she devoted herself to this task. She gave audiences the impression of someone thinking out loud in front of them.

More than the freedom at the RCA, though, Murdoch loved the people: the bohemian painters and sculptors and filmmakers and designers who were now her colleagues and students. And she loved the setting. Her husband John Bayley didn't care for cities; Murdoch loved them. So for the next half-decade, Murdoch spent two nights a week on her own in the heart of London—a weekly private holiday. She visited her mother in nearby Barons Court, she threw parties for students, she studied Russian, she exulted in being immersed in the museums and streets and people of *her* city for the first time since the war.

Her students didn't always respect her. Or more precisely, they didn't always respect General Studies: "the Department of Words," some of them called it. To complete their degree, they were required to produce a 12,000-word thesis, but most just wanted to refine their craft. The thesis requirement was there to ensure a reasonable degree of literacy among RCA graduates. Some had never read a book, though—or didn't care about the degree. They regarded their time at the RCA as an advanced apprenticeship and moved on. Murdoch, not easily offended, found them all delightful, even the scornful ones. She called them "wild," "utterly different from Oxford students."[18] She took notes on her students' speech, their clothing, their backgrounds—endless raw material for her fiction.

Some of her students, however, became deeply attached to her. Too deeply, some of them. Murdoch was never careful about emotional boundaries, and it was easy for needy students to seek more from her than it was wise to give. David Morgan, for instance—brilliant, but wounded and immature—entered into an emotionally and physically intense relationship with Murdoch soon after meeting her.[19] Murdoch was only saved from another scandal when Morgan bragged to a fellow student that he was Murdoch's favorite. When this got back to Murdoch, she was outraged and withdrew from Morgan for a time. True to character, though, she didn't drop him completely: "[h]aving taken you on as a friend," she wrote, "I can't go back on that."[20] She later helped Morgan find his feet as a young teacher at the Chelsea College of Art. Around that time, another student, sculptor Rachel Fenner (then Brown) became infatuated with Murdoch. Murdoch was wise enough now not to let the relationship turn into an affair, and she became one of Fenner's principal mentors over the following decade. She was remembered for her kindness even by students who didn't become close with her. She paid for an aspiring fashion designer from Detroit to go to Paris for the first time. She bought four early works by Bridget Riley, who became one of the leading figures of the Op Art movement. She always welcomed conversation.

The mid-to-late 1960s was an extraordinary period of creativity for Murdoch. Breaking with her St. Anne's colleague Margaret Hubbard and with Oxford was like breaking a chemical or even a nuclear bond: energy tied up was suddenly released. Murdoch produced six novels in seven years and published her three best-known philosophical essays. In one of these, "On 'God' and 'Good'," Murdoch wrote,

> Human beings are naturally "attached" and when an attachment seems painful or bad, it is most readily displaced by another attachment, which an attempt at attention can encourage. There is nothing odd or mystical about this, nor about the fact that our ability to act well "when the time comes" depends partly, perhaps largely, upon the quality of our habitual objects of attention.[21]

In the years before writing those words, she had *lived* this displacement, slowly acquiring projects and relationships that re-grounded her and gave new discipline and focus to her affections.

Murdoch's 1960s essays resonate with general readers in a way that contemporary philosophy rarely does. Their power lies partly in Murdoch's skill as a writer, which she brought to her nonfiction as well as her novels. But it also lies partly in how these essays emerged out of the suffering and striving of their author. Like ancient wisdom literature, they are full of vivid descriptions of how our lives go wrong, and how they can be set right:

> I am looking out of my window in an anxious and resentful state of mind, oblivious of my surroundings, brooding perhaps on some damage done to my prestige. Then suddenly I observe a hovering kestrel. In a moment everything is altered. The brooding self with its hurt vanity has disappeared. There is nothing now but kestrel. And when I return to thinking of the other matter it seems less important. And . . . this is something which we may also do deliberately: give attention to nature in order to clear our minds of selfish care.[22]

A central theme in these essays is the role of perception (or "vision") in moral self-transcendence. Often what hinders us from treating others well, Murdoch says, is a haze of self-concern that stops us from *apprehending* them: their thoughts, their longings, their histories, their characters. "Love," Murdoch writes, "is the perception of individuals." This thought is central not only to her moral philosophy but also to her fiction, which is full of characters living in fantasy worlds of their own making. "Love," she adds, "is the extremely difficult realisation that something other than oneself is real."[23]

Perhaps the most famous passage in any of Murdoch's post-Oxford essays is a novelist's thought-experiment on this theme. Murdoch imagines a mother ("M") who finds her daughter-in-law ("D") unrefined, loud, "tiresomely juvenile." But M is also self-critical: "I am old-fashioned and conventional. I may be prejudiced and narrow-minded. I may be snobbish. I am certainly jealous. Let me look again." Murdoch traces a possible vector of growth from this moment: "M observes D or at least reflects deliberately about D, until gradually her vision of D alters. . . . D is discovered to be . . . not undignified but spontaneous, not noisy but gay, not tiresomely juvenile but delightfully youthful, and so on."[24] Through sustained attention, M comes to see more and better. And thus she and her relationships are healed.

Not everyone admires Murdoch's later essays. Foot could never understand what people saw in the M and D fable and "sometimes spoke of [its] admirers . . . as if they must be feeble-minded."[25] All this talk of purified vision sounded religious—which Foot was resolutely *not*. She and Murdoch had inherited different things from their mentor, MacKinnon. MacKinnon had *converted* Murdoch—for a time, anyway—and imbued her permanently with his sense of the spiritual dimension of life. She got from MacKinnon her intense awareness of the dynamics of spiritual struggle—all the guilty contortions of the human soul. MacKinnon's legacy to Foot was different. It was his moral seriousness, his concern for the suffering of the world, that inspired her. Foot was a woman of action, sorting clothes and writing grants and running off flyers at midnight. She only wondered whether it still made rational *sense* to act virtuously if your virtuous behavior would destroy your happiness.

Foot came to feel about Murdoch the way she felt about Midgley—only more sharply, because Foot's friendship with Murdoch was more intimate. She felt slighted, dismissed. "Iris left us, in the end," Foot remarked.[26] She and Murdoch had taught together. They had worked together through some of the key ideas—about rudeness, about the impossibility of grounding ethics on arbitrary choice—that Foot had developed in her breakthrough articles. And then Murdoch had turned away, away from the arena in which Foot had finally distinguished herself. Though Foot loved her friend, this stung—especially when Murdoch's reputation began to soar. The first critical study of her fiction appeared in 1965. Murdoch was always in the papers; she spent hours each day personally answering fan mail. More than once, people cultivated Foot's acquaintance, hoping for an introduction to Murdoch.[27]

But Murdoch was no more at ease with Foot than Foot was with her. Murdoch didn't resonate with Midgley's sense of having *escaped* Oxford. Or if she did, she didn't think of it as an escape from an artificial set of constraints. It *was* freeing to traipse around London and teach feral young artists and concentrate on her novels. It was freeing above all to get away from Margaret Hubbard and to know that her marriage was no longer in danger. But it wasn't freeing to give up philosophy as she understood it—or to pursue philosophy in a way that she knew Foot didn't respect. Murdoch had internalized mid-century Oxford conceptions of philosophy. She had defended them in the face of Gellner's attack. Murdoch *venerated* Oxford philosophy. She just didn't think she had the ability for it. Foot was a *real* philosopher. She, Murdoch, was a dilettante: "a philosophical poet," as she said to Foot once.[28]

It was perhaps inevitable, then, that within a few years of Foot's divorce and the return of their former intimacy, Foot would become an object of erotic fascination to Murdoch, just like Anscombe in 1948. Foot embodied standards that Murdoch longed to attain. "I have always seen [Foot] as a judge," Murdoch wrote in her journal.[29] But the effect was attractive, not repulsive. Foot, Murdoch wrote, was "numinous, taboo."[30]

Around the beginning of May 1968, Murdoch proposed to Foot that they try sex. "I feel . . . about you," Murdoch wrote to Foot, "that I can't link expression and emotion . . . that no expression seems quite easy, adequate, right."[31] To herself, Murdoch wrote, "Philippa [is] the Sphinx. The Sphinx knew every man's secret, but did not always know that she knew."[32] Murdoch hoped for the revelation of a great secret, or at least to find a fitting expression for her devotion. Foot saw that this was important to Murdoch and played along. But over the course of a few days, it became clear that *this* expression was forced. Murdoch had hoped to dispel the awkwardness she felt before her friend. But the awkwardness was something they would have to live with, alongside love.

Foot, for her part, tried to be sensitive to her friend's insecurities— to make sure she didn't "act the tyrannical princess."[33] There was only one wrenching moment in the decades that followed. It was about philosophy again. In the early 1990s, some of Foot's former students were preparing a *Festschrift* for her. Anscombe contributed a piece. The editors asked Foot if she would solicit something from her friend Murdoch. It was well-meant. But nothing Murdoch had to offer was suitable for a collection of professionalized philosophical essays. She submitted the text of a lecture, riffing on Anselm's ontological argument for the existence of God: arguing that *Goodness*—the Platonic Ideal—has to exist. Foot didn't think the piece good enough to print but was ashamed to say so. She lamely suggested that it was too theological. It was awful for them both: for Foot to have to review—and reject—the work of her friend; for Murdoch to have confirmed what she always feared, that Foot didn't think her philosophical work any good.

Though Murdoch always felt that her philosophical work was desperately inadequate, she could never leave it alone, either. And she remained in demand as a lecturer. As the Romanes Lecturer at Oxford in 1976, she spoke about Plato's views of art. Her lecture was subsequently published as *The Fire and the Sun*. Then she was invited to give the 1982 Gifford Lectures.

This was a crisis. Burdened with a sense of the occasion, Murdoch set to work on a sprawling project, seemingly trying to summarize everything she thought about everything. The lecture titles convey the flavor and range: "Tragedy," "Consciousness," "Politics," "Must religion become prophecy?"[34] And so on. When John Bayley broke his ankle in the winter of 1981–82, Murdoch got most of a year's reprieve. But she only used the time to torture herself with alterations, becoming more dissatisfied the longer she worked. "I am just *not a philosopher*," she wrote to Foot.[35] And three months later: "if it hadn't been for John's mishap, the whole beastly thing would be over, I would have done it in a crazy, impetuous way! Now I see, as I laboriously rewrite, how *hopelessly* bad, indeed partly *senseless* it is!"[36]

Murdoch got through. Her talks resembled her 1964–65 series at the RCA in their open-ended, suggestive character. For all Murdoch's doubts, some in the audience were inspired. Peter Conradi, a "hungry and dissatisfied" seeker writing a dissertation on Murdoch, was enthralled.[37] What Plato found in Socrates, Conradi found in Murdoch: a proclaimer and embodiment of strange new ideals in a world where older ones seemed desiccated. They happened to get adjacent hotel rooms in Edinburgh and over the course of two weeks established a friendship that would become one of the most important of the next 15 years, for each of them: biographer and subject, disciple and master.

Most people didn't know what to make of the talks, though. Readers had no better idea when, after a decade of intermittent, fretful rewriting, Murdoch published the lectures under the title, *Metaphysics as a Guide to Morals*. The book was as disparate as the talks—though also equally packed with provocative observations and asides. "A great congested work, a foaming sourcebook," one reviewer called it. Murdoch dedicated the book to Anscombe. As the dedicatee, Anscombe had a steel-clad excuse for declining when she was asked to review it.

But Murdoch kept writing philosophy, right into her final decade. In 1987, she began a book on Martin Heidegger—another giant of twentieth-century continental thought ignored by most Anglophone philosophers. The book was in proofs in 1993 when she rejected it, judging it no good. This line from its opening page could be an epigraph for her career: "would one rather be damned with Schopenhauer, Bradley, Collingwood, and Simone Weil, than saved with Prichard, Ross, Hare . . . ?"[38]

Conradi rightly saw that Murdoch was offering new or reconstructed ideals to a world bereft. From early in her career, even as she criticized Sartre's picture of human nature and his ethics, she occasionally *talked* like him, or like Hare, about what "everyone now knows" or "everyone must think" in the disenchanted late-modern world.

After she abandoned Christianity, she gradually came to think of faith in the supernatural as doomed. As she wrote in 1966: "Morality has always been connected with religion and religion with mysticism. The disappearance of the middle term leaves morality in a situation which is . . . more difficult but essentially the same."[39] It was a recurring theme both in her philosophy and in her fiction: how to live without God. In the early 1990s, Anthony Kenny invited her to dine with a group of Rhodes Scholars. She scandalized them all, believers and unbelievers alike, by opening the conversation with this pronouncement: "As it is now impossible to believe in God, how can we preserve religion?"[40]

Murdoch came to resonate more and more with Sartre's Romantic talk about steeling ourselves to face a godless world. And really: in her repeated attacks on Sartre and other existentialist thinkers, in her insistence that they were posturing, she was taking a Sartrean idea one step further. Sartre understood authenticity as facing the void without consolations. Murdoch added that, if this is right, there is one last, hardest consolation to refuse: the consolation of thinking how grand you look as you refuse all consolations, the consolation of representing everything as tragic and yourself as Antigone. The consolation, in other words, of the Dawkins sublime. Better, she thought, to be a humble mystic on a quest for an ideal Goodness that we can recognize, God or no God.

A deep theme in Murdoch's fiction, drawn from Sartre, is that the stories we tell falsify reality. They are among the principal means by which people stop themselves from seeing truly. In the novel that finally won Murdoch the Booker prize—*The Sea, The Sea*—the protagonist, imperious retired stage director Charles Arrowby, imprisons himself (and others) in a story about his childhood girlfriend

Hartley and how they are destined for one another. The damage he does is incalculable and is only kept from being worse by the other-directed attentiveness of his mystical cousin, James. At the end of the book, Charles reflects, "Time, like the sea, unties all knots . . . Human arrangements are nothing but loose ends and hazy reckoning, whatever art may otherwise pretend in order to console us."[41]

In 1997, Murdoch was diagnosed with Alzheimer's. Already for a year or two, she had known she was "sailing away into darkness."[42] Her 1995 novel, *Jackson's Dilemma*, was a politely received failure. It grieved her that she could no longer write. At a party in 1996, she turned to a person next to her and said, "I used to write novels."[43] Her final journal entries, that same year, reflect both the tenderness and fear that accompanied her decline:

> Tiredness, weekness [sic]. . . . I feel exhausted. Grief. No, I am listening to the birds singing in the garden.
>
> We swam in the Thames, in our usual secret place, for the first time this year. Ducks, geese, swans—a delightful man comes swimming in—we talked—No one else in the whole huge area swimmed off he swimmed by, conversation, beautiful. The area: immense field, river, another further on immense field, no one, no sign of the road. On other side, cows wander. Poor cows! This is usual, actual, the way we go on—Absolute solitude.[44]

John Bayley didn't seek respite care until very late. Friends stepped up. Foot began having Murdoch over for lunch every Friday. Murdoch knew her friend to the last. But domestic life became difficult. Between the menial chores, Bayley began work on the first of three memoirs focused on Murdoch's decline, books that would frame public perceptions of her for years afterward. In her 2005 memoir, Midgley wrote, "to be remembered only—or even primarily—for the disease that destroyed one is surely a horrid misfortune, an especially unsuitable fate for someone the rest of whose life was as full and active as hers was."[45]

Foot, too, felt that Bayley's memoirs were a betrayal. She despised them, and did not watch the affecting film based on the first, *Elegy for Iris*. No elevated awareness of the realities of Alzheimer's, she thought, justified the infantilizing pictures of her friend absorbed in the Teletubbies or wandering into the street. She and Conradi cast about for explanations. Perhaps Bayley needed to do this to work through his grief. Perhaps it was unconscious revenge on his magnetically attractive wife, who always came home but never stopped giving herself away.

Murdoch died on February 8, 1999. On her last visit with Foot, Murdoch kissed her friend's hand. When the call came that afternoon, Foot was having tea with Conradi. As they parted, she half-quoted something MacKinnon had said to her years before, about the death of a friend: "you will never hear the way they call you by your first name again."[46]

GERTRUDE ELIZABETH MARGARET

Anscombe was enormously productive as the new holder of Wittgenstein's Professorship at Cambridge. But her work diverged from that of her friends. Apart from her interest in murder—that is, in the *concept* of murder, which she feared was being forgotten or minimized in the late-modern West—Anscombe's philosophical interests never centered on ethics. Lesley Brown, who studied with Anscombe in the 1960s, remarked that Anscombe's students at Oxford didn't think of her as working in ethics at all.[47] She lectured on Plato, Aristotle, Locke, Berkeley, Hume, Wittgenstein, and philosophical psychology. She never even repeated her lectures on intention.

Murder did remain a preoccupation, though, and she began teaching about it after she moved to Cambridge.[48] She defined it (subject
to minor qualifications) as the intentional killing of innocent human
beings, and thus stood with the Church, and against the rising tide of
late-modern Western culture, in condemning abortion and euthanasia as well as the killing of civilians in war (the case she had first discussed in print). Each of her first four autumns at Cambridge, from
1970 to 1973, she taught a class with "killing" in the title. She had
little interest in theories of ethics except as they bore on this central
question. As she wrote in 1981, "my interest in moral philosophy has
been more in particular moral questions than in what is now called
'meta-ethics.'"[49] She wrote mostly on other matters: the concept of
truth, the writings of past philosophers, and the topic that first pulled
her into philosophy, causation. Like Murdoch, she became intrigued
late in her career with Anselm's ontological argument for the existence of God.

By the time she moved to Cambridge, Anscombe had been out of
touch with Midgley and Murdoch for years.[50] Now that she and
Foot were no longer colleagues, they kept up less, too. There was
one occasion during Anscombe's first years at Cambridge when
Foot (between jobs) traveled to attend one of her friend's classes,
titled "Killing and Murder." It was like old times. They argued again,
this time over a hoary thought-experiment about a big spelunker
who gets stuck in the entrance to a cave, trapping his fellow adven-
turers inside. They happen to have a stick of dynamite with which
they could blow up their stuck companion before rising waters kill
them all. Different versions of the thought-experiment have the
big spelunker facing *out* (so he wouldn't drown with the others) or
facing *in* (so he would).[51] Foot journaled about the discussion. "If

the . . . man's head is inside the cave do we injure him in blowing him up?" Foot asked. "Suppose him unconscious, or if conscious frightened & in pain"? "PRF denies," she noted. But "G.E.M.A. asserts that we do injure him, doing him 'wrongful harm.'"[52] As ever, Foot puzzled over her friend's words, certain that there *must* be something there to consider. But when they weren't together, Anscombe was not as avid a correspondent as Murdoch.

Anscombe remained always, immovably, who she was: a person devoted to the Truth, to the Church, and to those in her circle of care—family, students, charity cases like the alcohol-addicted gardener she and Geach paid for puttering indifferently around their home.[53] Little else mattered. Anscombe's wardrobe changed on her accession to Wittgenstein's Chair, but wasn't any more stylish. In the stories told by pupils and colleagues at Cambridge, she was no longer wearing a duffel coat and trousers, but instead a cobbler's apron and clinging tights or a maroon track suit. She remained hard to place. When she first appeared at the Cambridge payroll office, the clerk asked her if she was one of the new cleaning ladies. Anscombe paused, then replied quietly, "No, I am the Professor of Philosophy."[54] On another occasion, following a panel discussion on abortion, a woman in the audience remarked that, as usual, the discussion was being carried on exclusively by men, none of whom knew what it was like to be pregnant. Anscombe, track-suited and smoking a cigar, was visibly amused.[55]

She shocked not only by her appearance but also by her convictions. She had known since her conversion that her beliefs would divide her from people around her. Her beliefs had divided her from her parents, recalling Jesus' difficult words: "Anyone who comes to me without hating father, mother, wife, children, brothers, sisters, yes and his own life too, cannot be my disciple."[56] They had divided her and Peter Geach from their fellow citizens (and even their archbishop) when they each declared their objection to Britain's conduct in the Second World War. They had divided her from most of her colleagues during the Truman controversy. And after her move to Cambridge, they divided her from the other Professor of Philosophy, fellow Oxford transplant Bernard Williams.

Colleagues and students of Anscombe and Williams from the 1970s readily perceived the animosity between them. Nicholas Denyer remembered them "bristling" at one another at a meeting of the B Club, the University's ancient philosophy society. The topic that day was Aristotle's account of material constitution.[57] But the ground of their mutual hostility was not their differing views of Aristotle, but their differing views of sex and religion. In 1972, a "review of English letters," *The Human World*, had published an essay by Anscombe explicating and defending the traditional Catholic objection to contraception. (Anscombe and Geach had held a party to celebrate the 1968 publication of the papal encyclical *Humanae Vitae*, which reiterated the Church's teaching after several years of intense discussion about whether it should change in light of the pill.)

In a subsequent issue of *The Human World*, Williams and fellow King's College philosopher Michael Tanner expressed their "outrage" at the "rotten thinking" Anscombe was defending. They called her arguments "offensive and absurd" and said she was "preach[ing] impoverishment of life."[58] For anyone familiar with the Church's view, there was nothing very surprising in what Anscombe wrote— though Williams and Tanner rightly noted the "relish" with which Anscombe attacked "the spirit of the age." They remarked that she "presumably intended to confirm the orthodox in their attitudes, to enrage the rest of her readers, and to render them incapable of rational reply."

Anscombe was invited to reply in the same issue. Addressing her colleagues ("my friendly neighborhood philosophers"), she said that outrage had put "blood in their eye and . . . blots in their piece." Most of her reply was dedicated to showing ("in the interests of better standards in controversy") that they had misread her arguments in various ways. But in her concluding paragraph, she took a different tone:

> [T]here is one thing that I don't count as a "blot." That is, when they accuse me of "preaching impoverishment of life." That is an honest accusation: it is something they really think about what I really think. It is an old and intelligible accusation against the Christian religion. That one must be prepared to lose one's life in order to save it, that "being poor in spirit" is blessed . . . all this Christianity has indeed taught.[59]

But, she added, "[a]t this point in time I look at that old accusation with rather wry feelings." What, after all, is "the thought of the most serious and alive writing and theatre" of the age?: "[t]hat we are all crawling around in shit, that all is hopeless and absurd." She concluded, "I feel mild surprise that anyone is angry with me for not much liking the spirit of the present age."

Anscombe was a woman of action as well as words. Twice she was arrested for blocking the entrance to an abortion clinic: the second time when she was entering her seventies.* But words remained her sharpest tools—and her most dangerous. Near the end of her life, Anscombe almost destroyed her friendship with Foot. On a spring

---

* Readers, I know, will divide over Anscombe's staunchness: some seeing in her an icon of moral courage, others a fanatic who could not intuit how the world appears to others. I hope I have made both reactions intelligible. I spoke to sources in the course of researching this book who revered Anscombe, and to sources who loathed her. I invoked Socrates once before in this chapter. Socrates and Anscombe are importantly alike; the same effort is needed to understand each. If you do not grasp how Socrates could inspire Plato and his friends to abandon their prospects as young aristocrats and devote their lives to his teaching, you have not understood. If you do not grasp why a majority of the Athenian jury would vote to put Socrates to death, you have not understood.

day in 1997, Anscombe burst in on her old colleague and began denouncing her. It was about Oxfam.

Anscombe knew Foot's history with Oxfam. With Foot gravitating toward the United States in 1972, she finally resigned from Oxfam's Council of Management. Her Oxfam colleagues pleaded with her not to leave the Council; she was a distinguished administrative talent and knew the organization top to bottom. Foot couldn't see how the distance could be managed, though. She regretfully walked away. But Foot believed in Oxfam as deeply as she believed in anything. She was *far* more moved when Oxfam invited her to deliver the biannual Gilbert Murray Memorial Lecture than when Downing Street approached her the following year (1993) to ask if she would let the Queen name her to the Order of the British Empire. (Foot declined.) Oxfam was a thread running through her whole adult life, a source of joy. In a journal entry in late 2000, she wrote, "Nanny and Michael: the two from whom my happiness has come." In a facing note, dated a few weeks later, she wrote, "As well as from philosophy, and from Oxfam."[60]

Anscombe had learned that Oxfam supported contraceptive campaigns as part of their development work, and that they promoted abortion as a fallback. She was appalled; now facing her former colleague, Anscombe raged against her for condoning evil. A friend and former student of Foot's had an appointment shortly after the encounter and found Foot beside herself with anger. Foot vowed she would never see Anscombe or speak to her again.[61]

Foot was a woman of principle. But this time, she broke her word. As I noted once before: Anscombe's rages burned hot, then flamed out. During the time Foot and Anscombe were estranged, Foot continued to visit Anscombe's eldest daughter, who had suffered a disabling accident. If Barbara did not insist, Foot wouldn't let the one rupture cause another. In fact, the opposite happened—the one connection led to the restoration of the other. In time, without any explicit reconciliation, Foot did see Anscombe again. And they did speak. When Foot learned of Anscombe's death in January 2001, she wrote in her journal,

> Now Elizabeth has died. I think about her life and, strangely for someone who so little courted <u>success</u> that it was a hugely successful life. A wonderful marriage. Seven devoted children. A marvellous body of work. And <u>many</u> Somervillians— undergraduates & graduates in her time—who say they owe her everything.[62]

In her obituary for Anscombe, Foot said *she* owed her everything, too.

A few months later, preparing to talk about Anscombe on the BBC's Women's Hour, Foot jotted down several pages of notes. She hunted for the right epithets to describe her closest colleague. She called her "civilised but totally unconventional" and "scornful." "Especially," she added, "of anyone who wanted a <u>Quick fix</u>" to some philosophical problem. She settled finally on "<u>Truthful. A lover of truth</u>."[63]

Anscombe died on the eve of the Feast of Epiphany, surrounded by her family. After kissing Peter Geach one last time, she sailed into her rest.[64] She was buried next to Wittgenstein, as she had requested, in the Ascension Parish cemetery in Cambridge.

Near the end of her life, Anscombe remarked to a mutual friend that she and Foot had never had a cross word.[65] By this time, Anscombe's memory was deteriorating. Still, Foot was surprised when she learned what Anscombe had said. Foot included the line in the obituary she wrote, framing it with characteristic delicacy and exactness: "she remarked once that she thought we never had a cross word."[66] But that was the impression of Foot that stayed with Anscombe: the devoted companion who had stood by her side against the whole world.

INTERLUDE: RICHARD MERVYN (II)

When he died in 2002, Richard Hare left behind a long, introspective "Philosophical Autobiography," which his son published on his father's behalf. It begins:

> I had a strange dream, or half-waking vision, not long ago. I found myself at the top of a mountain in the mist, feeling very pleased with myself, not just for having climbed the mountain, but for having achieved my life's ambition, to find a way of answering moral questions rationally. But as I was preening myself on this achievement, the mist began to clear, and I saw that I was surrounded on the mountain top by the graves of all those other philosophers, great and small, who had had the same ambition, and thought they had achieved it.[67]

Hare believed for a time that he had achieved his ambition. Though it must be said that he took a strange route up the mountain face. Over the course of the 1970s and 1980s, Hare slowly, gradually embraced utilitarianism: the Enlightenment-born theory that our actions should aim at producing as much satisfaction as possible. Given a choice between two (or three, or forty-two) alternatives, one should select whichever promises to make everyone affected as satisfied as possible, on the whole. The theory can be formulated in many different ways. (How do we define and measure satisfaction? does it matter whether satisfaction is reasonably well-distributed? do the satisfactions of horses and gorillas and fish count the same as those of humans? what about the potential satisfactions of generations yet unconceived?) Still, the gist is clear: the theory tells people to base their decisions on the best cost-benefit analyses they can manage, choosing whatever promises the best results, so far as they can foresee.

Hare regarded his final views, expressed in his 1981 book, *Moral Thinking*, as a direct outgrowth of his earlier ones. This was hard to accept. How could Hare, whose great theme had been *choice*, now turn around and say that there was *no* choice—that there was one correct set of principles, binding everyone? Hare insisted he hadn't changed his mind. In the opening chapter of *Moral Thinking*, he explains: utilitarianism is implied by "the language of morals." So *if you choose* to use universally prescriptive words like "ought," *then you must* be a utilitarian—on pain of contradicting yourself.[68]

No one has to use the language of morals. That language is a cultural construct, however firmly established in common discourse. So Hare remained true to his earlier views. The universe is billiard balls. There is no underlying ethical reality—only the way Hare (and, he presumes, his readers) happen to talk. They *could* talk differently—or at least try. So it's still technically a choice.

By the 1980s, though, Hare's earlier emphasis on freedom had receded far into the background. After the upheaval of the 1960s and 1970s, Hare's thought no longer centered on the brutalized prisoner of war standing alone, stripped of all supports, clinging to his commitments by force of will. Now his focus was on how warring parties— Irish and English, Pakistanis and Indians—could come to agree. It was on the power of reason. As he wrote, "[p]ractical issues are issues over which people are prepared to fight and kill one another; and it may be that unless some way is found of talking about them rationally and with hope of agreement, violence will finally engulf the world."[69]

But Hare continued to think Foot and her friends were wrong—indeed, utterly confused. Partly this was just deep-seated stubbornness. Even affectionate colleagues—Anthony Kenny, John Lucas—couldn't recall Hare ever conceding a point. (Over the years, Kenny learned to engage Hare on topics Hare had never thought about, like the nature of time. *Then*, without a position to defend, Hare could be marvelously inventive, and genuinely interested in the ideas of his conversation partner.)[70] Hare's dogged attempts to bring people around could be comic. In the summer of 1958, a year before they were supposed to teach together, Hare asked Foot if he could borrow the manuscripts of her ethics lectures. Over the course of a week, Hare typed twenty-one pages of critical commentary. Hare seemed to think that if he kept reiterating his position, eventually anyone honest and clear-headed would come around. He and Kenny once discussed a proposal to publish a volume including some of his work and the work of critics like Foot. "I would not wish to bestow immortality on such ephemera," Hare replied.[71]

Hare didn't merely think that he was right. He also thought, from almost as soon as he returned to Oxford, that *Ayer* was right. Not in his account of moral language, but in his fundamental picture of the world. Ethics can't be grounded in facts—in anything that merely *is*. Ethics is a construction. It is a creature of words, of language. It is artifice.

Hare died grieving his legacy. At the end, a stroke stopped him from continuing to articulate once more, and once more, in the face of obstinate critics what he knew—*knew*—was true. Though he inspired several enormously influential students—Peter Singer, Derek Parfit—after 1958, his views were never again an orthodoxy. Never again did most of his peers defer to him. In 1984, he wrote to

Foot, seizing on something she'd written that reminded him of his own views, and suggesting that maybe she was at last coming around. Could he have believed what he wrote? Foot replied: "As for the Hare-Foot axis, we could always try it, but I am not very hopeful."[72] Two years later, his former student and colleague John Lucas spoke to Hare on his birthday. Lucas found him despondent:

> Dick told me that his life had been a failure: he had converted nobody to his views, he had had no disciples. In vain I expostulated, pointing out that he had been the most influential moral philosopher in the second half of the twentieth century, whose arguments had had to be considered by everyone else who thought about the subject. Dick was determined to be disappointed.[73]

Hare had endured appalling physical suffering and carried no bitterness. He and his wife vacationed in Japan once, after he retired from Oxford. He delighted in the place, the people, the culture. The only allusion he made to what he had suffered in 1943 was a passing comment as they were hurrying with a lot of luggage to catch a train. Hare remarked that the last time he was in East Asia, he'd hauled heavier things each day, so he ought to be able to bear it.[74]

But he never stopped being galled by Foot's critique.

On May 10, 1994, Foot gave the annual H.L.A. Hart Memorial Lecture at Oxford. Foot's lecture, "Does Moral Subjectivism Rest on a Mistake?", was one of her first statements of the Midgley-esque view she would develop in *Natural Goodness*. It was a major occasion. Many of the University's philosophy faculty were in attendance. At the outset, as is customary, Foot praised the person in whose memory the lectures are held: her longtime colleague in jurisprudence, Herbert Hart. But after concluding her talk, Foot said there was someone else she wanted to acknowledge, someone who had had a tremendous impact on moral philosophy, someone richly worthy of recognition. She named Hare. Roger Teichmann, sitting in the audience, wasn't sure as Foot started this eulogy whom she meant—or perhaps he was so surprised, he couldn't believe it. There was a round of applause, which Hare received unsmilingly.[75] It wasn't enough.

Foot was a genius at reconciliation: with Murdoch, with Anscombe. Late in life, even she and Michael met and spoke warmly—though, after one of their conversations, she wrote in her journal, "lest I should have any regret for the loss of him he showed himself as much of an ass as ever," exulting "over . . . the genes of his grandson."[76] But with Hare she failed. She had supposed that the fundamental thing was their both being old Oxford philosophers, with a wealth of memories and friends in common. Let the young fight, she thought. We have seen fashions come and go. Let us remember what we share and part with good will.[77]

Some walls are too high.[78]

PHILIPPA RUTH

If there are few true-believing Hare disciples anymore, nonetheless the ethical naturalism developed in stages by Murdoch, Anscombe, Foot, and Midgley did not sweep everything before it. It has a hearing now. It is up for discussion. But both inside and outside the academy, Hare's deepest conviction endures.

One of the foremost schools of contemporary ethical theory is constructivism: an adaptation of the moral thought of Kant first articulated by Harvard philosopher John Rawls and most forcefully and elegantly argued in the work of his student, Christine Korsgaard. It is an existentialist theory.

Korsgaard doesn't speak, as Hare did, of "principles" and "duties." But she does speak of "obligations," and traces them to acts of self-commitment. We adopt "practical identities," she says—self-conceptions—and build our lives around them. Once we've done so, the burden falls on us to live up to our chosen identities. An obligation is the perception of a threat to some identity you've embraced. If you conceive of yourself as someone's friend, for example, you will have notions of what behavior fits or doesn't fit with that identity. The pained awareness that your friend's birthday is approaching and you haven't yet sent a card: that's the force of obligation. But all of this exists, Korsgaard insists, only from "the first-person perspective."[79] We cannot be wrong about ethics— only inconsistent. We can, at worst, fail to live up to the identities we've embraced.

Like Hare in the final phase of his career, Korsgaard tries to pinch readers with an appeal to consistency. She depicts as vividly as Sartre the situation of self-conscious, free beings in a valueless world. Our plight, she says, is that we each need *some* practical identity. We are condemned to be free—just as Sartre argued. But Korsgaard thinks that there are some very basic identities—the identity of *human being*, the identity of *animal*—that are inseparable from any more robust and particular identities we adopt. So to claim any identity is to claim these more basic identities, too. But behind Korsgaard's view is the familiar picture: the billiard-ball universe in which value does not exist unless we put it there.

And children around the world continue to be quizzed on their ability to distinguish facts from non-facts: to recognize and be on their guard against "biased" statements like "you're in great shape," or "education is important," or "murder is wrong."

Nonetheless, there is now a minority report. There is an alternative to explore for those who want to say, like Foot did in 1945, that the commandant at Bergen-Belsen was not just inconsistent, or devoted to different principles or self-conceptions, but wrong. Like a dissenting opinion from an appeals court, the naturalism that Foot and her friends developed is now *available*.

I noted already the emergence of "virtue ethics," a family of ethical theories inspired especially by the early work of Anscombe and Foot. There is something ironic about this. Anscombe never used the term "virtue ethics," and Foot disliked it. If you're going to ground ethics on anything, she thought, *don't* ground it on virtues and vices—important though they are. No, ground ethics on what Anscombe called "Aristotelian necessities": resources, traits, practices, *anything* necessary for the achievement of some good. Horses need exercise, and blueberries need iron. What do *people* need in order to succeed in characteristically human pursuits? Virtues, certainly, like justice and charity. But other things as well. Foot appreciated a line from Peter Geach: human beings "need virtues as bees need stings."[80] After publishing *Natural Goodness*, Foot worked for a while on a paper she never published. The working title was, "Against Virtue Ethics."[81] But she *was* responsible for a revolution in the academy. You can't control what people do with your teaching.

In any case, Anscombe and Foot's legacy went well beyond those who explicitly appropriated their ideas. Murdoch and Midgley were inspiring teachers, but were most influential through their writings. Again, it was Anscombe and Foot—especially Foot—who changed the face of the academy. Preparing her obituary for Anscombe, Foot tried counting the women who had come through Somerville and gone on to teaching positions in philosophy, in England and around the world: Sarah Broadie, Onora O'Neill, Rosalind Hursthouse . . . . Foot stopped when she got to 20. And this is not to mention non-Somervillians like Cora Diamond, who attended Foot's and

Anscombe's classes at Oxford. Or the men who visited Oxford and came under their influence (and Murdoch's), like Thomas Nagel and Charles Taylor. Or those Anscombe and Foot influenced at Cambridge and UCLA. Foot was proudest of the women, though. She and Anscombe hadn't had philosophical mentors at Somerville and St. Hugh's. They had done for a generation of Somervillians and others what no one had done for them: marked a path.

Midgley was the only one of the four who wrote at length about women and men, and about the place of women in the world. She concluded later that she had found her voice as a philosopher only because there were so few men at Oxford at the moment she began to study philosophy. She suspected that the same was true of her friends Foot and Murdoch. Quite apart from their getting more attention from mentors than they might have gotten a decade earlier, Midgley judged that the dearth of men during the war had atmospheric effects. Drawing on her immersion in animal-behavior studies, Midgley remarked, "[a]ny situation where a lot of young men are competing to form a dominance hierarchy, will produce cock-fights. But . . . these fights . . . interfere with philosophical work."[82] If there are people who like this sort of thing better than conversations where people try to understand and improve one another's thoughts, Midgley suggested they set up "Departments of Cognitive Poker."

Foot might have dissented from her friend's conclusions. At least, she did not like to be labeled a "woman philosopher." When Peter Conradi showed her a chapter in which he referred to her and Murdoch and their friends as "women philosophers," she said she preferred to be thought of as part of a generation.

But all four noticed the small slights—the missed invitations, the stereotypes—and were determined not to be messed with. Murdoch has a wonderful, painful line in her one historical novel, *The Red and the Green*; Frances Bellman, expected by everyone to marry British officer Andrew Chase-White but feeling acutely *unseen*, remarks, "I think being a woman is like being Irish .... Everyone says you're important and nice, but you take second place all the same."[83] I have noted that Anscombe went by "Miss Anscombe" her whole adult life—though this caused consternation among the staff at the Radcliffe Infirmary whenever she turned up to give birth. But on another occasion, in Cambridge, she spoke up when someone referred to her merely as "Miss Anscombe." She remarked that, while one might speak of a male Professor as "Mr. So-and-So," one would hasten to add that he was the Such-and-Such Professor of This-or-That.[84] Foot, for her part, said that she first reflected on her position as a woman in philosophy when she began traveling to the United States to lecture. She noticed that she was frequently introduced as "the first woman to give this lecture or that lecture." Her first thought was that it was "a funny thing to mention."[85] She thought, she'd rather they mention that she came from the north of England. But then she began to reflect and, in small ways, to resist. In 1976, an elegant-looking letter arrived, informing her of her election to the British Academy. A keepsake. Foot pulled out her typewriter and struck through the salutation—"Dear Sir"— with four x's. To the right, she typed "Madam". And when the same thing happened in 1983, on her election to the American Academy of Arts and Sciences (AAAS), she replied: "I was a little disconcerted to be addressed as 'Sir' in the invitation.... you would I think be surprised if I addressed you as 'Madam' and it is precisely the same for me to be addressed as 'Sir.'"[86]

None of this meant as much to her as the happiness or unhappiness of her students, though. And as with the AAAS invitation, Foot leveraged her status—her reputation—to make things better for others. Rosalind Hursthouse recalled Foot coming to her rescue once, in her first year of teaching. Hursthouse's advisor Anthony Kenny had drawn her attention to a temporary lectureship at Corpus Christi, one of Oxford's men's colleges. As a woman, she was ineligible for *membership* in Corpus, but—Kenny pointed out—the advertisement didn't specify that the successful candidate had to become a member. Whether or not they were caught off guard, the hiring committee acknowledged Hursthouse as the best candidate and duly hired her. Then the misery began. Her new colleagues treated her coldly from the day she appeared in the Senior Common Room and at high table. Foot was in the United States at the time, on her first short-term appointment after resigning from Somerville. On her return to Oxford that spring, she checked in on her former pupil and was outraged to hear of the treatment Hursthouse had endured. She insisted that Hursthouse invite her to the next formal dinner at Corpus.

Foot did nothing so direct or obvious as a dressing-down. At high table, she was seated opposite one of Hursthouse's tormentors, a well-known philosopher of Foot's generation. He and Foot fell into conversation about the recent shootings at Kent State University, and the man said he thought that the National Guard had acted appropriately. After all, he said, the students had been throwing rocks. Foot corrected him: in the United States, "rocks" doesn't mean great boulders, as it does in England. She noted that the protesters had been armed chiefly with flowers. Then there was a lull in the conversation and Foot saw the opening she had been looking for. In her perfect aristocratic accent, in ringing tones, she said, "I will grant you, they were being rude. They called the police 'motherfuckers'. But really! If I were to call *you* a 'motherfucker,' you wouldn't think you would be justified in shooting me, would you?" Such a thing had certainly never been said at high table in Corpus. And the message was received. Hursthouse was treated better from then on.[87]

Foot could be wickedly clever. But the personal quality that her friends most often remarked was a refusal to let polite forms come between them. "How are you *really*?" she would ask.[88] Not that Foot ever forgot her instinctive decorum. She was "a back-room person" by her own account. One of her teachers, Heinz Cassirer, characterized her as "pathologically discreet." And Midgley kidded Foot once that a graphologist's report on her would read, "a very secretive person."[89] This wasn't only a comment on her poor handwriting.

Especially for someone who routinely prodded others to open up, Foot *was* secretive. Conradi recalled her telling him once that she had just destroyed a load of personal documents. "That ought to throw them off the scent!" she said.[90] In the hunting metaphors she loved, she was now the fox. She told Conradi that she had likewise destroyed a suitcase full of letters from Donald MacKinnon—though she passed along a select few.[91]

We are, to a large degree, who our most significant friends and relations have made us. Like Murdoch, Foot venerated and brooded on her mentors to the end of her life. She venerated and brooded on Anscombe. And she venerated and brooded on MacKinnon. MacKinnon's place in Foot's imagination was as complex as Anscombe's. Foot told Murdoch once that MacKinnon had "put her [Foot] against Christianity."[92] Foot insisted, in a number of late interviews, that she had been firmly atheistic her whole adult life. But she did *ask* MacKinnon, early in their friendship, whether he thought she needed to become a Christian. And her remark to Murdoch suggests a moment of turning. In her final journal, from 1996 forward— one of the few she didn't destroy—few names appear as frequently as "Donald," who she once said "created" her, and also described as "holy." Though Foot was not a believer, she yearned toward the ritual and eternal contexts supplied by faith. She wrote in one of her journals of her longing to go to Chartres and spend several days immersed in the cathedral's rhythms of worship and prayer. She then did. In 1997, she records reading through the passion narrative of *John* on Good Friday. And in the 1980s, on a trip to the continent, she stopped in an old chapel and lit a candle for MacKinnon: "It was to burn for all time, in memory of all he did for me, and for his unhappy life."[93]

Whatever she made of his beliefs, MacKinnon was the person who had spoken to Foot most powerfully about grief and loss. As she walked forward into the 2000s without her closest friends, she recalled in her journal something MacKinnon had said to her: "I remember Donald saying of his friend . . . that he could <u>never ever</u> see him again. And as I write this Donald's great bulk and ever-so-distinctive voice come before me."[94] Her late journals are a catalog of such losses. Repeatedly she compares them to losing MacKinnon. On January 15, 2001: "Elizabeth died on Jan. 5th. Everything is done for the first time in the <u>different</u> world that is without her. (Like going to London for the first time after Donald had died. This time it was merely going, or looking, into the garden.)"

Foot died on her ninetieth birthday, October 3, 2010. She outlived Anscombe and Murdoch both. Foot had other old friends—Midgley, the Dummetts—but none so central to her life. How hard it is to go on alone. In her last decades, she became a more attentive mentor than Anscombe, Midgley, or even Murdoch. Her students were her children. Anscombe and Midgley had families. Murdoch had correspondents all over the world. Foot had Hursthouse and others. For years, former students routinely came and went from the house Foot took over when her *oldest* friend, Anne Cobbe, died. Foot became a model, too, of the devoted adoptive aunt. The Dummetts invited her to Christmas gatherings, and she bought gifts for each of the many Dummett grandchildren. But in the gaps between visits from students and others, the house grew quiet. She wrote to a friend of the "moments of slight desolation as one arrives [home] alone."[95]

Foot wrote, "It is not just that the dead are silent, that one can never ever hear their voice again. One's <u>own</u> voice is silent too."[96] In *The Epic of Gilgamesh*, Gilgamesh despairs over exactly this: if his friend and partner Enkidu is gone, if Enkidu's beauty and laughter are ended, how can he bear it? The poem itself is the poet's answer. It is represented as the testimony of Gilgamesh, carved on a stele for unseen generations to come and read. Recorded testimony, recorded narrative: these are painful second-bests to the living voice or embrace of the friend, "the pressure of [their] hand."[97] But they are not nothing. They honor; they preserve. They can even convey life. Tennyson wrote how, re-reading his friend Arthur's letters ("those fall'n leaves which kept their green"), it was like Arthur's "living soul" was present.

And we build on one another's work. We borrow from our foremothers, and leave things to our children. While the sun smiles on us, we collaborate with friends and see what we can do together. It is the kind of creature we are. After one of her visits to Barbara Geach, Foot visited Norwich Cathedral. She reflected in her journal afterward on the "glorious nave of Norman pillars and Gothic vaulting. And . . . the continuity of the place. So many generations of 'singing men' and monks and custodians and builders and cleaners. We keep things going—all of us who work in such places—and in Universities too!"[98]

NOTES

Prelims

1. Mary Midgley, *The Owl of Minerva*, 123–124.
2. Midgley, email correspondence with author, March 11, 2010.
3. R.M. Hare, quoted in A.W. Price, "Richard Mervyn Hare," *Proceedings of the British Academy* 124, 134.
4. Thomas Kuhn, *The Structure of Scientific Revolutions* (Chicago: University of Chicago, 1962).
5. Iris Murdoch to Leonie Cohn, October 9, 1951. BBC Written Archives Centre RCONT1 Iris Murdoch Talks File 1, 1946–1962.

Chapter 1

1. For the details surrounding this episode, I rely on Philippa Foot's archived papers and staff file at Somerville College, as well as on M.R.D. Foot, *Memories of an SOE Historian* (Barnsley: Pen and Sword, 2008) and correspondence with M.R.D. Foot.
2. For discussion of the deliberations that led to the publication of images from the camps, and of their impact, see Hannah Caven, "Horror in Our Time: Images of the concentration camps in the British media, 1945," *Historical Journal of Film, Radio and Television* 21: no 3 (2001): 205–253.

3. Again, see Caven, "Horror in Our Time." The newsreel itself can be viewed on the website of British Pathé. For further detail on the background and results of the parliamentary delegation, see Myfanwy Lloyd, "The Parliamentary Delegation to Buchenwald Concentration Camp—70 Years On," *The History of Parliament*, https://thehistoryofparliament.wordpress.com/2015/04/21/the-parliamentary-delegation-to-buchenwald-concentration-camp-70-years-on/. The quotation from Ranfurly is from her published diaries, *To War with Whitaker* (London: Bello, 2014).

4. She recounted this conversation many times, including to her friend Peter Conradi, who relayed it to me, as well as in an interview with Martin Gornall, available in the Foot Papers at Somerville (SC/LY/SP/PF/10). My description of MacKinnon's rooms is drawn from a short memoir by his pupil, Vera Crane, in the Iris Murdoch archive at Kingston (KUAS 6/11/1/12/1). All materials from the Somerville College Archives are used courtesy of the Principal and Fellows of Somerville College, Oxford.

5. Jenny Anderson, "Only 9 % of 15-year-olds Can Tell the Difference between Fact and Opinion," QZ, December 3, 2019, https://qz.com/1759474/only-9-percent-of-15-year-olds-can-distinguish-between-fact-and-opinion/.

6. Rhonda Dubec, "Fact v. Opinion Resource," Lakehead University Teaching Commons, July 22, 2019, https://teachingcommons.lakeheadu.ca/fact-vs-opinion-resource; Sharon Linde, "Facts vs Opinions," Study.com, December 28, 2018, https://study.com/academy/lesson/facts-vs-opinions-examples-games-activities.html.

7. Kevin Cummins, "Fact and Opinion Worksheets for Students," edgalaxy.com, March 31, 2013, https://www.edgalaxy.com/journal/2013/3/31/fact-and-opinion-worksheets-for-students; *Making Judgments and Drawing Conclusions* (lesson worksheet), Center for Humanities, 1977, https://www.bmcc.cuny.edu/wp-content/uploads/ported/lrc/studyskills/factsandopinions.pdf.

8. Horace Morse and George McCune, "Selected Items for the Testing of Study Skills," *Bulletin Number 15* (National Council for the Social Studies, 1940).

9. Shane Mac Donnchaidh, "A Teacher's Guide to Fact and Opinion," Literacy Ideas, https://www.literacyideas.com/teaching-fact-and-opinion.

10. Paul Blaschkow, "Let's Stop Hating On the Fact-Opinion Distinction," *Paul Blaschko* (blog), April 1, 2017, www.paulblaschko.com/blog/2017/4/1/lets-stop-hating-on-the-fact-opinion-distinction.

11. Among other problems, this makes it unclear how to classify fact-type statements that are false ("vaccines cause autism") or that cannot be proven ("there is a largest prime number"). Are these "opinions"? Not by the linguistic tests the authors put forward.

12. Sarah Sumnicht, "Fact & Opinion Statements with Adjectives," Education.com, n.d., https://www.education.com/download/lesson-plan/

el-support-lesson-fact-and-opinion-statements-with-adjectives/el-support-lesson-fact-and-opinion-statements-with-adjectives.pdf.

13. Charles Taylor makes this point in the opening chapter of *Sources of the Self: The Making of the Modern Identity* (Cambridge, MA: Harvard University Press, 1989).

14. Taylor (see previous note) has done as much as anyone to call attention to the character and operation of these frameworks.

15. See Armand Leroi, *The Lagoon* (New York: Viking, 2014).

16. See Frances A. Yates, "Giordano Bruno's Conflict with Oxford," *Journal of the Warburg Institute* 2, No. 3 (January 1939): 230. As Yates details, even after the works of the "School-men" mocked by Hobbes and others were banished from the university curriculum, a different kind of rigidity set in. From 1585/6, students at Oxford labored under the following statute: "all Bachelaurs and Undergraduats in their Disputations should lay their various Authors, such that caused many dissensions and strifes in the Schools, and only follow Aristotle and those that defend him . . . ."

17. Here and throughout this discussion, I draw on David Wootton, *The Invention of Science* (New York: Harper, 2015) and Robert Proctor, *Value-Free Science? Purity and Power in Modern Knowledge* (Cambridge, MA: Harvard University Press, 1991).

18. Francis Bacon, *The Advancement of Learning* (1605), I.v.11.

19. Gottfried Wilhelm Leibniz, *Discourse on Metaphysics* (trans. George Montgomery), XI.

20. This story is also told—from radically different perspectives—in Alasdair MacIntyre, *After Virtue* (Notre Dame: University of Notre Dame Press, 1981) and Christine M. Korsgaard, *The Sources of Normativity* (Cambridge, UK: Cambridge University Press, 1996).

21. Johannes Kepler, *Harmonices Mundi* (1618), V.

22. Charles Taylor, *A Secular Age?*, 549.

23. Edmund Burke, *A Philosophical Enquiry into the Origin of our Ideas of the Sublime and Beautiful* (1757), (Oxford: Oxford University Press, 2015).

24. Alfred Tennyson, *In Memoriam A.H.H.*, III, ed. Eric Gray, (New York: Norton, 2003).

25. Matthew Arnold, "Dover Beach," stanza IV, 1867, https://www.poetryfoundation.org/poems/43588/dover-beach.

26. Quoted in Taylor, *A Secular Age?*, 561.

27. Steven Weinberg, *The First Three Minutes*, second edition (New York: Basic Books, 1993), 154–155.

28. Philippa Foot, interview with Jonathan Ree, "Twenty Minutes—Philosophical Lives," September 19, 2000, BBC Radio 3 BBC, broadcast September 19, 2000.

Chapter 2

1. Peter Conradi, *Iris* (New York: W.W. Norton, 2001), 128. In recounting this episode, I draw on Conradi's account, on an interview he conducted with Foot, available in the Iris Murdoch archive at Kingston University, and on Foot's staff file at Somerville College. Conradi became close with Foot as well as with Murdoch while writing his biography of the latter. The detail about Foot's childhood tuberculosis is recounted in Conradi's memoir, *Family Business: A Memoir* (Bridgend: Seren, 2019), 177.

2. Pauline Adams, *Somerville for Women* (Oxford: Oxford University Press, 1996), 164, (quoting a letter from Annie Rogers to Emily Penrose).

3. Adams, *Somerville for Women*, 163–165.

4. Mary Midgley, *The Owl of Minerva* (New York: Routledge, 2005), 76. I draw pervasively in this section and throughout this chapter on Midgley's delightful memoir and on personal interviews and correspondence with her.

5. Nina Bawden, *In My Own Time* (New York: Clarion, 1994), 63–64. The entire passage is priceless.

6. Midgley, *The Owl of Minerva*, 76.

7. Foot and Murdoch likewise showed themselves philosophers long before they discovered philosophy, securing their scholarships with fine general papers.

8. Conradi, *Iris*, 86.

9. Bawden, *In My Own Time*, 68.

10. Midgley, *The Owl of Minerva*, 77.

11. Conradi, *Iris*, 85–86.

12. Conradi, *Iris*, 84. I rely throughout the following section on Conradi's fourth chapter and Midgley's *Owl of Minerva*, as well as on conversation and correspondence with each of them.

13. Philippa Foot, "Iris Murdoch," in *Oxford Today* (Hilary Term 1999), 58.

14. Conradi, *Iris*, 82.

15. *Somerville College Report*, 1938–1939.

16. Christopher Hobhouse, *Oxford* (London: B.T. Batsford, 1939), 101.

17. Quoted in Conradi, *Iris*, 83. From a contribution to the *Badminton School Magazine*.

18. Midgley, *The Owl of Minerva*, 89.

19. Quoted in Conradi, *Iris*, 90. The words are those of Murdoch's intimate friend Frank Thompson.

20. Iris Murdoch to Ann Leech, April 1939, in *Living on Paper: Letters from Iris Murdoch, 1934-1995*, ed. Avril Horner and Anne Rowe, (London: Chatto & Windus, 2015), 10–11.

21. Hobhouse, *Oxford*, 102.

22. Midgley, *The Owl of Minerva*, 95.

23. Iris Murdoch to David Hicks, 1941, in *A Writer at War*, ed. Peter Conradi (London, Short Books, 2010), 187.

24. Conradi, *Iris*, 115.
25. Midgley, *The Owl of Minerva*, 97–98.
26. Mary Warnock, *A Memoir: People and Places* (London: Duckbacks, 2002), 40.
27. Aeschylus, *The Oresteia*, trans. Fagles (New York: Penguin, 1977), 109.
28. Midgley, *The Owl of Minerva*, 98.
29. Conradi, *Iris*, 122.
30. Midgley, *The Owl of Minerva*, 123.
31. Adams, *Somerville for Women*, 164.
32. Midgley, *The Owl of Minerva*, 123.
33. The Vienna Circle, *The Scientific Conception of the World* (1929), in *Empiricism and Sociology*, by Otto Neurath (Dordrecht, Holland: D. Reidel Publishing, 1973). Emphasis original.
34. A.J. Ayer, *Language, Truth and Logic* (Minneola: Dover, 1952), 33.
35. Ayer, *Language*, 35.
36. Ayer, *Language*, 107.
37. Michael Ignatieff, *Isaiah Berlin: A Life* (New York: Metropolitan, 1998), 84–85.
38. Donald MacKinnon, *A Study in Ethical Theory* (London: A. & C. Black, 1957), ch. 3.
39. Nineham's reminiscence is recorded in Conradi (*Iris*, 125). I draw below also on notes from Nineham and others in the Iris Murdoch archive at Kingston University, as well as from Conradi's synthetic account and from Midgley's *The Owl of Minerva* and Bawden's *In My Own Time*.
40. Midgley, *The Owl of Minerva*, 116.
41. Midgley, *The Owl of Minerva*, 117.
42. Conradi, *Iris*, 127.
43. Iris Murdoch to David Hicks, November 6, 1945, in *Living on Paper*, 256.
44. The description is from the recognizable portrait of her father in her Booker-winning novel, *The Sea, the Sea* (New York: Vintage, 1999), 30.
45. Iris Murdoch to Frank Thompson, January 29, 1942 in *Living on Paper*, 105.
46. Iris Murdoch to Frank Thompson, December 24, 1941 in *Living on Paper*, 102.
47. There is a document comparing the two in the staff archives at Somerville College (SC/AO/AA/FW/Anscombe). Writing a reference for Anscombe in 1946, Wykeham Professor of Logic H.H. Price highlighted two of her qualities especially: one, the depth of her knowledge of canonical philosophers ("much more thorough and extensive than is usual even among the best greats students"), and two, her "grasp of modern Symbolic Logic and of the rather difficult and subtle techniques of philosophical analysis which are associated with it." It was an unusual combination, he notes: "the only parallel I can think of is Mr. MacKinnon of Keble." All materials from the Somerville College Archives are used courtesy of the Principal and Fellows of Somerville College, Oxford.
48. Midgley, *The Owl of Minerva*, 113.

Chapter 3

1. The details in this section are drawn from a variety of sources: interviews with Anscombe's daughter Mary Geach Gormally, family friend Roger Teichmann, Mary Midgley, and Baroness Mary Warnock; materials from Anscombe's file in the St. Hugh's College archives; Jenny Teichman's memoir of Anscombe in the *Proceedings of the British Academy* 115 (2001), and Anscombe's own remarks in the introduction to Volume II of her *Collected Philosophical Papers* (Minneapolis: University of Minnesota Press, 1981).

2. Notes from an interview with Mary Mothersill, published in Amélie Okenberg Rorty, *The Many Faces of Philosophy* (Oxford: Oxford University Press, 2003), 502.

3. J.R.H. Moorman, *A History of the Church in England* (London: A & C Black, 1973), 391–392.

4. Mary Geach, "Introduction," in *Faith in a Hard Ground* (Exeter: Imprint Academic, 2008), xxi.

5. Anscombe dates her conversion to 1935 in her earliest known publication: "I am Sadly Theoretical: It is the Effect of being at Oxford," in *The Catholic Herald*, July 8, 1938. The essay was a response to a call for testimonials from young Catholics, articulating their hopes and fears for the future. The call went out the very day Anscombe was received into the Church. John Berkman recently unearthed and republished the essay, with illuminating commentary. See Berkman, "G.E.M. Anscombe's 'I am Sadly Theoretical: It is the Effect of being at Oxford' " (1938): A newly discovered article by Anscombe edited and with an editor's introduction," in *New Blackfriars* (September 2021).

6. Mary Midgley, *The Owl of Minerva* (New York: Routledge, 2005), 24. Midgley's memoir is my principal source in this section, supplemented by conversations and correspondence with her.

7. Midgley, *The Owl of Minerva*, 19.

8. Midgley, *The Owl of Minerva*, 23.

9. Midgley, *The Owl of Minerva*, 79–80.

10. Peter J. Conradi, *Iris* (New York: W.W. Norton, 2001). Childhood information on Murdoch is drawn from Conradi.

11. Quoted in Conradi, *Iris*, 33.

12. Conradi, *Iris*, 44.

13. Conradi, *Iris*, 59.

14. Conradi, *Iris*, 60.

15. Conradi, *Iris*, 66.

16. Conradi, *Iris*, 66.

17. Quoted in Conradi, *Iris*, 72.

18. Richard Overy, *The Morbid Age: Britain between the Wars* (London: Penguin 2010). The following discussion draws on Overy throughout.

19. Midgley, *The Owl of Minerva*, 83.
20. Midgley, *The Owl of Minerva*, 84.
21. Irish Nationalist Constance Markievicz had won a Dublin seat the year before, but unsurprisingly refused to take the Oath of Allegiance. Thus she never joined the Commons.
22. Not only the direct quotations but most of the other details adduced in the following paragraphs come from documents in Philippa Foot's papers at Somerville College. I have also drawn on conversation and correspondence with Peter Conradi, on correspondence with M.R.D. Foot (April 11, 2011) and on correspondence with Jan Hawthorn, friend of both Foot and her sister Marion.
23. Interview with Martin Gornall, SC/LY/SP/PF/10, Philippa Foot Papers, Somerville College Archives.
24. Friedrich Nietzsche, *Twilight of the Idols*, trans. Walter Kaufmann, "Maxims and Arrows," in *The Portable Nietzsche* (New York: Penguin, 1954), 467.
25. Journal entry for January 4, 1998, Foot Journals, SC/LY/SP/PF/3, Foot Papers, Somerville Archives.
26. Journal entry for December 5, 2000, SC/LY/SP/PF/6/1, Foot Papers, Somerville Archives.
27. Peter Conradi, conversation with author, March 10, 2011.
28. Philippa Bosanquet to Esther Bosanquet, undated, SC/LY/SP/PF/1/6e, Foot Papers, Somerville Archives.
29. Journal entry for August 5, 1996, SC/LY/SP/PF/6/1, in Foot Papers, Somerville Archives.
30. Tom and Mary story, SC/LY/SP/PF/3, Foot Papers, Somerville Archives.
31. Alex Voorhoeve, "The Grammar of Goodness: An Interview with Philippa Foot" in *The Harvard Review of Philosophy* XI (2003), 33.
32. Peter Conradi and Gavin Lawrence, "Professor Philippa Foot" (obituary), *The Independent*, October 19, 2010.
33. Voorhoeve, "The Grammar of Goodness," 33.
34. For richly detailed discussions of the formative influence of the Blackfriars community on Anscombe's thought and the background to her early pamphlet, "The Justice of the Present War Examined" (see below), see John Berkman, "Justice and Murder: The Background to Anscombe's 'Modern Moral Philosophy,'" in Roger Teichmann, ed., *The Oxford Handbook of Elizabeth Anscombe* (Oxford: Oxford University Press, 2022) and John Haldane, "Anscombe: Life, Action, and Ethics in Context," in *Philosophical News* 18 (June 2019), 45–75.
35. St. Hugh's College archive.
36. Evidently Anscombe did not tell her tutor what had happened. Indeed, she did not even tell one of her closest friends. Somervillian Jean Coutts (later Austin), in Anscombe's year and also reading Greats, was with her constantly.

She learned from me in 2012 that Anscombe's father had died in 1939. Coutts too lost her father in her undergraduate years; she said it would have been a comfort to talk with someone who understood what this meant. Whatever she thought or felt, Anscombe kept her loss private.

37. "The Justice of the Present War Examined." Anscombe's contribution is reprinted in G.E.M. Anscombe, *The Collected Philosophical Papers of G.E.M. Anscombe, Vol. 3: Ethics, Religion and Politics* (Minneapolis: University of Minnesota Press, 1981), 72–81.

38. The following term, MacKinnon tutored Anscombe once more. Though he remained impressed, he observed that "she would gain by being more tentative in her conclusions." Anscombe does not seem to have been as affected by MacKinnon as the three Somervillians were. She evidently worked hard for him, and in 1946 named him as a reference in a job application. But she does not mention him in her scattered reminiscences about her undergraduate years.

39. St. Hugh's College archive.

40. In Roger Teichmann, *The Philosophy of Elizabeth Anscombe* (Oxford, 2008), 3.

41. G.E.M. Anscombe, "Introduction," in *The Collected Philosophical Papers of G. E. M. Anscombe, Vol. 2: Metaphysics and the Philosophy of Mind* (Minneapolis: University of Minnesota Press, 1981), vii.

42. Anscombe, *Metaphysics and the Philosophy of Mind*, vii.

43. Anscombe, *Metaphysics and the Philosophy of Mind*, viii.

Chapter 4

1. I have drawn the specific details in this section from R.M. Hare, "A Philosophical Autobiography," in *Utilitas* 14, no. 3 (November 2002); from his son John Hare's "R.M. Hare: A Memorial Address" in the same issue, and from the "Postscript" to *An Essay in Monism*, the (unpublished) book Hare wrote while imprisoned. In "A Philosophical Autobiography," Hare singles out E.E. Dunlop, *The War Diaries of Weary Dunlop* (ed. New York: Penguin, 2010) as "the only completely truthful account of these experiences I have read" (from "A Philosophical Autobiography"). For general descriptions of conditions in the railway camps during these months, I have drawn on Dunlop. Groups of forced laborers were sent up from Singapore in waves in the spring of 1943. In his "Autobiography," Hare only says that he was sent to the railway camps that spring and was there about eight months. An Imperial Japanese Army record book, available at www.forces-war-records.co.uk, lists Hare and many others as having been sent "Overland" on May 17, 1943.

2. Hare, "Philosophical Autobiography," 282.

3. Hare, "Philosophical Autobiography," 282.

4. Hare, "Philosophical Autobiography," 281.

5. Archilochus, fragment, translated for the author by Morgan Flannery.

6. Sources for the following section include an obituary by Philippa Foot in the *Somerville College Report* (1999), 135–138; Conradi's biography of Murdoch, *Iris* (Norton, 2001); Midgley's memoir, *The Owl of Minerva* (Routledge, 2005); and letters and notebooks in Philippa Foot's papers in the Somerville College Archives.

7. Iris Murdoch to Marjorie Boulton, August 16, 1942, in *Living on Paper*, ed. Avril Horner and Anne Rowe (London: Chatto & Windus, 2015), 27.

8. Midgley, *The Owl of Minerva*, 134.

9. In Murdoch, *Living on Paper*, 30, 32.

10. In Murdoch, *Living on Paper*, 25.

11. Sometime late in the war, or perhaps after traveling to eastern Europe with the United Nations Relief and Rehabilitation Administration and seeing what the Soviets had done, Murdoch finally became disillusioned with communism. Around this time, she also began to explore Christianity. Her biographer Peter Conradi sees a connection, one faith displacing another. See *Iris Murdoch: A Life* (New York: W.W. Norton, 2001).

12. Philippa Bosanquet to Esther Bosanquet, undated, SC/LY/SP/PF/3, Foot Papers, Somerville Archives.

13. Nina Bawden, *In My Own Time* (New York: Clarion 1994), 71, 91.

14. Midgley, *The Owl of Minerva*, 123–124.

15. See Bawden, *In My Own Time*.

16. Mary Warnock, *A Memoir: People and Places* (London: Duckbacks, 2002), 42.

17. This profile of Ryle as "academic politician" is drawn from Hare's "A Philosophical Autobiography," and from conversations with Mary Midgley and Mary Warnock.

18. "Introduction" to *The Revolution in Philosophy* (London: Macmillan & Co, 1956).

19. Hare, "Philosophical Autobiography," 284.

20. Warnock, *A Memoir*, 49.

21. This anyway is how Murdoch and Scrutton's classics tutor, Mildred Hartley, recalled the topic in a May 15, 1969 letter to Somerville Principal Barbara Craig (Foot Staff File, SC/AO/AA/FW/Foot, Somerville College Archives, used by permission of Hartley's executor, Alan Poulter). Hartley was reminiscing on the occasion of Anscombe's and Foot's departures from Somerville about how she (Hartley) and a colleague had been on a university-wide committee in 1941, reviewing candidates for the Gilchrist studentship, and had independently converged on Anscombe as the best candidate.

22. What were Geach's objections? He never published them. In the pamphlet Anscombe co-authored with Norman Daniel, she argued that although there were just grounds for war, the British government had made clear that it would not refrain from unjust tactics: for example, from carpet bombing

German cities. It seems that Geach, too, thought that there were just grounds for war. As Anthony Kenny reports in his 2014 memoir of Geach in the *Proceedings of the British Academy*, Geach attempted unsuccessfully to join the Polish army.

23. Mary Geach Gormally, conversation with author, July 13, 2012.

24. In a 1946 letter, applying for a position at Bedford College, London, Anscombe mentions that she had received a grant from Newnham College, Cambridge, each of the previous two years. It was something, but cannot have been as valuable as the competitive Smithson studentship. (Box no. 10, File no. 370, Anscombe Papers, Collegium Institute)

25. Conradi, *Iris*, 283.

26. Letters from C.H.M. Waldock to Janet Vaughan (January 18, 1948), and from Vaughan back to Waldock (February 21, 1948), both in Anscombe's staff file in the Somerville College Archives (SC/AO/AA/FW/Anscombe). Quotations from the papers of Professor G.E.M. Anscombe are with the permission of the copyright holder Mrs. M.C. Gormally.

27. March 29, 1946 letter from Anscombe to Janet Vaughan, applying for the Fellowship, in the Mary Somerville Research Fellowship file (SC/AO/FS/MSRF) in the Somerville College Archives.

28. Warnock, *A Memoir*, 46.

29. A quip attributed to Frank Ramsay.

30. C.K. Ogden and I.A. Richards, *The Meaning of Meaning: A Study of the Influence of Language Upon Thought and of The Science of Symbolism*, 3rd ed. (London: Kegan Paul, Trench, Trubner, and Co., 1930), 149.

31. Warnock, *A Memoir*, 44.

32. R.M. Hare, "Postscript" to *An Essay in Monism* (unpublished manuscript, 1940–1945), typed manuscript. Reference 0.1, Philosophical Papers, held in the Hare Papers in the Balliol College Historic Collections. All quotations from Professor R.M. Hare's unpublished papers are used by permission of the copyright holder, Dr. John Hare.

33. Charles Stevenson, *Ethics and Language* (New Haven: Yale University Press, 1944), 21.

34. To adopt the preferred expression of Justin Tosi and Brandon Warmke, in their *Grandstanding: The Use and Abuse of Moral Talk* (Oxford: Oxford University Press, 2020). Tosi and Warmke's book highlights aspects of contemporary moral discourse that fit an emotivist analysis, in hopes of persuading readers to *reject* these ways of talking.

35. Readers of Alasdair MacIntyre's *After Virtue* (Notre Dame: Notre Dame University Press, 1981) will readily perceive how indebted I am to his analysis of emotivism. My debt to Charles Taylor's *Sources of the Self* (Cambridge, MA: Belknap, 1989) is subtler, but no less significant.

36. R.M. Hare, *The Language of Morals* (Oxford: Oxford University Press, 1952). The preceding several paragraphs are a summary of the principal doctrines of the book.

37. John Lucas, "A Memoir of Professor R.M. Hare, FBA," in *The Balliol College Annual Record* (2002).

38. Hare, "Philosophical Autobiography," 273.

39. Rugby School Report, Biographical and Autobiographical Materials, Hare Papers, Balliol College Historic Collections. Used by permission of Rugby School.

40. Lucas, "A Memoir of Professor R. M. Hare."

41. Hare, *The Language of Morals*, 69.

42. Hare, "Postscript" to *An Essay in Monism* (unpublished).

43. Catherine Hare, conversation with author, August 1, 2012.

44. William Shakespeare, *Othello*, Act I, scene iii, lines 190–191.

45. Hare, "Philosophical Autobiography," 272.

46. Midgley, *The Owl of Minerva*, 148.

47. Midgley, *The Owl of Minerva*, 147.

48. Julie Jack, conversation with author, July 2, 2012.

49. Janet Vaughan (?) to Philippa Foot, November 25, 1948. Foot Staff File, Somerville College Archives.

50. Journal 6, June 12, 1948, KUAS 202/1/6. Murdoch's journals are held at the Kingston University Archives. All quotations from Iris Murdoch's unpublished papers are used by permission of Kingston University.

51. Hare, "Philosophical Autobiography," 286.

52. Late in his career, Hare argued that the logic of moral language commits anyone who uses it unironically to utilitarian conclusions. He insisted, though, that these conclusions could be rationally avoided by talking differently. See *Moral Thinking* (Oxford: Oxford University Press, 1981), chapter 1.

Chapter 5

1. I draw in this opening section—indeed, throughout this chapter—on a variety of letters in two collections of Murdoch's letters, *A Writer at War* and *Living on Paper* (both cited previously), as well as on Peter Conradi's *Iris* (London: W.W. Norton, 2001). Concerning Murdoch's address in Brussels: written on the inside of the notebook I mention later, dated October 1945, is the inscription, "Iris Murdoch Brussels Rue Neuve." In her first letter from Brussels to her undergraduate friend Leo Pliatzky, she lists her "home address" as "c/o Agence Continentale et Anglaise, 32 Rue Picard," just west of the canal in Molenbeek.

The Agence was a travel agency, though, and appears from a later letter to have been appropriated as a local HQ for the UNRRA. The notebook address, though not precise, seems likely to have been correct at the time of writing.

2. Iris Murdoch to Leo Pliatzky, June 17, 1944, in *Living on Paper*, ed. Avril Horner and Anne Rowe (London: Chatto & Windus, 2015), 37.

3. Iris Murdoch to David Hicks, September 4, 1944, in *Living on Paper*, 38.

4. Iris Murdoch to Leo Pliatzky, October 30, 1945, in *Living on Paper*, 50.

5. Iris Murdoch to Leo Pliatzky, September 4, 1945, in *Living on Paper*, 47.

6. Iris Murdoch to David Hicks, September 16, 1945, in *A Writer at War*, ed. Peter Conradi (Short Books, 2010), 242.

7. W.H. Auden, *Collected Poems*, ed. Edward Mendelson (London: Vintage, 1991), 179.

8. Iris Murdoch to David Hicks, September 16, 1945 in *A Writer at War*, 237.

9. Iris Murdoch to David Hicks, September 16, 1945 in *A Writer at War*, 237.

10. Iris Murdoch to David Hicks, October 4, 1945 in *A Writer at War*, 244.

11. Iris Murdoch to Leo Pliatzky, October 30, 1945, in *Living on Paper*, 50.

12. Iris Murdoch to Leo Pliatzky, October 30, 1945, in *Living on Paper*, 50.

13. Iris Murdoch to David Hicks, November 3, 1945 in *A Writer at War*, 251. I have gathered incidental details about the talk from coverage in *La Lanterne* from October 23–25, 1945, from Catherine Lanneu, *L'inconnue Française* (Brussels: Peter Lang, 2008), 258–262, and from the testimony of another attendee, Jacques Taminaux. See "The Phenomenological Movement," in *Tradition and Renewal*, Vol. 3 (1993), 110.

14. A historiographical note: it is commonplace in sketches of Sartre's life, and of postwar existentialism, to cite the lecture Sartre gave at the Club Maintenant five days later as the unveiling of Sartre's great manifesto. The lecture was soon published as "Existentialism is a Humanism," and scholarly introductions routinely point to the Paris lecture as its origin. Perhaps the published version is closer to the text of the Paris lecture. But as Murdoch's notes show, the talk Sartre gave in Brussels was essentially the same, from the early comparison between Christian and atheistic existentialism to the "parable" (as Murdoch calls it in her notes) of the young man who approached Sartre for guidance.

15. Iris Murdoch, IML 682, Kingston University Archives.

16. Iris Murdoch, unpublished interview with Richard Wollheim, KUAS 6/6/4/5, Kingston University Archives.

17. Murdoch, "Midnight Hour," in *Adelphi*, January-March 1943, 62.

18. Iris Murdoch to David Hicks, January 25, 1946, in *A Writer at War*, 288.

19. Iris Murdoch to Philippa Foot, undated (probably early 1947), KUAS 100/1/9, Kingston University Archives.

20. Iris Murdoch to David Hicks, November 6, 1945, in *A Writer at War*, 254.

21. Philippa Foot, interview with Peter Conradi, 1998, KUAS6/4/2/1, audio file held by the Kingston University Archives.

22. Philippa Foot, interview with Peter Conradi, 1998, KUAS6/4/2/1, audio file held by the Kingston University Archives.

23. Iris Murdoch to David Hicks, November 6, 1945, in *A Writer at War*, 255.

24. Iris Murdoch to Philippa Foot, October 10, 1946, in *Living on Paper*, 83.

25. Iris Murdoch to Philippa Foot, undated, in *Living on Paper*, 85.

26. Newnham College Archives, AC/5/2/1.

27. It didn't make Murdoch's homecoming any easier that she and her father had argued over her decision to leave the UNRRA. The relief organization was steady employment. See Valerie Purton, *An Iris Murdoch Chronology* (New York: Palgrave Macmillan, 2007), 45.

28. Murdoch to David Hicks, November 6, 1945, in *Living on Paper*, 53.

29. She would later incorporate many observations from her three visits to Malling Abbey into her novel, *The Bell*.

30. Conradi, *Iris*, 243.

31. Newnham College Archives, AC/5/2/10.

32. Conradi, *Iris*, 258.

33. Iris Murdoch to Philippa Foot, undated, KUAS 100/1/27, Kingston University Archives.

34. Iris Murdoch to Philippa Foot, August 5, 1947, KUAS 100/1/24, Kingston University Archives.

35. Newnham College Archives, AC/5/2/10.

36. Newnham College Archives, AC/5/2/20.

37. Ved Mehta, *Fly and the Fly-Bottle* (Boston: Little Brown, 1962), 55.

38. Iris Murdoch, Journal 4, October 23, 1947, KUAS 202/1/4, Kingston University Archives.

39. Mehta, *Fly and the Fly-Bottle*, 55.

40. Ray Monk, *Wittgenstein: The Duty of Genius* (New York: Penguin, 1991), 260–261.

41. Ludwig Wittgenstein, *Philosophical Investigations*, section 12, 7.

42. Ludwig Wittgenstein, *Philosophical Investigations*, section 241, 88.

43. Mary Midgley, *The Owl of Minerva* (Routledge, 2005), 159.

44. Bernard Williams, *Ethics and the Limits of Philosophy* (Cambridge, MA: Harvard University Press, 1985), 218.

45. In a single-subject biography, more would have to be mentioned, including at least Raymond Queneau, Franz Steiner, and Elias Canetti. See Peter Conradi, *Iris* (London: W.W. Norton, 2001).

46. Iris Murdoch, Journal 4, July 25, 1947, KUAS 202/1/4, Kingston University Archives.

47. Iris Murdoch, Journal 7, June 15, 1949, KUAS 202/1/7, Kingston University Archives.

48. Iris Murdoch, Journal 6, December 13, 1948, KUAS 202/1/6, Kingston University Archives.

49. Iris Murdoch, Journal 6, December 13, 1948, KUAS 202/1/6, Kingston University Archives.

50. Iris Murdoch, Journal 9, February, 1959, KUAS 202/1/9, Kingston University Archives.

51. Iris Murdoch, Journal 6, December 12, 1948, KUAS 202/1/6, Kingston University Archives.

52. Anscombe Papers, Collegium Institute, box 6, no. 212.

53. Iris Murdoch, Journal 7, February 26, 1949, KUAS 202/1/7, Kingston University Archives.

54. Iris Murdoch, Journal 7, March 1, 1949, KUAS202/1/7, Kingston University Archives.

55. Elizabeth Anscombe and Peter Geach, interview with Peter Conradi, April 17, 1998, KUAS6/4/1/9 Iris Murdoch archive, Kingston University.

56. Iris Murdoch, "On 'God' and 'Good'" in *The Sovereignty of Good* (London: Routledge, 1970), 51–52.

57. Ayer, quoted in Iris Murdoch, "The Novelist as Metaphysician," in *Existentialists and Mystics*, ed. Peter Conradi (New York: Penguin, 1999), 105.

58. Murdoch, "The Novelist as Metaphysician," 105.

59. Iris Murdoch, "The Existentialist Hero," in *Existentialists and Mystics*, ed. Peter Conradi (New York: Penguin, 1999), 110.

60. Iris Murdoch, *Sartre: Romantic Rationalist* (New York: Viking, 1987), 111.

61. Murdoch "The Novelist as Metaphysician," 50.

62. "L'Angoisee, snobisme moderne," May 2, 1950, Murdoch, Talks File I, 1946-1962, BBC Written Archives Centre.

63. Iris Murdoch, "Metaphysics and Ethics," in *Existentialists and Mystics*, ed. Peter Conradi (New York: Penguin, 1999), 75.

64. "Under the net," that is, of language. One of Murdoch's abortive titles for the book gestures toward the billiard-ball picture that was on her mind throughout this period: "In Solemn Stillness All." The reference is to Joseph Addison's austere eighteenth-century Deist hymn, praising the Creator of a silent, lifeless mechanism.

65. *Living on Paper* 169–170.

66. Austin, "A Plea for Excuses" in *Philosophical Papers*, ed. J.O. Urmson and G.J. Warnock (Oxford: Oxford University Press, 1961), 123.

67. Austin, "A Plea for Excuses", 129.

68. Mehta, *The Fly and the Fly-Bottle*, 51.

69. Conradi, *Iris*, 302.

70. Mary Warnock, conversation with author, February 28, 2011.

71. Murdoch, "On 'God' and 'Good,'" 46.

72. Iris Murdoch to Raymond Queneau, undated, quoted in Conradi, *Iris*, 285.

Chapter 6

1. For more on this story, see either Fiona McCarthy, *Eric Gill* (London: Faber and Faber, 1989) or Malcolm Yorke, *Eric Gill: Man of Flesh and Spirit* (London: Constable, 1981), as well as one of their sources, longtime BBC producer D.G. Bridson's memoir, *Prospero and Ariel: The Rise and Fall of Radio* (London: Victor Gollancz, 1971), 41, from which the headmaster's quote is taken.

2. The two were involved with several of the same organizations for the promotion of Catholic social teaching, like the peace organization, Pax. Indeed, Gill was chair of the national Pax organization in 1939–40, during Anscombe's most intense period of engagement with the Oxford Pax group. John Berkman, who has gone more deeply than anyone into Anscombe's association with Pax, called this to my attention.

3. This tale is as well-confirmed as any. Nicholas Denyer related that he and some other graduate students at Cambridge were sitting around with Anscombe one day and began asking whether this or that legend was true: did she really take off her trousers in a Boston restaurant? "Oh, no, it was nothing like that!" she said. "It was a bar, and it was in Toronto!" (Nicholas Denyer, conversation with author, June 29, 2012).

4. A recording of her 1953 broadcast about the life and thought of her mentor Wittgenstein survives in the BBC Sound Archives ("Ludwig Wittgenstein," 9 July 1953, BBC Third Programme).

5. Rosalind Hursthouse, correspondence with author, September 6, 2012.

6. Roger Teichmann, conversation with author, July 24, 2012.

7. Thomas Aquinas, *Summa Theologiae* Part I, Question 16, Article 5. (Cincinnati: Benzinger Brothers, 1947)

8. G.E.M. Anscombe, "War and Murder," in *The Collected Philosophical Works of G.E.M. Anscombe, Vol. 3: Ethics, Religion, and Politics* (Minneapolis: Minnesota University Press, 1981), 61.

9. Conradi, *Iris*, 283.

10. G.E.M. Anscombe, "Introduction," in *The Collected Philosophical Works of G.E.M. Anscombe, Vol. 2: Metaphysics and the Philosophy of Mind* (Minnesota, 1981), viii.

11. Ludwig Wittgenstein, *Philosophical Investigations*, trans. G.E.M. Anscombe (London: Basil Blackwell, 1958), s. 115.

12. Wittgenstein, *Philosophical Investigations*, s. 309.

13. G.E.M. Anscombe, "Introduction," in *Metaphysics and the Philosophy of Mind*, viii–ix.

14. G.E.M. Anscombe, Wittgenstein notebook, Box no.7, Fle no. 529, Anscombe Papers, Collegium Institute.

15. Anthony Kenny, *Brief Encounters: Notes from a Philosopher's Diary* (London: SPCK, 2018), 91.

16. G.E.M. Anscombe, Wittgenstein notebook, Box no.7, File no. 529, Anscombe Papers, Collegium Institute.

17. Elizabeth Anscombe, "Ludwig Wittgenstein," July 9, 1953, BBC Third Programme, BBC Sound Archives.

18. Anscombe, notes on Wittgenstein, Box no. 7, File no. 259, Anscombe Papers, Collegium Institute. "Not house-trained" was Wittgenstein's dismissive verdict on Anscombe's abandoned doctoral thesis. Or this is what he said to her face. In her reminiscences about Wittgenstein, Anscombe appears to quote him characterizing her work as "shit on the floor," but adds that "not house-trained" was "how he put [it] to me." Luke Gormally suggested to me that "shit on the floor" was Anscombe's "translation" of Wittgenstein's more genteel remark. In any case, that was how she labeled the file where she stored the thesis. (Luke Gormally, correspondence with author, December 31, 2020).

19. Anscombe, "The Reality of the Past," in *Metaphysics and the Philosophy of Mind*, 114n.

20. Philippa Foot, "Obituary of Elizabeth Anscombe", *Somerville College Review* (2001), 120.

21. Kenny, *Brief Encounters*, 91.

22. Mary Warnock, *A Memoir: People and Places* (London: Duckbacks 2002), 65.

23. John Searle, "Oxford Philosophy in the 1950s," in *Philosophy* 90 (2015), 180.

24. Wittgenstein, *Philosophical Investigations*, section 66, 31.

25. Mary Warnock, *A Memoir*, 65.

26. Searle, "Oxford Philosophy in the 1950s," 184.

27. Warnock, *A Memoir*, 68.

28. Max Deutscher, "Some Reflections of Ryle and Remarks on His Notion of Negative Action," in *Australasian Journal of Philosophy* 60 (1982), 254.

29. Mehta, *Fly and the Fly-Bottle*, 62.

30. Geoffrey Warnock, "Saturday Mornings," in *Essays on J.L. Austin* (Oxford: Oxford University Press, 1973), 33.

31. Conversations with John Lucas ("negative," "frightening") (July 18, 2012) and Mary Midgley ("captious," "dismissive") (March 7, 2011).

32. John Lucas, conversation with author, July 18, 2012.

33. Anthony Kenny, conversation with author, July 12, 2012.

34. Iris Murdoch, *Sartre: Romantic Rationalist* (New York: Viking, 1987), 78–79.

35. Mary Warnock, *A Memoir*, 68.

36. For a fuller account of the debate and its aftermath, as well as relevant background information, see Christopher W. Mitchell, "University Battles: C.S. Lewis and the Oxford University Socratic Club," in *C.S. Lewis: Lightbearer in the Shadowlands*, ed. Menuge (Wheaton: Crossway, 1997), 329–352. My remarks on the origins of the Club draw on Mitchell's account, as well as from conversation with Jim Stockton.

37. Iris Murdoch, foreword to Stella Aldwinckle, *Christ's Shadow in Plato's Cave* (Oxford: Amate Press, 1990), 7.

38. C.S. Lewis, *Miracles* (London: Geofrey Bles, 1947). In the 1960 edition, the title was revised to "The Cardinal Difficulty of the Naturalist."

39. Elizabeth Anscombe to Ludwig Wittgenstein, February 3, 1948, Box no. 12, File no. 537, Anscombe Papers, Collegium Institute. The complete letter appears, together with several other newly available documents about the debate, in Jim Stockton and Benjamin J. B. Lipscomb, "The Anscombe-Lewis Debate: New Archival Sources Considered," in *Journal of Inklings Studies* 11.1 (April 2021), 35–57. Anscombe may have picked up her taste for vulgarity in Wittgenstein's circle, where it seems to have been part of a general atmosphere of "ruthless authenticity." No reminiscences from her undergraduate years recount her talking like this. By the late 1940s, though, it was part of her persona. Anscombe's daughter Mary Geach Gormally suggested to me that Anscombe's vocabulary was influenced by Fowler and Fowler's *The King's English*, with its counsel to "Prefer the Saxon word to the Romance." (Mary Geach Gormally, correspondence with author, July 24, 2020). I take the suggestion seriously, but don't think it explains enough. For one thing, Anscombe's crudities were as often Latinate ("bastard," "piss") as they were Germanic. Moreover, a preference for "shit" over "defecate" does not explain a penchant for bringing excrement into conversation in the first place.

40. Elizabeth Anscombe, "A Reply to Mr. C.S. Lewis's Argument that 'Naturalism' is Self-Refuting," in *Metaphysics and Philosophy of Mind*, 225.

41. Elizabeth Anscombe to Ludwig Wittgenstein, February 3, 1948, Box no. 12, File no. 537, Anscombe Papers, Collegium Institute.

42. A.N. Wilson contended in his biography of Lewis (London: W.W. Norton, 1990) that the experience put Lewis off Christian apologetics for good. Wilson went so far as to suggest that the chapter in Lewis's fantasy novel, *The Silver Chair*, in which the Green Lady bewitches Eustace and Jill, befuddling them until they no longer know how to defend obvious truths, is a recasting of the Socratic Club debate in the mode of nightmare. Critics of Wilson, like Alan Jacobs in *The Narnian* (New York: HarperCollins, 2005), observe that Lewis did plenty of apologetic writing after 1948, and side with Anscombe's own response to such legends: "I am inclined to construe the odd accounts of the matter by some of [Lewis's] friends . . . as an interesting example of the phenomenon called 'projection'" (introduction to *Metaphysics and the Philosophy of Mind*, x). But this doesn't show that Lewis wasn't humiliated. Nor does Anscombe's recollection that they had dinner together at a colleague's house a few weeks later, apparently without incident. All it shows is that Lewis could behave himself in the presence of someone who had vanquished him.

43. Mary Geach, "Introduction," in Mary Geach and Luke Gormally, eds., *From Plato to Wittgenstein: Essays by G.E.M. Anscombe* (Exeter: Imprint Academic, 2011), xiv.

44. Alex Voorhoeve, "A Mistrustful Animal: An Interview with Bernard Williams," in *Harvard Review of Philosophy*, 12 (2004), 81.

45. G.E.M. Anscombe, "Causality and Determination," in *Metaphysics and the Philosophy of Mind*, 146.

46. G.E.M. Anscombe, "Introduction," in *Metaphysics and Philosophy of Mind*, x.

47. Jenny Teichman, "Gertrude Elizabeth Margaret Anscombe, 1919-2001," in *Proceedings of the British Academy* 115 (2001), 34. Teichman attributes this expression to Anscombe and Geach. Mary Geach Gormally, though, attributes it to Bernard and Shirley Williams and denies that her parents used it (correspondence with author, December 13, 2020).

48. My descriptions of life at 27 St. John Street and of Anscombe's tutorial style are drawn from the published reminiscences already cited, by Anthony Kenny and John Searle, as well as from correspondence with Rosalind Hursthouse and Miranda Villiers and conversation and correspondence with Mary Geach Gormally. Also worth anyone's time is the newspaper profile mentioned below (Ann Chesney, "Don, philosopher, and happy mother of six" in *The Manchester Guardian*, June 1, 1959), which Rachael Wiseman drew to my attention.

49. Rosalind Hursthouse, correspondence with author, September 6, 2012.

50. Philippa Foot, "Obituary of Elizabeth Anscombe", *Somerville College Review* (2001), 120.

51. Michael Dummett, obituary in *The Tablet*, January 13, 2001.

52. Quoted in Conradi, *Iris*, 581.

53. John Searle, "Oxford Philosophy in the 1950s," 181.

54. John Carey, "Down with Dons," in *Original Copy* (London: Faber and Faber, 1987), 14.

55. John Searle, "Oxford Philosophy in the 1950s," 181.

56. Jenny Teichman, obituary in *The Independent*, January 10, 2001.

57. Jimmy Altham, conversation with author, July 31, 2012.

58. Rosalind Hursthouse, correspondence with author, September 6, 2012.

59. Obituary in *The Tablet*, January 13, 2001.

60. Jane O'Grady, obituary in *The Guardian*, January 10, 2001.

61. Rosalind Hursthouse notes that she could be gentler with inexperienced interlocutors, showing a nurturing interest in Hursthouse's Open University students when she visited their class one summer. If she judged that someone could handle brutal contradiction, though, she did not restrain herself. Conversation with author, March 19, 2012.

62. Mary Warnock, *A Memoir*, 68.

63. Jean Coutts Austin, conversation with author, July 13, 2012.

64. Isaiah Berlin to Anna Kallin, May 9, 1951, in Isaiah Berlin, *Enlightening: Letters 1946-1960*, ed. Hardy and Holmes (London: Chatto & Windus, 2009), 229. Berlin had not always felt this way about Anscombe, or anyway had not always discouraged the BBC from giving her a platform. According to a note in Anscombe's file at the BBC Written Archives Centre, he recommended in late 1950 that Kallin try to secure Anscombe as a broadcaster.

65. Mary Geach Gormally, conversation with author, July 13, 2012.

66. Iris Murdoch, Journal 6, December 13, 1948, KUAS 202/1/6, Kingston University Archives.

67. Midgley, *The Owl of Minerva*, 115-16.

68. If this conversation took place in late 1948 or early 1949, when Anscombe and Murdoch's friendship was at its most fraught, it adds a layer to the anecdote.

69. C.S. Lewis to Stella Aldwinckle, quoted in Mitchell, "University Battles: C.S. Lewis and the Oxford University Socratic Club."

70. Jim Stockton, who is writing a book on the Socratic Club, has a complete index of speakers. Though Anscombe went on attending, she was not a featured speaker between 1948 and when Lewis left Oxford in 1954.

71. Mary Midgley, correspondence with author, August 7, 2011.

72. Elizabeth Anscombe to Ludwig Wittgenstein, February 3, 1948, Box no. 12, File no. 537, Anscombe Papers, Collegium Institute.

73. Anscombe, "Mr. Truman's Degree," in *Ethics, Religion, and Politics*, 65. The minutes of the Hebdomadal Council, then the chief executive body of the University, record the Vice-Chancellor's proposal that if the protest seemed to be gaining traction, he should adjourn the meeting—but that the Council should do all in their power to make this unnecessary.

74. Anscombe, "Mr. Truman's Degree," in *Ethics, Religion, and Politics*, 65.

75. Anscombe, "Mr. Truman's Degree," in *Ethics, Religion, and Politics*, 70.

76. Anscombe, "War and Murder," in *Ethics, Religion, and Politics*, 61.

77. A.E. Harvey to Elizabeth Anscombe, July 18, 1956, BBC WAC RCONT3 Elizabeth Anscombe, BBC Written Archives Centre.

78. John Lucas, conversation with author, July 18, 2012.

79. As Anscombe wrote of P.H. Nowell-Smith in a letter to the editor of *The Listener* 1460 (March 21, 1957), 478.

80. Elizabeth Anscombe, "Does Oxford Moral Philosophy Corrupt Youth?," *The Listener* 1455 (February 14, 1957), 271.

81. Anscombe, "Does Oxford Moral Philosophy Corrupt Youth?," 266–267.

82. R.M. Hare, *Freedom and Reason* (Oxford: Clarendon Press, 1963), 2.

83. R.M. Hare, *The Language of Morals* (Oxford: Clarendon Press, 1952), 78.

84. Anscombe, "Does Oxford Moral Philosophy Corrupt Youth?", 267.

85. T.S. Gregory to Elizabeth Anscombe, December 5, 1956, BBC WAC RCONT3 Elizabeth Anscombe, BBC Written Archives Centre.

86. And they had ample reason to respond. In 1957, according to the annual *BBC Handbook*, *The Listener* averaged sales of more 120,000 copies per week.

87. G.E.M. Anscombe, Letter to the Editor, *The Listener* 1457, (February 28, 1957), 349.

88. T. A. Burkill, Letter to the Editor, *The Listener* 1459, (March 14, 1957), 427.

89. Anscombe, "Does Oxford Moral Philosophy Corrupt Youth?," 267.

90. G.E.M. Anscombe, Letter to the Editor, *The Listener* 1457, (February 28, 1957), 349.

91. R.M. Hare, Letter to the Editor, *The Listener* 1456 (February 21, 1957), 311.

92. R.M. Hare to T.S. Gregory, January 17, 1957, BBC WAC RCONT1 R M Hare Talks File 1, 1951-1962, BBC Written Archives Centre.

93. R.M. Hare to T.S. Gregory, February 6, 1957, BBC WAC RCONT1 R M Hare Talks File 1, 1951–1962, BBC Written Archives Centre.

94. Elizabeth Anscombe to T.S. Gregory, undated, BBC WAC RCONT3 Elizabeth Anscombe, BBC Written Archives Centre.

95. G.E.M. Anscombe, Letter to the Editor, *The Listener* 1459 (March 14, 1957), 427.

96. T.S. Gregory to Elizabeth Anscombe, March 7, 1957, BBC WAC RCONT3, Elizabeth Anscombe BBC Written Archives Centre.

97. The timing fits. "Modern Moral Philosophy" appeared in the January 1958 issue of *Philosophy*. The editor would likely have worked a couple of issues ahead, so the article was probably submitted by late spring. When it first appeared, it contained a footnote explaining that it had initially been delivered to the Voltaire Society, a then-popular venue for discussions among Oxford outsiders: a more secular Socratic. (For more on the Voltaire Society, see John Haldane, "Anscombe: Life, Action and Ethics in Context," in *Philosophical News* (2019).) The talk that was to become "Modern Moral Philosophy" was probably delivered in late winter or early spring, then: just after Anscombe's second script was rejected. Moreover, "Modern Moral Philosophy" contains numerous one-liners reminiscent of her first script. It reads in places like a broadcast talk.

98. Many Hume scholars now reject this way of interpreting Hume. See, for instance, Annette Baier, "Hume's Own 'Ought' Conclusions," in Pigden, ed., *Hume on Is and Ought* (Basingstoke, England: Palgrave Macmillan, 2010), 49–64. But I am concerned with "the history of effects." The target of Anscombe's attack was what we could call the "received reading" of Hume: received particularly in mid-twentieth-century England.

99. David Hume, *A Treatise of Human Nature*, Book III, Part I, Section I, (Garden City, NY: Dover Publications 2003).

100. G.E.M. Anscombe, Letter to the Editor, *The Listener* 1462 (April 4, 1957), 564.

101. G.E.M. Anscombe, "Modern Moral Philosophy," in *Ethics, Religion, and Politics*, 26.
102. Microfilm script, discussion on "The Sanctity of Life and the Criminal Law," July 10, 1958, BBC Written Archives Centre.
103. G.E.M. Anscombe, "Introduction," in *Ethics, Religion, and Politics*, vii.

Chapter 7

1. This vignette is based on conversation and correspondence with colleagues and students of Foot's, including Lesley Brown, Gaby Charing, Miriam Griffin, Rosalind Hursthouse, and Julie Jack, but above all Barbara Harvey.
2. Barbara Harvey, correspondence with author, July 24, 2011.
3. Gaby Charing, quoting another student, unpublished memoir.
4. Gaby Charing, unpublished memoir.
5. Rosalind Hursthouse, correspondence with author, January 19, 2012.
6. Mary Midgley, *The Owl of Minerva*, 125.
7. Or it *was*. The room has recently been refurbished.
8. Foot described these afternoon discussions both in a September 19, 2000 interview with Jonathan Ree on BBC Radio 3 and in her obituary for Elizabeth Anscombe in the *Somerville College Report* (2001), 120.
9. Philippa Foot, journal entry for July 28, 2001, SC/LY/SP/PF/6/1, with notes toward a BBC Woman's Hour profile on Anscombe, Foot Papers, Somerville College Archives.
10. There are conflicting reports about whether Foot was invited to Austin's Saturday mornings. In a late interview, she said that women were excluded. But Mary Warnock attended and recalled Foot being there too. It is noteworthy that no women appear in any of the stories that have come down about Austin's "playgroup" (as it was also called). Perhaps Foot received an invitation but, out of loyalty to Anscombe, (mostly) stayed away. Neither Anscombe nor Murdoch were invited.
11. Barbara Harvey, conversation with author, June 22, 2012.
12. Miranda Villiers, correspondence with author, July 12, 2012.
13. M.R.D. Foot, *Memories of an SOE Historian* (Barnsley: Pen & Sword Military, 2009), 124.
14. Peter Conradi, *Iris* (New York: Norton, 2001), 169.
15. Mary Warnock, *A Memoir* (London: Duckbacks, 2002), 52.
16. Alex Voorhoeve, "The Grammar of Goodness: An Interview with Philippa Foot," *Harvard Review of Philosophy* XI (2003), 33.
17. Philippa Foot, interview with Martin Gornall, SC/LY/SP/PF/10, Philippa Foot Papers, Somerville College Archives.

18. Philippa Foot, "Moral Arguments," in *Virtues and Vices* (New York: Oxford University Press, 2002), 102–103.

19. In 1948 and 1963, at least. Foot Staff File, Somerville College Archives.

20. In my discussion of Foot's involvement with Oxfam, I draw on several documents in the Philippa Foot Papers at Somerville, above all on her lengthy interview with Martin Gornall, SC/LY/SP/PF/10.

21. Interview with Martin Gornall, SC/LY/SP/PF/10, Philippa Foot Papers, Somerville College Archives.

22. Interview with Martin Gornall, SC/LY/SP/PF/10, Philippa Foot Papers, Somerville College Archives.

23. Philippa Foot to Janet Vaughan, January 27, 1947, SC/AO/AA/FW/Anscombe, in Anscombe Staff File, Somerville College Archive.

24. They may both have been applying for the Mary Somerville Research Fellowship. Anscombe's first term was ending that spring, and Foot, as we saw, was seeking more support so that she could begin to write without compromising her and Michael's domestic future.

25. Gilbert Ryle to Janet Vaughan, November 10, 1948, SC/AO/AA/FW/Anscombe, in Anscombe Staff File, Somerville College Archives.

26. If there is any figure with whom Foot would have been associated in the first half-decade of her career, it wouldn't have been Aristotle or Wittgenstein, but rather Kant. In the Fall of 1949, when Foot debuted as a lecturer in Schools, her topic was "Some Problems in Kantian Philosophy." And in Murdoch's journals from the late 1940s, when she recounted a philosophical conversation with Foot, the subject was almost always Kant.

27. John Campbell, correspondence with author, September 4, 2011.

28. As we saw in chapter 4, Hare, too, was interested early on in "thick" concepts, like "friend." In a journal entry for January 28, 1950, Murdoch recounts a talk in which Hare tried to "steer bet[ween] intuitionism, emotionism & naturalism," arguing that "Good is both descriptive & evaluative." KUAS 202/1/7.

29. Voorhoeve, "The Grammar of Goodness," 34.

30. Voorhoeve, "The Grammar of Goodness," 34–35.

31. Voorhoeve, "The Grammar of Goodness," 35.

32. Philippa Foot, *Natural Goodness* (Oxford: Clarendon Press, 2001), 1.

33. R.M. Hare, *The Language of Morals* (Oxford: Clarendon Press, 1952), 69.

34. Supplement to the *Proceedings of the Aristotelian Society* 28, (1954), 97.

35. Supplement to the *Proceedings of the Aristotelian Society* 28, (1954), 105.

36. It seems likeliest that she took her sabbatical in Michaelmas term. The *Somerville College Report* for 1957 (covering events through December 1957), notes that Foot "has been working in Oxford on philosophical problems." That isn't conclusive, as all three of the College's 1957 sabbaticals are described in the same tense. But Michaelmas was the only term in which Foot did not lecture.

37. Voorhoeve, "The Grammar of Goodness," 35.

38. Mary Geach Gormally, conversation with author, July 13, 2012. Anscombe's approach to Aquinas is reminiscent of Kierkegaard's approach to Kant. Confronting his Hegelian contemporaries, most of them arrogantly convinced that they had transcended Kant, Kierkegaard deployed Kantian ideas throughout his writings, but almost never mentioned Kant by name. See Ronald M. Green, *Kierkegaard and Kant: The Hidden Debt* (Albany: State University of New York Press, 1992). It is possible that Anscombe would have recognized and welcomed this comparison. In her reminiscences on Wittgenstein, she mentions conversations between them about Kierkegaard and his method of "indirect communication."

39. An undated letter from Anscombe to Foot, preserved in Foot's papers at Somerville, conveys the intensity of their conversations about Aquinas: "It is evident that 'material object' means what we thought. From the Q.D. De Veritate [Disputed Questions on Truth]—But no, I'll bring it round! . . . It might be useful to refer to Intention p. 65 . . . to elucidate St. Thos. use of 'material object' . . . or to use St. Thos. to elucidate me!" (file ID SC/LY/SP/PF/12).

40. Voorhoeve, "The Grammar of Goodness," 35.

41. Philippa Foot, "Immoralism," BBC Third Programme, September 22, 1957.

42. Foot, "Moral Arguments," 103.

43. Foot, "Moral Beliefs," in *Virtues and Vices* (New York: Oxford University Press, 2002), 114–115.

44. Foot, "Moral Beliefs," 115.

45. Foot, "Moral Arguments," 107.

46. Miriam Griffin studied with Foot in the late 1950s (later, they became colleagues); her husband Jasper studied with Hare. Miriam deputized Jasper to ask Hare questions that were really Foot's, and vice-versa. Conversation with author, July 23, 2012.

47. Rosalind Hursthouse, conversation with author, March 19, 2012.

48. Anthony Kenny, conversation with author, March 19, 2011.

49. Foot, "Immoralism," BBC Third Programme, September 22, 1957.

50. Mary Warnock, conversation with author, February 28, 2011.

51. Mary Warnock, *A Memoir*, 50.

52. Philippa Foot, interview with Jonathan Ree, *Twenty Minutes—Philosophical Lives*, BBC Radio 3, September 19, 2000.

53. Conradi, *Iris*, 174.

54. Philippa Foot to Elizabeth Anscombe, February 19, 1964, Box 14, File 580, Anscombe Papers, Collegium Institute.

55. Peter Conradi, conversation with author, July 20, 2012.

56. Iris Murdoch, Journal 7, October 31, 1949, KUAS 202/1/7, Kingston University Archives.

57. Foot to Vaughan, November 1957, SC/AO/AA/FW/Anscombe, Anscombe Staff File, Somerville College Archives.
58. Philippa Foot to R.M. Hare, March 24, 1959, in R.M. Hare Papers, Balliol College archives.
59. M.R.D. Foot, *Memories of an SOE Historian*, 130.
60. Miriam Griffin, conversation with author, July 23, 2012.
61. The letter is undated. Out of touch and outside Oxford, Murdoch seems not to have learned of the Foots' separation for several weeks. She records it in her journal on April 29: "Pip & Michael are parting. This was almost incredible news. I had thought of them as so indissolubly connected–& somehow of that part of my history concerning them as . . . ended. (How immediately one falls into egoism.) I feel extremely disturbed. . . . An extraordinary sense of time rolling backward. And honestly a certain sense of relief at the removal of the barrier between P & me which M. constituted. I wrote at once to P. saying I sent my old love–& she replied quickly saying this meant a lot." (Journal 9, Kingston University Archives, KUAS202/1/9).
62. Iris Murdoch to Philippa Foot, KUAS100/1/37; drawing (on postcard), Murdoch to Foot, KUAS100/1/38.
63. Foot Papers, SC/LY/SP/PF/3, Somerville College Archives.
64. Foot, "Moral Beliefs," 129.
65. Philippa Foot, "Morality as a System of Hypothetical Imperatives," in *Virtues and Vices* (New York: Oxford University Press, 2002), 167.
66. Philippa Foot, "The Problem of Abortion and the Doctrine of the Double Effect," in *Virtues and Vices* (New York: Oxford University Press, 2002).

Chapter 8

1. The opening section draws on Mary Midgley's memoir, *The Owl of Minerva* (New York: Routledge, 2005), but also and especially on conversation and correspondence with her middle son, David Midgley. There is some imaginative reconstruction in the vignette about the broken windowpanes, but I have checked the results with David to make sure it doesn't contradict his memory. Source-confirmed details: the time of day, everyone's locations in the house, David's destruction of the two windowpanes with an arch-shaped block, the overheard dialogue on the homemade radio, the way the boys talked as young children.
2. Geoffrey Midgley collaborated in designing the radar systems that helped hold off the Luftwaffe in the Battle of Britain.
3. Mary Scrutton, "On Being Reformed," *The Listener* 1428, 196.
4. Mary Midgley to Anna Kallin, undated, BBC Written Archives Centre RCONT1, Mary Scrutton Talks File 1, 1942-1962, BBC Written Archives Centre.

5. Mary Midgley, *The Owl of Minerva* (New York: Routledge, 2005), 188.

6. Midgley, *The Owl of Minerva*, 189.

7. David Edmonds, *Would You Kill the Fat Man?* (Princeton: Princeton University Press, 2014).

8. *Radio Times* 1707 (July 27, 1956), 36.

9. Iris Murdoch, Journal 6, June 12, 1948, KUAS 202/1/6. Kingston University Archives.

10. Midgley, *Beast and Man: The Roots of Human Nature* (London: Routledge 2002), xxxv.

11. Midgley, *Utopias, Dolphins, and Computers: Problems in Philosophical Plumbing* (London: Routledge, 1996), 1–14. Foot later began using the same comparison.

12. Some readers of Murdoch will be surprised at my linking her to such a project, given the wistful fascination with which she wrote, starting in the 1960s, about the Platonic Idea of Goodness. There are crucial differences between her vision and Anscombe's, Foot's, or Midgley's. And the contribution she made to their work—her *diagnosis*—would stand, even if she had opposed their Aristotle-inspired reflections. But the affinity between them goes deeper. Consider one of the main points in Murdoch's attack on Sartrian existentialism: that it does not take seriously enough our nature and its *inertia*. What does she recommend instead? An inquiry into our nature and its defects, and into the techniques of attention and habituation that might assist us in overcoming these defects. In one of her later essays, she praises Freud for appreciating the mechanism of the human psyche, and suggests that for anyone who takes Freud's point, the question is how to reorient and purify our psychic energies "in such a way that when moments of choice arrive we shall be sure of acting rightly." See "On 'God' and 'Good,'" in *The Sovereignty of Good*. Or see "Metaphysics and Ethics" in *Existentialists and Mystics*—in which Murdoch repeatedly contrasts her own view with what she calls "anti-naturalism." I do not want to overstate the affinity between Murdoch and her friends. Murdoch makes no positive use of Aristotle in her philosophy, in marked contrast to Anscombe, Foot, and Midgley. But neither did her friends have to reject anything she had said, in developing their Aristotle- and Aquinas-inspired thoughts. And as I will show, Murdoch was enthusiastically supportive of Midgley's project as it emerged. I am grateful to Kieran Setiya for pressing me on this. I suspect I have not satisfied him, but his objection made me think harder.

13. Midgley, *The Owl of Minerva*, 162.

14. Jane Heal, conversation with author, July 31, 2012.

15. Midgley, *The Owl of Minerva*, 161.

16. Midgley, *The Owl of Minerva*, 168.

17. Midgley, "The Month," *The Twentieth Century* 156 (May 1959), 507.

18. Jane Heal, conversation with author, July 31, 2012.

19. Mary Scrutton to Anna Kallin, December 29, 1951, BBC Written Archives Centre. RCONT1, Mary Scrutton Talks File 1, 1942-1962, BBC Written Archives Centre.

20. Jane Heal, conversation with author, July 31, 2012.

21. David Midgley, correspondence with author, August 3, 2020.

22. Mary Scrutton to Anna Kallin, August 5, 1961, BBC Written Archives Centre RCONT1, Mary Scrutton Talks File 1, 1942-1962, BBC Written Archives Centre.

23. Midgley, *The Owl of Minerva*, 195.

24. Mary Midgley, "A Letter to Posterity," *The Listener*, March 27, 1952, 510.

25. Mary Midgley, "A Letter to Posterity," *The Listener*, March 27, 1952, 510.

26. Mary Midgley, "A Letter to Posterity," *The Listener*, March 27, 1952, 510.

27. This began with her unfinished thesis on Plotinus. Recollecting later, Midgley praised Plotinus for his attempt "to find a wider, more inclusive perspective which could bring together" the physical and the spiritual. Midgley, *The Owl of Minerva* (New York: Routledge, 2005), 157.

28. Mary Scrutton to Anna Kallin, July 17, 1952, BBC Written Archives Centre RCONT1, Mary Scrutton Talks File 1, 1942-1962, BBC Written Archives Centre.

29. I am grateful to Mary Midgley for lending me this script and for permission to quote it. "Rings and Books," unpublished radio script, MID/C/3, Mary and Geoff Midgley Papers, Durham University Library and Collections.

30. Anna Kallin to Mary Scrutton, June 16, BBC Written Archives Centre RCONT1, Mary Scrutton Talks File 1, 1942-1962, BBC Written Archives Centre.

31. Midgley, "Bishop Butler: A Reply," *The Twentieth Century* 152, no. 95 (July 1952), 61.

32. Interview with Jonathan Ree, *Twenty Minutes—Philosophical Lives*, BBC Radio 3, September 19, 2000.

33. Midgley, *The Owl of Minerva*, 159.

34. Mary Midgley, "Newcastle: Comments on a Case History," *The Twentieth Century* 59 (February, 1956), 160.

35. Midgley, "Newcastle: Comments on a Case History," 160–161.

36. Midgley, "Newcastle: Comments on a Case History," 161–162.

37. Midgley, *The Owl of Minerva*, 188.

38. Stewart Sutherland, "Donald Mackenzie MacKinnon," *Proceedings of the British Academy* 97 (1998), 3830–3834.

39. Ernest Gellner, "Reflections on Linguistic Philosophy—I," *The Listener* 1480 (August 8, 1957), 205–207.

40. If Gellner thought he was disagreeing with Anscombe: he wasn't. Anscombe's thesis, as we saw in chapter 6, was that Oxford moral philosophy merely channeled the spirit of the age.

41. Ernest Gellner, "Reflections on Linguistic Philosophy—II," *The Listener* 1481 (August 15, 1957), 240.

42. Murdoch's review, "Words and Ideas," appeared in Volume 27, Number 2 (Spring 1960) of *The Partisan Review*, 348–353. The two other epithets are quoted in T.P. Uschanov, "The Strange Death of Ordinary Language Philosophy," June, 2006, https://www.mv.helsinki.fi/home/tuschano/writings/strange/. Uschanov's paper is the most in-depth discussion one could wish of the Gellner affair and its consequences for Austin's legacy.

43. Mehta, *Fly and the Fly-Bottle* (Little, Brown, 1962), 13–14.

44. Gellner, "Reflections on Linguistic Philosophy—II," 240.

45. Midgley, *The Owl of Minerva*, 118.

46. *Beyond the Fringe*, at https://www.youtube.com/watch?v=KUd1OxPbKk4, beginning at 32:45.

47. "The Moral Philosopher's Job," BBC Third Programme, broadcast January 19, 1955.

48. Midgley, *Beast and Man*, xii.

49. Mary Scrutton to Anna Kallin, October 7, 1951, BBC Written Archives Centre RCONT1, Mary Scrutton Talks File 1, 1942-1962, BBC Written Archives Centre.

50. Mary Midgley, "The Concept of Beastliness," *Philosophy* 48, no. 184 (April, 1973), 114.

51. Midgley, *The Owl of Minerva*, 191.

52. Midgley, *Beast and Man*, xxxiii.

53. Midgley, *Beast and Man*, 50-2.

54. Charles Darwin, *The Descent of Man* (Princeton, NJ: Princeton University Press, 1981), 71–72.

55. Midgley, *Beast and Man*, 248.

56. Helmut Gollwitzer, Käthe Kuhn, and Reinhold Schneider, eds., *Dying We Live: The Final Messages and Records of the Resistance* (New York: Pantheon, 1956), 51.

57. Foot, *Natural Goodness* (Oxford: Clarendon, 2001), 10.

58. Midgley, *Beast and Man*, 251.

59. Midgley, *Beast and Man*, 249.

60. Midgley, "The Concept of Beastliness," 113.

61. W. David Solomon, conversation with author, May 27, 2014.

62. Andrew Brown. "Mary, Mary, Quite Contrary," *The Guardian*, January 13, 2001.

63. Midgley, *Beast and Man*, xxxiv.

64. Peter Conradi, correspondence with author, November 19, 2010.

65. Rosalind Hursthouse, conversation with author, September 6, 2012.

66. Midgley, "Newcastle: Comments on a Case History," 162.

67. Mary Midgley, correspondence with author, June 27, 2014.

68. Iris Murdoch to Mary Midgley, undated, MID/E/60, in the Mary and Geoff Midgley Papers at the Durham University Library and Collections.

69. Iris Murdoch to Philippa Foot, July 28, 1978 in *Living on Paper*, ed. Horner and Rowe (London: Chatto & Windus, 2015), 459.

Chapter 9

1. Iris Murdoch, "Metaphysics and Ethics," in *Existentialists and Mystics*, 75.

2. Alasdair MacIntyre, *After Virtue*, 3rd ed. (Notre Dame, IN: Notre Dame University Press, 2007).

3. Andrew Brown, "Mary, Mary, Quite Contrary," *The Guardian*, January 13, 2001.

4. As usual, background details on Midgley's life are drawn from conversation with her and her son, and on her memoir, *The Owl of Minerva* (New York: Routledge, 2005).

5. Mary Midgley, *Beast and Man* (London: Routledge, 1995), 92–93.

6. Midgley, *Beast and Man*, xvi.

7. Midgley, *Beast and Man*, 99.

8. J. L. Mackie, "The Law of the Jungle," *Philosophy* 53 (October, 1978).

9. As she would write: "in the absence of a serious and realistic psychology of motive, people will clutch at straws. Moral philosophers, in particular, have so thoroughly and deliberately starved themselves of the natural facts needed to deal with their problems that many of them are reduced to a weak state in which they lack resistance to even the most obvious absurdities" Mary Midgley, "Gene-Juggling," *Philosophy* 54 (October, 1979), 458n.

10. Midgley, "Gene-Juggling," 439.

11. Midgley, "Gene-Juggling," 449.

12. Richard Dawkins, "In Defense of Selfish Genes," *Philosophy* 56, (October, 1981), 556. It did not help that a journalist who spoke with Midgley and Dawkins about the *contretemps* reported to Dawkins—falsely—that Midgley hadn't read his book. (What Midgley *said* was that she hadn't read the book until well after it appeared.) When Midgley learned that Dawkins had been told this and was spreading it around, she wrote to him to clarify. He apologized. They met only once, years later—crossing paths in a stairwell. They had a brief, amicable exchange.

13. He was aggravated too by Midgley's most insulting remarks. For example, "Up till now, I have not attended to Dawkins, thinking it unnecessary to break a butterfly upon a wheel" ("Gene-Juggling," 458n).

14. Mary Midgley, "Selfish Genes and Social Darwinism," *Philosophy* 58 (July, 1983), 365.

15. Richard Dawkins, *The Selfish Gene* (Oxford: Oxford University Press, 1976), 3.

16. Midgley, *Beast and Man*, 124.

17. Except as noted, details of Murdoch's life are drawn from Peter Conradi's *Iris* (New York: Norton, 2001) and Valerie Purton's *An Iris Murdoch Chronology* (New York: Palgrave Macmillan, 2007).

18. Conradi, *Iris*, 476.

19. David Morgan, *With Love and Rage* (London: Kingston University Press, 2010).

20. Morgan, *With Love and Rage*, 143.

21. Murdoch, "On 'God' and 'Good'," in *The Sovereignty of Good* (London: Routledge, 1970), 56.

22. Murdoch, "The Sovereignty of Good Over Other Concepts," in *The Sovereignty of Good* (London: Routledge, 1970), 84.

23. Murdoch, "The Sublime and the Good," in *Existentialists and Mystics*, ed. Peter Conradi (New York: Penguin, 1997), 215.

24. Murdoch, "The Idea of Perfection," in *The Sovereignty of Good* (London: Routledge, 1970), 17–18.

25. Peter J. Conradi, *Family Business: A Memoir* (Bridgen, Wales: Seren Books, 2019), 181.

26. Conradi, *Family Business*, 181.

27. Conradi, *Family Business*, 181.

28. Iris Murdoch, Journal 10, October 27, 1969, KUAS 202/1/10, Kingston University.

29. Iris Murdoch, Journal 10, December 9, 1967, KUAS 202/1/10, Kingston University.

30. Iris Murdoch, Journal 10, May 18, 1968, KUAS 202/1/10, Kingston University.

31. Iris Murdoch to Philippa Foot, early May 1968, in Anne Rowe and Avril Horner, eds., *Living on Paper* (Chatto & Windus, 2015), 363.

32. Iris Murdoch, Journal 10, October 5, 1968, KUAS 202/1/10, Kingston University.

33. Iris Murdoch, Journal 10, May 3, 1968, KUAS 202/1/10, Kingston University.

34. Peter Conradi passed along to me a copy of the handout he received, accompanying the lectures.

35. Iris Murdoch to Philippa Foot, January 7. 1982, in *Living on Paper*, 489.

36. Iris Murdoch to Philippa Foot, April 20, 1982, in *Living on Paper*, 490.

37. Conradi, *Family Business*, 86.

38. Murdoch, "*Sein und Zeit*: Pursuit of Being" from *Heidegger*, in Justin Broakes, ed., *Iris Murdoch: Philosopher* (Oxford: Oxford University Press, 2012), 94.

39. Murdoch, "On 'God' and 'Good'," 74.

40. Anthony Kenny, conversation with author, March 18, 2011.

41. Iris Murdoch, *The Sea, The Sea* (London: Vintage Books, 1999), 512.

42. Conradi, *Iris*, 589.

43. Conradi, *Iris*, 588.

44. Iris Murdoch, Journal 15, KUAS202/1/15, Kingston University Archives.

45. Midgley, *The Owl of Minerva*, 85–86.

46. Peter Conradi, conversation with author, July 20, 2012.

47. Lesley Brown, conversation with author, March 2011.

48. For a deep, nuanced discussion of Anscombe's unfolding thought on the concept of murder, see John Berkman, "Justice and Murder: The Background to Anscombe's 'Modern Moral Philosophy'," in Roger Teichmann, ed., *The Oxford Handbook of Elizabeth Anscombe* (Oxford: Oxford University Press, 2022).

49. Anscombe, "Introduction," in *Ethics, Religion and Politics*. (Minneapolis: University of Minnesota Press, 1981), viii.

50. Murdoch did send Anscombe tickets to her second play, *The Three Arrows*, which debuted in Cambridge in 1972 (Elizabeth Anscombe and Peter Geach, interview with Peter Conradi, April 17, 1998, Iris Murdoch archive, Kingston University).

51. Foot referenced the case in her famous article on abortion, the one in which she also introduced the first trolley case. See "The Problem of Abortion and the Doctrine of the Double Effect," in *Virtues and Vices* (New York: Oxford University Press, 2002), 21.

52. Philippa Foot, journal entry for October 29, 1972, SC/LY/SP/PF/6/1, Foot Papers, Somerville College Archives.

53. Nicholas Denyer, conversation with author, June 29, 2012.

54. Teichman, Jenny. "Gertrude Elizabeth Margaret Anscombe," *Proceedings of the British Academy* 115 (2001), 37–38.

55. Jimmy Altham, conversation with author, July 31, 2012. Altham had the story from a mutual colleague.

56. Luke 14:26, New Jerusalem Bible, (Garden City, NY: Doubleday 1985).

57. Nicholas Denyer, conversation with author, June 29, 2012.

58. Bernard Williams and Michael Tanner, *The Human World* 9 (November 1972), 42–48.

59. G.E.M. Anscombe, in *The Human World* 9 (November 1972), 48–51.

60. Philippa Foot, journal entries, December 5, 2000 and January 10, 2001, SC/LY/SP/PF/6/1, Philippa Foot Papers, Somerville College Archives.

61. Gaby Charing, conversation with author, May 14, 2020. It is worth noting that Anscombe was badly injured the year before in a car accident. Anthony Kenny, who had by then been named one of Wittgenstein's literary executors, recalled that she was not the same afterward. But it was in character for Anscombe to turn on a friend like this over a conflict of convictions. Kenny himself, for instance: when he left the priesthood and then married without a papal dispensation, Anscombe told him, "our dearest wish for you must be that you will be desperately unhappy in your marriage." They scarcely spoke for the next three decades. (Kenny, *Brief Encounters*, 94.)

62. Philippa Foot, journal entry for January 10, 2001, SC/LY/SP/PF/6/1, Foot Papers, Somerville College Archives.

63. Journal entries for July 27-28, 2001. SC/LY/SP/PF/6/1, Foot Papers, Somerville College Archives.

64. Christopher Coope, correspondence with author, September 16, 2012.

65. Christopher Coope, conversation with author, July 21, 2012.

66. Foot, "Obituary of Elizabeth Anscombe," *The Somerville College Record* (2001), 119.

67. R.M. Hare, "A Philosophical Autobiography," *Utilitas* 14 (November, 2002), 269.

68. In slightly more detail: to issue a universal prescription is to declare what everyone should do, every time (that's what "universally" means) when faced with the situation you're prescribing for. But to declare *that* is to say that everyone should perform that action (call it A) no matter *who* is *where* in the situation. As you consider whether to issue such a prescription, if you're being honest with yourself, you must ask, "can I prescribe this *if I'm the person doing A?* Now how about *if I'm a beneficiary of A?* Or *if I'm a victim?*" To conclude, "yes, I *universally* prescribe A for this situation" is to take all of that into account. That is, it is to consider everyone affected by A and how well satisfied they are by it.

69. R.M. Hare, *Moral Thinking: Its Levels, Method, and Point* (Oxford: Oxford University Press, 1981), v.

70. Anthony Kenny, conversation with author, March 18, 2011.

71. Anthony Kenny, conversation with author, March 2011.

72. Philippa Foot to R.M. Hare, August 26, 1984, Hare Papers, Balliol College Archives.

73. John Lucas, "A Memoir of Professor R.M. Hare, FBA," *The Balliol College Annual Record* (2002), 32.

74. Catherine Hare, conversation with author, August 1, 2012.

75. Roger Teichmann, conversation with author, July 24, 2012. Rosalind Hursthouse was not present, but Foot spoke with her beforehand about her intentions.

76. Philippa Foot, journal entry, December 3, 2000, SC/LY/SP/PF/6/1, Foot Papers, Somerville College Archives.

77. Rosalind Hursthouse, correspondence with author, October 18, 2012.

78. Catherine Hare survived her husband by over a decade, and was still living when Foot died. She would have liked to attend the memorial but checked herself, worrying that her presence might stir unhappy memories.

79. Christine M. Korsgaard, *The Sources of Normativity* (Cambridge, UK: Cambridge University Press, 1996), 257.

80. Peter Geach, *The Virtues* (Cambridge, UK: Cambridge University Press, 1977), 17. Quoted in Foot, *Natural Goodness*, 35.

81. Draft, "Against Virtue Ethics," SC/LY/SP/PF/3, Foot Papers, Somerville College Archives.

82. Midgley, *The Owl of Minerva*, 162.

83. Iris Murdoch, *The Red and the Green* (Harmondsworth: Penguin, 1967), 31–32.

84. Nicholas Denyer, conversation with author, June 29, 2012.

85. Philippa Foot, interview with Jonathan Ree, *Twenty Minutes–Philosopohical Lives*, BBC Radio 3, 19 September 2000.

86. Letter to Manfred Karnovsky, SC/LY/SP/PF/5, Foot Papers, Somerville College Archives.

87. Rosalind Hursthouse, conversation with author, September 6, 2012.

88. Peter Conradi, conversation with author, July 20, 2012.

89. Conradi, *Family Business*, 176.

90. Peter Conradi, conversation with author, July 20, 2012.

91. Conradi, *Family Business*, 176.

92. Iris Murdoch, Journal 10, February 17, 1968, KUAS 202/1/10, Kingston University Archives.

93. Philippa Foot, journal entry for July 5, 2003, SC/LY/SP/PF/6/1, Foot Papers, Somerville College Archives.

94. Philippa Foot, journal entry for November 7, 1997, SC/LY/SP/PF/6/1, Foot Papers, Somerville College Archives.

95. Conradi, *Family Business*, 175.

96. Philippa Foot, journal entry for June 9, 1997, SC/LY/SP/PF/6/1, Foot Papers, Somerville College Archives.

97. Tennyson, *In Memoriam A.H.H.*, CXIX.

98. Philippa Foot, journal entry for March 15, 1997, SC/LY/SP/PF/6/1, Foot Papers, Somerville College Archives.

IMAGE CREDITS

1. Courtesy of Jan Hawthorn.
2. Photo by Laird Parker. Originally published by the British Academy, 1998. Used by permission.
3. Used by kind permission of the Principal and Fellows of St. Hugh's College, Oxford.
4. Used by permission of the Principal and Fellows of Somerville College, Oxford.
5. Photo by Frances White, 2012. Used by permission.
6. Used by permission of Kingston University. File number KUAS164.
7. Public domain. Held by the Austrian National Library. Inventory number Pf 42.805: C (1).
8. Originally published by the British Academy, 2004. Used by permission.
9. Photo by Anna Schilke, 2021. Used by permission.
10. Photo by Anna Schilke, 2021. Used by permission.
11. Photo by Geoff Midgley. Originally published in *The Owl of Minerva*, by Mary Midgley, Routledge, 2005. Used by permission of David Midgley.

12. Photo by George Douglas, 1952. Used by permission of Getty Images.
13. Photo by Toblu, 2018. Creative Commons Attribution-Share Alike 4.0 International License. https://commons.wikimedia. org/wiki/File:Senior_Common_Room,_Somerville_ College.jpg
14. Photo by Elijah Tangenberg, 2021. Used by permission.
15. Used by permission of Kingston University. File number KUAS100/1/38
16. Used by permission of Kingston University. File number KUAS083/4. Of unknown provenance.
17. Originally published by the British Academy, 2002. Used by permission.
18. Originally published by the British Academy. Used by permission.
19. Used by permission of David Midgley.
20. Photo by Peter Conradi, 1998. Used by permission.

BIBLIOGRAPHY

Adams, Pauline. *Somerville for Women: An Oxford College.* Oxford: Oxford University Press, 1996.

Aeschylus. *The Oresteia.* Translated by Robert Fagles. New York: Penguin, 1977.

Anderson, Jenny. "Only 9% of 15-Year-Olds Can Tell the Difference between Fact and Opinion." https://qz.com/1759474/only-9-percent-of-15-year-olds-can-distinguish-between-fact-and-opinion/.

Anscombe, G.E.M. "Does Oxford Moral Philosophy Corrupt Youth?" *The Listener* 1455 (February 14, 1957): 266.

Anscombe, G.E.M. *Intention.* Oxford: Basil Blackwell, 1957.

Anscombe, G.E.M. "Modern Moral Philosophy." *Philosophy* 33, no. 124 (January 1958): 1–19.

Anscombe, G.E.M. *The Collected Philosophical Papers of G.E.M. Anscombe. Vol. 2, Metaphysics and the Philosophy of Mind.* Minneapolis: University of Minnesota Press, 1981.

Anscombe, G.E.M. *The Collected Philosophical Papers of G.E.M. Anscombe. Vol. 3, Ethics, Religion, and Politics.* Minneapolis: University of Minnesota Press, 1981.

Anscombe, G.E.M. Correspondence and comments in *The Human World* 9 (November 1972): 48–51.

Archilochus. Untitled fragment, in *Greek Iambic Poetry*, edited by Douglas Gerber, 67. Cambridge, MA: Harvard University Press, 1999.

Arnold, Matthew. "Dover Beach." 1867. https://www.poetryfoundation.org/poems/43588/dover-beach.

Aristotle. *Complete Works of Aristotle, Volume I.* Edited by Jonathan Barnes. Princeton, NJ: Princeton University Press, 1984.

Aquinas, Thomas. *Summa Theologiae*. Translated by the Fathers of the English Dominican Province. Cincinnati: Benziger Brothers, 1947.

Auden, W.H. *Collected Poems*. Edited by Edward Mendelson, 179. London: Vintage Books, 1991.

Austin, J.L. "A Plea for Excuses," in *Philosophical Papers*, edited by J.O. Urmson and G.J. Warnock, 123–152. Oxford: Oxford University Press, 1961.

Ayer, A.J. *Language, Truth and Logic*. Mineola: Dover Books, 1952.

Bacon, Francis. *The Advancement of Learning*. Edited by G. W. Kitchen. Philadelphia: Paul Dry Books, 2001.

Baier, Annette. "Hume's Own 'Ought' Conclusions," in *Hume on Is and Ought*, edited by Charles R. Pigden. Basingstoke, England: Palgrave Macmillan, 2010.

Bawden, Nina. *In My Own Time: Almost an Autobiography*. New York: Time Warner Book Group, 1995.

Berkman, John. "G.E.M. Anscombe's 'I Am Sadly Theoretical: It Is the Effect of Being at Oxford' (1938): A newly discovered article by Anscombe edited and with an editor's introduction." *New Blackfriars* 102 (2021): 1101.

Berkman, John. "Justice and Murder: The Background to Anscombe's 'Modern Moral Philosophy'," in *The Oxford Handbook of Elizabeth Anscombe*, edited by Roger Teichmann. Oxford: Oxford University Press, 2022.

Berlin, Isaiah. *Enlightening: Letters 1946-1960*. Edited by Henry Hardy and Jennifer Holmes. London: Chatto & Windus, 2009.

Bernays, Edward. *Crystallizing Public Opinion*. New York: Boni and Liveright, 1923.

Bernays, Edward. *Propaganda*. New York: Boni and Liveright, 1928.

Blaschko, Paul. "Let's Stop Hating on the Fact-Opinion Distinction." http://www.paulblaschko.com/blog/2017/4/1/lets-stop-hating-on-the-fact-opinion-distinction.

Bolieu, David A., and John A. Dick. "The Phenomenological Movement." *Tradition and Renewal: Philosophical Essays Commemorating the Centennial of Louvain's Institute of* Philosophy 3 (1993):110–115.

Bridson, D.G. *Prospero and Ariel: The Rise and Fall of Radio*. London: Gollancz, 1971.

Burke, Edmund. *A Philosophical Enquiry into the Origin of our Ideas of the Sublime and Beautiful*. 1757. Oxford: Oxford University Press, 2015.

Carey, John. *Original Copy: Selected Reviews and Journalism, 1969-1986*. London: Faber and Faber, 1987.

Caven, Hannah. "Horror in Our Time: Images of the Concentration Camps in the British Media, 1945." *Historical Journal of Film, Radio and Television* 21:3 (2001), 205–253.

Center for Humanities, Inc. *Making Judgements and Drawing Conclusions*. Lesson worksheet, 1977. https://www.bmcc.cuny.edu/wp-content/uploads/ported/lrc/studyskills/factsandopinions.pdf.

Chesney, Ann. "Don, Philosopher, and Happy Mother of Six." *The Manchester Guardian*. June 1, 1959.

Clark, Kelly James, ed. *Philosophers Who Believe: The Spiritual Journeys of 11 Leading Thinkers*. Downers Grove: InterVarsity Press, 1993.

Conradi, Peter J. *Family Business: A Memoir*. Bridgen, Wales: Seren Books, 2019.

Conradi, Peter J. *Iris Murdoch: A Life*. New York: W.W. Norton, 2001.

Conradi, Peter J., and Gavin Lawrence. "Professor Philippa Foot." *The Independent*. October 19, 2010.

Cummins, Kevin. "Fact and Opinion Worksheets for Students." https://www.edgalaxy.com/journal/2013/3/31/fact-and-opinion-worksheets-for-students.

Czernin, Ferdinand. *Europe: Going, Going, Gone!* London: Peter Davies, 1939.

Darwin, Charles. *The Descent of Man*. Princeton, NJ: Princeton University Press, 1981.

Dawkins, Richard. "In Defense of Selfish Genes." *Philosophy* 56, no. 218 (October 1981): 556–573.

Dawkins, Richard. *The Selfish Gene*. Oxford: Oxford University Press, 1976.

Deutscher, Max. "Some Recollections of Ryle and Remarks on His Notion of Negative Action." *Australasian Journal of Philosophy* 60, no. 3 (1982): 254–264.

Dubec, Rhonda. "Fact v. Opinion Resource." https://teachingcommons.lakeheadu.ca/fact-vs-opinion-resource.

Dunlop, E.E. *The War Diaries of Weary Dunlop*. New York: Penguin Books, 2010.

Edmonds, David. *Would You Kill the Fat Man?* Princeton, NJ: Princeton University Press, 2013,

Foot, M.R.D. *Memories of an SOE Historian*. Barnsley: Pen and Sword Military, 2009.

Foot, Philippa. Interview by Jonathan Ree. *BBC Radio 3*, BBC, September 19, 2000.

Foot, Philippa. *Natural Goodness*. Oxford: Clarendon, 2001.

Foot, Philippa. *Virtues and Vices: And Other Essays in Moral Philosophy*. New York: Oxford University Press, 2002.

Forbath, Alex. *Europe Into the Abyss: Behind the Scenes of Secret Politics*. London: Pallas, 1938.

Geach, Peter. *The Virtues: The Stanton Lectures 1973-4*. Cambridge, UK: Cambridge University Press, 1977.

Geach, Mary. Introduction to *Faith in Hard Ground: Essays by G.E.M. Anscombe*, ix–xxvi. Exeter, UK: Imprint Academic, 2008.

Geach, Mary. Introduction to *From Plato to Wittgenstein: Essays by G.E.M. Anscombe*, xiii–xx. Exeter, UK: Imprint Academic, 2010.

Gellner, Ernest. "Reflections on Linguistic Philosophy—I." *The Listener* 1480 (August 8, 1957): 205–207.

Gellner, Ernest. "Reflections on Linguistic Philosophy—II." *The Listener* 1481 (August 15, 1957): 237, 240–241.

Gellner, Ernest. *Words and Things: An Examination of, And an Attack on, Linguistic Philosophy*. London: Gollancz, 1959.

Gibbs, Phillip. *The Day After Tomorrow: What is Going to Happen to the World?* London: Hutchinson, 1928.

Gill, Eric. *Autobiography*. New York: Biblo and Tannen, 1968.

Glaser, Edward M. *An Experiment in the Defense of Critical Thinking*. New York: Teachers College, Columbia University, 1941.

Gollwitzer, Helmut, Käthe Kuhn, and Reinhold Schneider, eds. *Dying We Live: The Final Messages and Records of the Resistance*. New York: Pantheon, 1956.

Green, Ronald M. *Kierkegaard and Kant: The Hidden Debt*. Albany: State University of New York Press, 1992.

Haldane, John. "Anscombe: Life, Action and Ethics in Context." *Philosophical News* 18 (2019): 45–75.

Hare, R.M. "A Philosophical Autobiography." *Utilitas* 14, no. 3 (November 2002): 269–305.

Hare, R.M. *Freedom and Reason*. Oxford: Clarendon Press, 1963.

Hare, R.M. *Moral Thinking: Its Levels, Meaning, and Point*. Oxford: Oxford University Press, 1981.

Hare, R.M. "Nothing Matters," in *Applications of Moral Philosophy*. London: Palgrave, 1972, 32–47.

Hare, R.M. "Postscript." In *An Essay in Monism* (unpublished).

Hare, R.M. *The Language of Morals*. Oxford: Clarendon Press, 1952.

Hitchcock, David. "Critical Thinking," in *The Stanford Encyclopedia of Philosophy*, edited by Edward N. Zalta. https://plato.stanford.edu/archives/fall2018/entries/critical-thinking/.

Hobhouse, Christopher. *Oxford: As It Was & As It Is Today*. London: B.T. Batsford, 1940.

Hume, David. *A Treatise of Human Nature*. 1747. Garden City, NY: Dover Publications 2003.

Ignatieff, Michael. *Isaiah Berlin: A Life*. New York: Metropolitan Books, 1998.

Jacobs, Alan. *The Narnian: The Life and Imagination of C. S. Lewis*. New York: HarperCollins Publishers, 2005.

Kenny, Anthony. *Brief Encounters: Notes from a Philosopher's Diary*. London: Society for Promoting Christian Knowledge, 2018.

Kenworthy, J.M., and H.G. Wells. *Will Civilisation Crash?* London: Ernest Benn, 1927.

Kepler, Johannes. *Harmonices mundi libri V*. 1619.

Korsgaard, Christine M. *The Sources of Normativity*. Cambridge, UK: Cambridge University Press, 1996.

Kuhn, Thomas. *The Structure of Scientific Revolutions*. Chicago: University of Chicago Press, 1962.

Lanneu, Catharine. *L'inconnue Française*, 258–262. Brussels: Peter Lang, 2008.

Leibniz, Gottfried Wilhelm. *Discourse on Metaphysics*. Translated by George Montgomery. Chicago: Open Court Publishing Company, 1973.

Leroi, Armand. *The Lagoon: How Aristotle Invented Science*. New York: Viking Penguin, 2014.

Lewis, C.S. *Miracles*. London: Geofrey Bles, 1947.

Linde, Sharon. "Facts vs. Opinions." https://study.com/academy/lesson/facts-vs-opinions-examples-games-activities.html.

Lippman, Walter. *Public Opinion*. New York: Harcourt, Brace and Co., 1922.

Lloyd, Myfanwy. "The Parliamentary Delegation to Buchenwald Concentration Camp—70 Years On." https://thehistoryofparliament.wordpress.com/2015/04/21/the-parliamentary-delegation-to-buchenwald-concentration-camp-70-years-on/.

Lorenz, Konrad. *King Solomon's Ring: New Light on Animal Ways*. New York: Time Life Books, 1952.

Lorenz, Konrad. *On Aggression*. London: Methuen and Co., 1966.

Lucas, John. "A Memoir of Professor R.M. Hare, FBA." *The Balliol College Annual Record*, 2002, 30–32.

Mac Donnchaidh, Shane. "A Teacher's Guide to Fact and Opinion," *Literacy Ideas*. https://www.literacyideas.com/teaching-fact-and-opinion.

MacIntyre, Alasdair. *After Virtue*. Notre Dame: University of Notre Dame Press, 1981.

Mackie, J.L. "The Law of the Jungle: Moral Alternatives and Principles of Evolution." *Philosophy* 53, (October 1978): 455–464.

MacKinnon, Donald M. *A Study in Ethical Theory*. London: A. & C. Black, 1957.

McCabe, Joseph. *Can We Save Civilisation?* London: Search Publishing, 1932.

McCarthy, Fiona. *Eric Gill*. London: Faber and Faber, 1989.

Mehta, Ved. *The Fly and the Fly-Bottle: Encounters with British Intellectuals*. Boston: Little Brown, 1962.

Midgley, Mary. "A Letter to Posterity." *The Listener* 1204 (March 27, 1952): 510–511.

Midgley, Mary. *Beast and Man: The Roots of Human Nature*, revised edition. London: Routledge, 2002.

Midgley, Mary. "Bishop Butler: A Reply." *The Twentieth Century* 152 no. 95 (July 1952): 55–62.

Midgley, Mary. *Can't We Make Moral Judgements?* New York: St. Martin's Press, 1991.

Midgley, Mary. *Dolphins, Utopias, and Computers: Problems in Philosophical Plumbing*. London: Routledge, 1996.

Midgley, Mary. "Gene-Juggling." *Philosophy* 54, (October 1979): 439–458.

Midgley, Mary. *Heart and Mind: The Varieties of Moral Experience*. New York: St. Martin's Press, 1981.

Midgley, Mary. "Newcastle: Comments on a Case History." *The Twentieth Century* 59 (May 1956): 159–168.

Midgley, Mary. "Selfish Genes and Social Darwinism." *Philosophy* 58 (July 1983): 365–377.

Midgley, Mary. *Science as Salvation: A Modern Myth and Its Meaning*. London: Routledge, 1992.

Midgley, Mary. "The Concept of Beastliness: Philosophy, Ethics and Animal Behaviour." *Philosophy* 48, no. 184 (1973): 111–135.

Midgley, Mary. *The Essential Mary Midgley*. Edited by David Midgley. New York: Routledge, 2005.

Midgley, Mary. *The Ethical Primate: Humans, Freedom, and Morality*. London: Routledge, 1994.

Midgley, Mary. "The Month." *The Twentieth Century* 156, (May, 1959): 105–110.

Midgley, Mary. *The Owl of Minerva: A Memoir*. New York: Routledge, 2005.

Midgley, Mary. *Wickedness*. London: Routledge and Kegan Paul, 1984.

Midgley, Mary, and Judith Hughes. *Women's Choices: Philosophical Problems Facing Feminism*. New York: St. Martin's Press, 1984.

Midgley, Mary. *What is Philosophy For?* London: Bloomsbury Academic, 2018.

Milner, Gamaliel. *The Problems of Decadence*. London: Williams & Norgate, 1931.

Mitchell, Christopher W. "University Battles: C.S. Lewis and the Oxford University Socratic Club," in *C.S. Lewis: Lightbearer in the Shadowlands*, edited by Angus J. L. Menuge. Wheaton, IL: Crossway Books, 1997, 329–352.

Monk, Ray. *Wittgenstein: The Duty of Genius*. New York: Penguin, 1991.

Moorman, J.R.H. *A History of the Church in England*. London: A. & C. Black, 1973.

Morgan, David. *With Love and Rage: A Friendship with Iris Murdoch*. London: Kingston University Press, 2010.

Morrison, Toni. *Beloved: A Novel*. New York: Random House, 1986.

Morse, Horace, and George McCune. "Selected Items for the Testing of Study Skills." *Bulletin Number 15* (1940). National Council for the Social Studies.

Murdoch, Iris. *Existentialists and Mystics*. Edited by Peter J. Conradi. New York: Penguin Books, 1999.

Murdoch, Iris. Forward to *Christ's Shadow in Plato's Cave*, by Stella Aldwinkle. Oxford: Amate Press, 1990.

Murdoch, Iris. *Jackson's Dilemma*. London: Chatto & Windus, 1995.

Murdoch, Iris. *Living on Paper: Letters from Iris Murdoch, 1934–1995*. Edited by Avril Horner and Anne Rowe. London: Chatto & Windus, 2015.

Murdoch, Iris. "Midnight Hour," *The Adelphi*, January-March 1943, 62.

Murdoch, Iris. *Sartre: Romantic Rationalist*. New York: Viking, 1987.

Murdoch, Iris. "*Sein und Zeit*: Pursuit of Being," in *Iris Murdoch: Philosopher*, edited by Justin Broakes. Oxford: Oxford University Press, 2012.

Murdoch, Iris. *The Nice and The Good*. New York: Viking Press, 1967.

Murdoch, Iris. *The Red and The Green*. Harmondsworth: Penguin, 1967.

Murdoch, Iris. *The Sea, The Sea*. London: Vintage Books, 1999.

Murdoch, Iris. *The Sovereignty of Good*. London: Routledge, 1970.

Murdoch, Iris. *Under the Net*. London: Chatto & Windus, 1954.

Murdoch, Iris. "Words and Ideas." *The Partisan Review* 27, no. 2 (Spring 1960): 348–353.

Murdoch, Iris. *Writer at War*. Edited by Peter J. Conradi. London: Short Books, 2010.

Nietzsche, Friedrich. "Maxims and Arrows." In *The Portable Nietzsche*, translated by Walter Kaufmann, 466–473. New York: Viking, 1977.

Ogden, C.K., and I.A. Richards. *The Meaning of Meaning: A Study of the Influence of Language Upon Thought and of The Science of Symbolism*. London: Kegan Paul, Trench, Trubner, and Co., 1930.

Overy, Richard. *The Morbid Age: Britain between the Wars*. London: Penguin Books, 2010.

Price, A.W. "Richard Mervyn Hare." *Proceedings of the British Academy* 24 (2004): 117–137.

Proctor, Robert N. *Value-Free Science?: Purity and Power in Modern Knowledge*. Cambridge, MA: Harvard University Press, 1991.

Purton, Valerie. *An Iris Murdoch Chronology*. New York: Palgrave Macmillan, 2007.

Ranfurly, Hermione. *To War with Whitaker: Wartime Diaries of the Countess of Ranfurly, 1939-45*. London: Bello, 2014.

Rorty, Amélie Okenberg. *The Many Faces of Philosophy*. Oxford: Oxford University Press, 2003.

Ryle, Gilbert. Introduction to the *The Revolution in Philosophy*, by W.C. Kneale, A.J. Ayer, G.A. Paul, D.F. Pears, P.F. Strawson, G.J. Warnock, and R.A. Wollheim. London: Macmillan & Co, 1956.

Schweitzer, Albert. *The Decay and Restoration of Civilization*. London: A. & C. Black, 1923.

Scrutton, Mary. "On Being Reformed." *The Listener* 1428 (August 9, 1956): 196–197.

Searle, John R. "Oxford Philosophy in the 1950s." *Philosophy* 90, no. 2 (2015): 173–193.

Shakespeare, William. *The Complete Works of Shakespeare, 7th Edition*. Edited by David Bevington. London: Pearson, 2013.

Stockton, Jim, and Benjamin J.B. Lipscomb. "The Anscombe-Lewis Debate: New Archival Sources Considered." *Journal of Inklings Studies* 11, no. 1 (April 2021): 35–57.

Shotwell, James T. *On the Rim of the Abyss*. New York: Garland, 1936.

Spengler, Oswald, and Charles Francis Atkinson. *The Decline of the West*. New York: Knopf, 1926.

Stevenson, Charles L. *Ethics and Language*. New Haven: Yale University Press, 1944.

Styron, William. *Sophie's Choice*. New York: Random House 1976.

Sumnicht, Sarah. "Fact & Opinion Statements with Adjectives." https://www.education.com/lesson-plan/el-support-lesson-fact-and-opinion-statements-with-adjectives/.

Sutherland, Stewart. "Donald Mackenzie MacKinnon." *Proceedings of the British Academy* 97 (1998): 3830–3834.

Taylor, Charles. *Sources of the Self: The Making of the Modern Identity*. Cambridge, MA: Belknap University Press, 1989.

Taylor, Charles. *A Secular Age?* Cambridge, MA: Harvard University Press, 2007.

Teichman, Jenny. "Gertrude Elizabeth Margaret Anscombe." *Proceedings of the British Academy* 115 (2001): 31–50.

Teichmann, Roger. *The Philosophy of Elizabeth Anscombe*. Oxford: Oxford University Press, 2008.

Tennyson, Alfred. *In Memoriam A. H. H.*. Edited by Eric Gray. New York: W.W. Norton, 2003.

Tossi, Justin, and Brandon Warmke. *Grandstanding: The Use and Abuse of Moral Talk.* Oxford: Oxford University Press, 2020.

Uschanov, T.P. "The Strange Death of Ordinary Language." Last modified June 2006. https://www.mv.helsinki.fi/home/tuschano/writings/strange/.

Voorhoeve, Alex. "A Mistrustful Animal: An Interview with Bernard Williams." *The Harvard Review of Philosophy,* XII (2004): 80–91.

Voorhoeve, Alex. "The Grammar of Goodness: An Interview with Philippa Foot." *The Harvard Review of Philosophy,* XI (2003): 32–44.

Vienna Circle. *The Scientific Conception of the World.* In *Empiricism and Sociology,* by Otto Neurath. Dordrecht, Holland: D. Reidel Publishing, 1973.

Warnock, Geoffrey. "Saturday Mornings," in *Essays on J.L. Austin,* edited by Isaiah Berlin, 31–45. Oxford: Clarendon Press, 1973.

Warnock, Mary. *A Memoir: People and Places.* London: Duckbacks, 2002.

Wittgenstein, Ludwig. *Philosophical Investigations.* Translated by G.E.M. Anscombe. Oxford: Basil Blackwell, 1958.

Weinberg, Steven. *The First Three Minutes: A Modern View of the Origin of the Universe.* Second Edition. New York: Basic Books, 1993.

Wells, H.G. *The Salvaging of Civilisation.* New York: Macmillan, 1921.

Williams, Bernard. *Ethics and the Limits of Philosophy.* Cambridge, MA: Harvard University Press, 1985.

Williams, Bernard, and Michael Tanner. Correspondence and comments in *The Human World* 9 (November 1972): 42–48.

Wilson, A.N. *C.S. Lewis: A Biography.* London: W.W. Norton and Company, 1990.

Wilson, A.N. *Iris Murdoch as I Knew Her.* London: Hutchinson, 2003.

Wilson, E.O. *Sociobiology: The New Synthesis.* Cambridge, MA: Belknap, 1975.

Wootton, David. *The Invention of Science: A New History of the Scientific Revolution.* New York: Harper Perennial, 2015.

Yorke, Malcolm. *Eric Gill: Man of Flesh and Spirit.* London: Constable, 1981.

Archival Sources

BBC Sound Archives. Recording of talk by Elizabeth Anscombe on Ludwig Wittgenstein. Broadcast July 9, 1952. File number LP 24423. Accessed through the British Library, London, UK.

BBC Written Archives Centre. RCont Talks Anscombe. Reading, UK.

BBC Written Archives Centre. Mary Scrutton. Talks File 1–1942-1962. Reading, UK.

BBC Written Archives Centre. Iris Murdoch. Talks File 1–1942-1962. Reading, UK.

Elizabeth Anscombe File. St. Hugh's College Archive. Oxford University.

Elizabeth Anscombe Staff File. Somerville College Archives. Oxford University.

Iris Murdoch Archive. Kingston University Archives. Kingston on Thames.

Iris Murdoch's Journals 4, 6, 7, 9, 10, and 15. Kingston University Archives. Kingston on Thames.

Iris Murdoch's Personal File. St. Anne's College Archives. Oxford University

Mary Somerville Research Fellowship File. Somerville College Archives. Oxford University.

Newnham College Archives. AC/5/2/13. Murdoch on Hitler. Cambridge, UK.

Newnham College Archives. AC/5/2/13. Donald Mackenzie MacKinnon. Reference for Iris Murdoch. Cambridge, UK.

Newnham College Archives. AC/5/2/13. Iris Murdoch application for graduate study.

Philippa Foot Papers. Somerville College Archives. Oxford University.

Philippa Foot Staff File. Somerville College Archives. Oxford University.

R. M. Hare Papers. Balliol College Archives. Oxford University.

St. Anne's College Archives. Oxford University.

INDEX

Addison, Joseph, 290n64
Aldwinckle, Stella, 145, 145n*, 155
Anscombe, Allen, 50–55
Anscombe, Gertrude Elizabeth Margaret
    (G.E.M.), 40, 48, 281n47, 284n38,
    291n3, 294n61
  and Aquinas, 54, 87, 138, 167n*,
    185–188, 299n38, 299n39
  and Aristotle, 89, 164–167, 167n*, 186,
    260
  and Austin, 142–144, 153, 175, 192
  on abortion and contraception, 258–262,
    261n*, 169–170
  and the BBC, 135–136, 153, 155, 158–164,
    169–170
  conversion to Catholicism, 50–54, 138–139,
    259, 282n5
  debate with C.S. Lewis, 145–148, 155,
    180, 293n39, 293n42
  early life and family, 50–55, 72, 283n36
  end of life, 263–264
  friendship with Foot, 48–49, 173, 179,
    182–185, 193–195, 258–259, 261–264,
    299n39
  friendship with Midgley, 48–49, 154–155,
    203, 210, 258
  friendship with Murdoch, 48, 109, 117–125,
    130, 252, 254, 306n50
  and Hare, 83, 160–169, 192
  influence of Wittgenstein, 88, 90, 109,
    118–119, 121, 123–124, 139–144, 146,
    148–150, 153–154, 169, 174, 179, 185,
    197, 216, 263, 292n18
  later career, 168–171, 257–259
  life at 27 St. John Street, 148–151, 194, 196
  marriage to Peter Geach, 88, 137–138,
    148, 153, 161, 259, 270, 285n22
  and Truman's honorary degree, 155–158,
    162, 186, 260, 295n73
Anscombe, Gertrude Thomas, 51–53
Anscombe, John, 50
Anscombe, Tom, 50
Anselm of Canterbury, 253, 258
Aquinas, Thomas
  and early-modern universities, 11
  influence on Anscombe, 54, 87, 138,
    167n*, 185–188
  influence on Foot, 185–188, 191, 198
Aristotle, 238, 260, 279n16, 301n12
  influence on Anscombe and Foot, 89,
    164–167, 167n*, 180, 186–188,
    190–191, 257, 270
  influence on Midgley, 205, 214, 218, 220,
    224, 260
  world picture, 9–12, 14–16
Arnold, Matthew, 19–20, 211

Astor, Nancy, 66
Attenborough, David, 220
Auden, Wystan Hugh (W.H.), 104–105
Austin, Jean Coutts, 40, 48, 72, 153, 283n36
Austin, John Langshaw (J.L.), 44, 85, 147,
    153, 175, 220
  in contrast with Murdoch, 132–133
  and his "Kindergarten," 143, 174, 192,
    217, 235, 297n11
  personality, 223, 142–144, 147, 192, 216–217
Ayer, Alfred Jules (A.J.), 47, 171n*
  emotivism and anti-naturalist ethics,
    41–45, 90–93, 137n*, 266
  ongoing influence, 75, 85, 90, 110, 113,
    121, 127–128, 142–144, 161–162, 181,
    192, 223–224, 245

Bacon, Francis, 12, 14
Badminton School, 33, 60–62, 105
Bain, Ethel, "King," 60
Baker, Beatrice May, 61–62, 64
Balliol College, Oxford, 33, 77, 86, 95, 221
Balogh, Thomas, 80, 111
Bawden, Nina (Mabey), 26–28, 83
Bayley, John, 62, 130–131, 247, 253, 255–257
Baxter, Jennie, "Nanny," 68–70, 262
Beauvoir, Simone de, 106–107, 109, 119, 127
Bennett, Alan, 223–225
Bennett, William, 239
Bergen-Belsen concentration camp, 2–4, 21,
    46, 270
Berkeley, George, 257
Berlin, Isaiah, 41, 44, 133, 153, 295n64
Berlioz, Hector, 18
Bernays, Edward, 6–7
Black, Max, 228–229
Boedder, Bernard, 52–54, 73–74, 138–139
Bosanquet, Esther (Cleveland), 67–68,
    70, 175
Bosanquet, Marion, 68–70
Bosanquet, Philippa. See Foot, Philippa
Bosanquet, William, 67–68
Bradley, Francis Herbert (F.H.), 254
Broadie, Sarah, 270
Brontë, Charlotte, 129
Brown, Lesley, 257
Browning, Robert, 210

Buchenwald concentration camp, 2–4, 46
Bullock, Alan, 157
Burke, Edmund, 17–18
Burkill, T. Alec (T.A.), 161
Butler, Joseph, 44, 215–216, 218, 220
Byron, George Gordon, 129

Camus, Albert, 105, 127, 188n*
Canetti, Elias, 131, 131*, 289n45
Carey, John, 150–151
Carroll, Lewis, 60
Cassirer, Heinz, 274
Challoner, Richard, 50–52, 54, 138
Chesterton, G.K., 51, 54
Christ Church College, Oxford, 41, 85
Cobbe, Anne, 1, 23, 71, 177, 196, 275
Collet, Ernest, 105–106
Collingwood, Robin George (R.G.), 254
Conradi, Peter, 47, 59, 193–194, 253–255,
    257, 271, 274, 280n1
Cook, Peter, 223–224
Coope, Christopher, 150, 171n*
Corpus Christi College, Oxford, 35–36,
    272–273
Coutts, Jean, see Austin, Jean Coutts

Daniel, Norman, 73, 155–156, 285n22
Darbishire, Helen, 27, 35
Darwin, Charles, 219, 232
Dawkins, Richard,
  and the "Dawkins sublime," 1, 17, 43, 92,
    97, 128, 167, 255
  and The Selfish Gene, 241–244, 304n12,
    304n13
Denyer, Nicholas, 260, 291n3
Descartes, René, 12
Diamond, Cora, 270
Dobzhansky, Theodosius, 203
Dodds, Eric Robertson (E.R.), 35, 207
Dostoevsky, Fyodor, 45, 80
Dover, Kenneth, 37
Downe House School, 26, 28, 35, 58, 80,
    226, 245
Dummett, Michael, 73, 141, 152, 275–276

Edmonds, David, 204
Emmet, Dorothy, 74

Farnell, Vera, 31, 33, 71
Fenner, Rachel, 248
Flew, Anthony, 161, 208
Foot, Michael, 46, 75, 98–101, 111–112,
  156, 175–176, 195–196, 268
Foot, Philippa, 298n26, 299n39, 306n51
  and Aquinas, 185–188, 191, 198
  and Hare, 188–193, 195–196, 198–199,
    265–269, 307n78
  early life and family, 54–55, 68–71,
    175–176
  friendship with Anscombe, 48–49,
    157–158, 173, 179, 182–185, 193–195,
    261–264, 272, 299n39
  friendship with Midgley, 172, 199, 204,
    213, 233–237, 301n12
  friendship with Murdoch, 22–23, 34,
    79–83, 110–113, 176, 196, 234,
    250–254
  influence of MacKinnon, 22–23, 44–48,
    71, 172–173, 176–177, 185, 193, 257,
    274–275
  influence of Wittgenstein, 150, 182–184, 187
  legacy and end of life, 270–273, 274–276
  marriage to Michael Foot, 1–2, 98–101,
    111–112, 175–176, 179, 195–196, 268
  relief work, 175, 177–179, 262
  return to Oxford after the war, 75, 86–88,
    98–101, 177
  at Somerville, 20–21, 39–40, 71, 121,
    171–173
Fraenkel, Eduard, 35–37
Franco, Francisco, 44
Freud, Sigmund, 7, 182, 301n12
Friedrich, Caspar David, 128
Froebel Demonstration School, 60
Fromm, Eric, 210

Galilei, Galileo, 13, 15
Geach, Barbara, 88, 262–263, 276
Geach, Peter, 88, 137–138, 148, 153, 161,
  259, 270, 285n22
Gellner, Ernest, 221–223, 251–252, 302n40
Gide, André, 181
Gill, Eric, 135–136, 136n*, 291n2
Glover, Mary, 72, 74
Goethe, Johann Wolfgang von, 129

Goodall, Jane, 219–220, 240
Gore, Victoria, 68
Gormally, Luke, 292n18
Gormally, Mary Geach, 150, 212n*, 293n39
Gould, Steven Jay, 19, 240
Gracq, Julien, 105
Gregory, Theophilus Stephen (T.S.),
  161–164, 221
Griffin, Jasper, 299n46
Griffin, Miriam, 299n46
Gwyer, Barbara, 72

Hare, Catherine (Verney), 98, 307n78
Hare, Richard Mervyn (R.M.)
  and Anscombe, 83, 160–169, 192
  early life and family, 96, 98
  and Foot, 187–193, 195–196, 265–269
  influence of war, 76–79, 96–97, 119–120
  later career and end of life, 264–268
  marriage, 98
  philosophical project, 91, 94–95, 101–102,
    133, 165, 183, 188–189, 188n*, 225,
    287n52, 298n28, 307n68
  post-war return to Oxford, 83–84, 86
Hartley, Mildred, 30, 34–35, 71, 285n21
Harvey, Anthony Ernest (A.E.), 158
Harvey, Barbara, 171, 174–175, 179
Heal, Jane, 210
Heckstall-Smith, Hugh, 168
Hegel, Georg Wilhelm Friedrich, 115, 208
Heidegger, Martin, 254
Henderson, Isobel, 35, 36n*
Hicks, David, 48
Hitler, Adolf, 33, 44, 63, 64, 113, 156
Hobbes, Thomas, 41, 48, 73, 215,
  279n16
Hobhouse, Christopher, 32–35
Hogg, Quinton, 33
Housman, Alfred Edward (A.E.), 211
Hubbard, Margaret, 131, 157, 248, 251
Hume, David, 41, 146, 164–165, 257,
  296n98
Hursthouse, Rosalind, 137, 172, 191, 270,
  272–273, 275, 294n61

Ibbotson, Alan, 227
Ibbotson, Eva, 227

Jackson-Cole, Cecil, 177–179
Jacobs, Alan, 293n42
Jerusalem family, 64–65
Jowett, Benjamin, 28

Kallin, Anna, 153, 155, 201–202, 210,
    213–215, 227, 295n64
Kant, Immanuel, 44–45, 94, 115, 119,
    180–181, 185, 234, 268, 299n38
Keble College, Oxford, 4, 21, 44–46
Kehoe, Richard, 52–53
Kenny, Anthony, 141, 152, 255, 266,
    272–273, 306n61
Kepler, Johannes, 15–16
Kermode, Frank, 208
Kierkegaard, Søren, 82, 113, 115, 119, 126,
    182, 299n38
King's College, Newcastle. See Newcastle
    University.
Kipling, Rudyard, 211
Kneale, Martha, 73–74, 153
Kokoschka, Oscar, 215
Koestler, Arthur, 82, 210
Korsgaard, Christine, 268–269
Kramer, Joseph, 21

Lady Margaret Hall (LMH), Oxford, 23–24,
    72, 176
Leibniz, Gottfried, 14
Lenin, Vladimir, 126
Lewis, Clive Staples (C.S.), 145–148, 155,
    180, 293n39, 293n42
Lewontin, Richard, 240
Lindsay, Alexander Dunlop (A.D.), 33
Lloyd-Jones, Hugh, 37
Locke, John, 4, 41, 180–181
Lorenz, Konrad, 218–220, 228, 236, 240, 244
Lucas, John, 266, 267

MacIntyre, Alasdair, 238–239
Mackie, John Leslie (J. L.), 241–242
MacKinnon, Donald Mackenzie, 221
    cutting ties with Murdoch, 114–116
    influence on the four women, 44–48, 99,
        109–110, 215, 250–251, 257, 281n47,
        284n38
    ongoing help and support, 114, 116–117

MacKinnon, Lois, 114–115
Marcel, Gabriel, 144
Markievicz, Constance, 283n21
Martin, Ann, 207
Marx, Karl, 182
McCune, George, 7
Mead, Margaret, 210
Mehta, Ved, 222
Midgley, Geoffrey, 201n*
    marriage to Mary and life with children,
        200–203, 206–210
    career at Newcastle, 226, 245
Midgley, Mary, 121, 302n27, 304n9
    admission to Somerville and early days at
        Oxford, 25–31, 33–37, 39–40
    and Dawkins, 241–244, 304n12, 304n13
    early life and family, 54–58, 201
    end of life, 246
    friendship with Anscombe, 48–49, 154–155,
        203, 210, 258
    friendship with Foot, 172, 199, 204, 213,
        233–237
    friendship with Murdoch, 29–32, 33–37,
        47–48, 80, 98–99, 98n*, 116, 145n*,
        236–237
    and MacKinnon, 46–48, 215
    return to Oxford after the war, 87,
        98–101
    marriage to Geoff Midgley and life with
        children, 200–203, 206–210
    and ethology, 203, 226, 244
    unusual career path, 199, 203–206, 213,
        216–220, 225–227, 239–245
    on gender and marriage, 211–215, 271
    visit to Austria during Anschluss, 64–65
    writings on "Beastliness," 227–234,
        236–237, 239–240
Miller, Jonathan, 223–225
Mitchell, Basil, 131n*, 184, 192
Montaigne, Michel de, 12
More, Thomas, 138
Morgan, David, 248
Moore, Dudley, 223–224
Morse, Horace, 7
Mothersill, Mary, 169
Muir, Mrs., 23, 71
Murdoch, Hughes, 58–61, 281n44

Murdoch, Jean Iris, 145, 285n11
  at Somerville, 29–31, 33–37, 39–40, 145
  early life and family, 54–55, 58–62
  end of life, 256–257
  friendship with Anscombe, 48, 117–124,
    130, 164, 306n50
  friendship with Foot, 22–23, 79–83,
    110–113, 176, 196–197, 250–253,
    300n61
  friendship with Midgley, 29–32, 33–37,
    47–48, 80, 98–99, 98n*, 116, 145n*,
    236–237
  and MacKinnon, 46–48, 114–117,
    250–251
  leaving Oxford for the Royal College of
    Art, 130–134, 246, 248–250
  marriage to John Bayley, 62, 130–131,
    247, 253, 255–257
  post-war period, 87, 98, 103–108,
    113–119, 145, 287n1, 289n27
  scholarship on French existentialism and
    British thought, 105–110, 126–130,
    160, 255
Murdoch, Irene (Rene) Richardson, 59–61
Murray, Gilbert, 87, 262

Nanny, see Baxter, Jennie
Nagel, Thomas, 271
Newby, Percy Howard (P.H.), 210
Newcastle University, 199, 201n*, 204, 208,
  217, 220, 226, 236, 245
Newnham College, Cambridge, 88
Nietzsche, Friedrich, 69, 180–181, 188,
  199, 238
Nightingale, Florence, 210
Nineham, Dennis, 45
Nowell-Smith, Patrick Howard (P.H.), 161,
  163, 225

Ogden, Charles Kay (C.K.), 91
O'Neill, Onora, 270
Overy, Richard, 63

Plato, 6, 35, 58, 73, 87, 119, 125, 153, 187,
  212–214, 224–226, 253–254, 257,
  261n*, 301n12
Plotinus, 87, 207, 302n27

Plumer, Eleanor, 116n*
Popov, Linda Kavelin, 239
Price, Anthony (A.W.), 97
Price, Henry Haberly (H.H.), 74, 281n47
Proust, Marcel, 82, 181

Queneau, Raymond, 289n45
Quinn, Warren, 234

Rawls, John, 268
Reith, John, 136
Richards, Ivor Armstrong (I.A.), 91
Riley, Bridget, 248
Rowntree, Jean, 58, 64
Rugby School, 27, 37, 77, 96
Russell, Bertrand, 40, 114, 186, 222
Russell, David, 226–227
Ryle, Gilbert, 41, 131–133, 85–87, 97, 144,
  180–181, 181n*, 185, 222, 224

Sartre, Jean-Paul, 106–108, 113, 117, 119,
  125, 127–130, 254–255, 269, 287n14,
  301n12
Sayers, Dorothy, 30
Schopenhauer, Arthur, 254
Schweitzer, Albert, 63
Scrutton, Leslie Hay, 55–58, 64–65, 202
Scrutton, Mary. See Midgley, Mary
Scrutton, Thomas, 55–58, 64–65, 202
Shakespeare, William, 14, 14n1, 135, 184
Shaw, George Bernard, 54
Shawn, William, 222
Shorten, Monica, 145
Smith, Janet Adam, 210
Smith, Prudence, 127, 155
Smythies, Yorick, 123, 146
Somerville College, Oxford, 22–27, 31,
  35, 44, 71, 171–177, 185, 194–195,
  270–271
Spengler, Oswald, 63
Stebbing, Susan, 74
Steiner, Franz, 289n45
Stevenson, Charles, 91–94, 100, 127, 181
Stevenson, Robert Louis, 60
St. Anne's College, Oxford, 87, 98, 100,
  116n*, 126, 130–131, 207, 246, 248
St. George's School, Ascot, 68

St. Hilda's College, Oxford, 25, 25n*
St. Hugh's College, Oxford, 25, 40, 48, 52, 72, 87–88, 271
Swift, Jonathan, 169–170
Sydenham High School, 51

Tanner, Michael, 260
Taylor, Charles, 17, 271, 279n14
Teichmann, Roger, 268
Tennyson, Alfred, 18–19, 276
Thatcher, Margaret, 244, 245
Thomas, Dylan, 82
Thompson, Frank, 47–48, 81
Tinbergen, Nikolaas, 203, 218–219, 236
Tod, Marcus, 73
Toulmin, Roger, 211
Toynbee, Arnold, 63
Truman, Harry S., 155–158, 162, 186, 260
Turgenev, Ivan, 181

University of Birmingham, 148
University of Cambridge, 24–25, 40–41, 86, 88, 115–119, 139, 169, 257–259
University of Oxford
   and degrees for women, 23–32, 271
   and WWII, 38–40
   post-war changes, 83–86
   and mid-century philosophy, 85–87, 131–133, 221–22, 245–246
University of Reading, 100, 204, 207–208

Vane, Rosemary, 68
Vassar College, 113–115

Vaughan, Janet, 89, 114, 177, 179–180, 195
Verney, Catherine. see Hare, Catherine
Verney, Stephen, 98
Villiers, Miranda, 25n*

Waismann, Friedrich, 181
Warnock, Geoffrey, 143–144, 153
Warnock, Mary, 37, 84–85, 90–91, 133, 139–144, 153, 193, 297n11
Weil, Simone, 119, 126, 130, 133, 254
Wells, Herbert George (H.G.), 63
Whitehead, Alfred North, 40
Williams, Bernard, 145n*, 147, 154, 184, 260
Williams, Charles, 58
Williams, Glanville, 169, 171n*
Willis, Olive, 58, 61
Wilson, Andrew Norman (A.N.), 131n*, 293n42
Wilson, Angus, 210
Wilson, Edward Osborne (E.O.), 230, 239–243
Wittgenstein, Ludwig, 40, 101, 118–120, 184, 187
   and Austin, 142–144, 216
   influence on Anscombe, 88–90, 109, 122–124, 139–142, 144, 146–150, 152–155, 164, 169, 174–175, 179, 182, 257, 292n18
   influence on Murdoch, 118–120, 129
   influence on Foot, 150, 182–184, 187
Woolf, Virginia, 212–213
Wright, Joseph of Derby, 18

Zvegintzov, Diana, 29